THE ORIGIN OF
THE DISTINCTION OF RANKS

NATURAL LAW AND
ENLIGHTENMENT CLASSICS

Knud Haakonssen
General Editor

John Millar

NATURAL LAW AND
ENLIGHTENMENT CLASSICS

The Origin of the Distinction of Ranks:

*Or, An Inquiry into the Circumstances
Which Give Rise to Influence and Authority,
in the Different Members of Society*

John Millar

Edited and with an Introduction
by Aaron Garrett

The Works and Correspondence of John Millar

LIBERTY FUND
Indianapolis

This book is published by Liberty Fund, Inc., a foundation established
to encourage study of the ideal of a society of free and responsible individuals.

The cuneiform inscription that serves as our logo and as the design motif for
our endpapers is the earliest-known written appearance of the word
"freedom" (*amagi*), or "liberty." It is taken from a clay document written
about 2300 B.C. in the Sumerian city-state of Lagash.

10 09 08 07 06 C 5 4 3 2 1
10 09 08 07 06 P 5 4 3 2 1

Frontispiece: Portrait of John Millar by James Tassie. Copyright Scottish
National Portrait Gallery; reprinted by permission.

Library of Congress Cataloging-in-Publication Data
Millar, John, 1735–1801.
The origin of the distinction of ranks, or,
An inquiry into the circumstances which give rise to influence and authority,
in the different members of society/John Millar;
edited and with an introduction by Aaron Garrett.
p. cm.—(Natural law and enlightenment classics)
Includes bibliographical references and index.
ISBN-13: 978-0-86597-476-0 (hardcover: alk. paper)   ISBN-10: 0-86597-476-4 (hardcover: alk. paper)
ISBN-13: 978-0-86597-477-7 (pbk.: alk. paper)   ISBN-10: 0-86597-477-2 (pbk.: alk. paper)
1. Social classes—History—Early works to 1800.
2. Women—History—Early works to 1800.   3. Women—Social conditions—Early works to 1800.
4. Primitive societies—Early works to 1800.   5. Parent and child—Early works to 1800.
6. Master and servant—Early works to 1800.
I. Garrett, Aaron.   II. Title.   III. Title: Origin of the distinction of ranks.
IV. Title: Inquiry into the circumstances which give rise to influence and authority,
in the different members of society.   V. Series.
HT607.M545 2006
305.5'12—dc22   2005022900

LIBERTY FUND, INC.
8335 Allison Pointe Trail, Suite 300
Indianapolis, Indiana 46250-1684

CONTENTS

INTRODUCTION

What is the nature of authority? How does it change and why? *The Origin of the Distinction of Ranks* is John Millar's[1] concise but trenchant answer to these questions via an empirical analysis of three so-called adventitious[2] personal rights and one adventitious "governmental right" of natural law theory: the right of husband over wife, father over children, master over servants, and chief or sovereign over tribesmen or citizens. These rights are of obvious interest for a social philosopher since all have a degree of authority built into them—the right of the father over the child, for example, presumes the father's authority to appropriately discharge his role and the duties incumbent to it. Yet, when these four rights are examined compar-

---

1. There is a growing secondary literature on Millar. In preparing this edition I have benefited particularly from, and drawn extensively on, Knud Haakonssen, *Natural Law and Moral Philosophy* (Cambridge: Cambridge University Press, 1996), chap. 5; William Lehmann, *John Millar of Glasgow 1735–1801: His Life and Thought and His Contributions to Sociological Analysis* (Cambridge: Cambridge University Press, 1960); John Cairns, "John Millar's Lectures on Scots Criminal Law," *Oxford Journal of Legal Studies* 8.3 (1988): 364–400; Michael Ignatieff, "John Millar and Individualism," in *Wealth and Virtue,* Istvan Hont and Michael Ignatieff, eds. (Cambridge: Cambridge University Press, 1983), 317–43; Duncan Forbes, "'Scientific Whiggism': Adam Smith and John Millar," *Cambridge Journal* 7 (1953–54): 643–70; Knud Haakonssen, *The Science of a Legislator: The Natural Jurisprudence of David Hume and Adam Smith* (Cambridge: Cambridge University Press, 1985).

2. The distinction between natural and adventitious states, duties, and rights was common in natural law, adventitious rights being "those which arise or are made out of some human institution." See Francis Hutcheson, *Philosophia Moralis Institutio Compendiaria* (translated as *A Short Introduction to Moral Philosophy*), II.5.1. The *Institutio* was the textbook for Hutcheson's moral philosophy courses and was used also by Smith for his first course in 1751–52 when he filled in for the ailing Thomas Craigie (Ian S. Ross, *The Life of Adam Smith* [Oxford: Clarendon Press, 1995], 111–12). In his biography of Millar, John Craig notes that Millar attended these lectures; see pp. 8–9 below.

atively and historically, from Aragon to Zeeland, from ancient Rome to Georgian Glasgow, drastic differences appear in the authority appropriate to the exercise of the right. And this is not just a problem of comparing European and non-European societies. The Roman law, the backbone of much European legal and moral thinking, allowed the head of the household to treat wife, children, and servants as property and to expose infants.[3] The authority appropriate for the exercise of the right by early Romans (and Greeks) is completely at odds with the authority proper to a progressive eighteenth-century society. Millar's *Ranks* provides an empirical account of how rights arise and how they change, and a means to understand historical discrepancies in the scope of authority. It also attempts to draw some limited normative consequences and thus offer the elements of an empirical moral theory.

The Argument of the *Ranks*

It is not surprising that the *Ranks* turns on rights, considering that the three most important influences on Millar's thinking all stressed that evolving systems of justice and rights were the backbone of morals and human nature. In *Treatise* III.2 David Hume argued that justice is an artificial human creation that guides and serves human utility. In his seminal essay, "The Rise and Progress of the Arts and Sciences," Hume discussed the history of the authority of husband over wife—the subject of the first long section of the *Ranks*—as an index of the progress of manners in society.[4] Adam Smith presented his historical theory of justice and rights in a series of lectures on moral philosophy that Millar attended in 1751. Student transcripts from Smith's lectures from the 1760s include extensive treatment of the rights Millar later considered in the *Ranks,* rooted in a stadial division between the ages of "Hunters," "Shepherds," "Agriculture," and "Com-

---

3. The question was debated in natural law theory (see p. 171 note). Hume discussed it in "A Dialogue" (David Hume, *Enquiries,* 3rd ed., ed. L. A. Selby-Bigge and P. H. Nidditch [Oxford: Clarendon Press, 1975], 324–28), Smith in *The Theory of Moral Sentiments* (V.2.15).

4. David Hume, *Essays Moral, Political, and Literary,* rev. ed., ed. Eugene V. Miller (Indianapolis: Liberty Fund, 1985), 131–34.

merce."[5] Lord Kames treated the historical evolution of different aspects of the law, including criminal law and property law, in his *Historical Law-Tracts* (1758), connecting legal obligation, moral duty, and social progress.[6]

Justice, law, and rights were also central to Millar's pedagogy. When the first edition of the *Ranks* appeared in 1771—*Observations Concerning the Distinction of Ranks in Society*—Millar had held the Regius Chair of Civil Law at the University of Glasgow for ten years. His primary teaching duty had been lecturing on Justinian's *Institutes* and *Digest* with the aid of Heineccius's commentaries.[7] The combination of Smith's jurisprudence and variations in rights within the *Digest* itself—for example, changes in the Roman *peculium* (*Ranks,* <132–33>)—must have set Millar thinking about the history of adventitious rights. Furthermore, in addition to his regular course Millar undertook a series of "private" "Lectures on Government." These lectures, which he continued for the rest of his life, were the source of his two major works: the *Ranks* and the *Historical View* (see appendix 3). Given the connection between the government lectures and the course on Roman law, it is unsurprising that the *Ranks*—the first part of the "Government" course—is infused with justice and rights.

The *Ranks*'s treatment of rights and their order was likely derived from Smith; likewise the division of human history into the four "ages" distinguished by population, wealth, the needs these engendered, and the ways those needs were satisfied.[8] Man's earliest stages were characterized almost wholly by attempts to satisfy simple needs. As basic needs were satisfied more efficiently and population grew, wealth resulting from the satisfaction

---

5. Smith, *Lectures on Jurisprudence,* ed. R. L. Meek, D. D. Raphael, and P. G. Stein (Oxford: Oxford University Press, 1978), LJ (A), i.27. Following standard practice, Smith's Lectures of 1762–63 are abbreviated "LJ (A)," and Smith's Lectures of 1766 "LJ (B)."

6. "Moral duties, originally weak and feeble, acquire great strength by refinement of manners in polished societies." Henry Home, Lord Kames, *Historical Law-Tracts* (Edinburgh: A. Kincaid and J. Bell, 1758), I:92.

7. Johann Gottlieb Heineccius (1681–1741) was a widely read and erudite natural lawyer. Millar used two works by Heineccius in structuring his civil law course: *Elementa juris civilis secundum ordinem Institutionem* (1725) and *Elementa juris civilis secundum ordinem Pandectarum* (1727).

8. Smith, *Lectures on Jurisprudence,* LJ (A), i.27, iv–v, 200–330. Kames also used a stadial scheme in the *Historical Law-Tracts* (I:28).

of needs allowed for leisure, the rise of human institutions, and more complex desires—the arts and sciences, taste, and love.

Romantic love provides a good illustration of how successive stages multiply needs. In the earliest stages of mankind commerce between the sexes
was a ubiquitous function of animal need and so considered of little import
in comparison with the acquisition of food (<28>). When men moved to
the pastoral stage, food supplies became more regular and the labor in acquiring them less:

> The leisure, tranquillity, and retirement of a pastoral life, seem calculated,
> in a peculiar manner, to favour the indulgence of those indolent gratifi-
> cations . . . and mere animal pleasure is more frequently accompanied
> with a correspondence of inclination and sentiment. (<58>)

The transition to the pastoral stage also initiated the system of ranks,[9]
as families acquired surplus wealth and power. When families separated due
to growing estates and retinues, the resultant rivalries between different
families seeking prominence in the order of ranks led to the suppression
of sexual desires and "animal" commerce between the sexes. At the same
time, increased leisure allowed young men and women to fixate more on
desires that had been considered unimportant in the previous stage of society. Consequently, "the inclinations of individuals . . . will break forth
with greater vigor, and rise at length to a higher pitch, in proportion to the
difficulties which they have surmounted" (<61>). With this structural explanation (and much comparative empirical evidence) Millar showed how
romantic love arose as a passion and became an important motive for action.
For example, interfamilial contests over women gave rise to chivalric combat mediated by elites dispensing justice and thus avoiding feuds through
a courtly system of ranks. These changes resulted in human beings with
more complex social codes and more varied emotional lives that they
needed to satisfy.[10]

For Millar, different historical stages were not just distinct but *progressive:*

---

9. "Ranks" means not just social or economic classes but any consistent, enduring
ordering recognized and approved of by spectators.
10. Hume had stressed, as well, the rise of romantic love in connection with the
progress of society (Hume, "Rise and Progress," *Essays,* 131–34).

"There is . . . in human society, a natural progress from ignorance to knowledge, and from rude to civilized manners, the several stages of which are usually accompanied with peculiar laws and customs" (<4>). Each succeeding stage satisfies needs in a prior stage while developing new needs and the means to satisfy and express them through science ("knowledge") and art ("civilized manners"). Stages were also progressive in another sense: our present stage of commerce has far less brutality than the first stage and less romantic extravagance than the later stages and thus allows women to be "more universally regarded upon account of their useful or agreeable talents" (<89>). Millar clearly viewed the unbigoted meritocracy and personal liberty appropriate to the fourth stage of society as desirable, and slavery and domestic tyranny as inappropriate to a progressive society insofar as it thwarted liberty and merit. In other words, unlike Rousseau and like Smith and Hume, Millar considered liberty and equality to be social achievements:[11]

> Whereever men of inferior condition are enabled to live in affluence by their own industry, and, in procuring their livelihood, have little occasion to court the favour of their superiors, there we may expect that ideas of liberty will be universally diffused. This happy arrangement of things is naturally produced by commerce and manufactures; but it would be as vain to look for it in the uncultivated parts of the world, as to look for the independent spirit of an English waggoner among persons of low rank in the highlands of Scotland. (<241–42>)

This stress on progress was not an unbridled advocacy of wealth. Much like Smith, Millar viewed stagnant luxury as a dangerous corruptor of morals that stopped "useful and agreeable" talents from being recognized.[12]

---

11. This point was so important for Millar that he changed the neat rights-centered chapter structure of the first two editions of *Ranks* and added a separate chapter on the subject (chap. V).

12. "The excessive opulence of Rome, about the end of the Commonwealth, and after the establishment of the despotism, gave rise to a degree of debauchery of which we have no example in any other European nation" (<103>). It is notable that Millar's main objection to debauchery in this context was that it restricts women to being viewed as sexual objects, a criticism possible only from an enlightened stage of commerce. Millar criticized "the voluptuousness of Eastern nations" (<102>) for reducing women to a state

Wealth is desirable only insofar as it gives rise to liberty and historical progress.

The scientist of human nature arrives at regularities that differentiate these stages through cross-cultural and comparative historical study. Millar's conclusions were tempered by the circumspect attitude toward evidence that he had learned from Hume.[13] In the later chapters of *Ranks* on government he made much use of Montesquieu's comparisons of legal codes and constitutions in *The Spirit of the Laws.* But Millar presumed, following Hume and *contra* Montesquieu, that mores or "moral causes," as opposed to physical causes such as climate, are responsible for characteristic differences in human population. Customs and mores arise from the aggregate actions of individuals. But individuals differ widely in their behavior, and the comparison of a few human individuals is not sufficient to educe general rules of human nature. By comparing many individuals, or different societies composed of many individuals, one can find consistent patterns of behavior. And by comparing regularities across historical periods the human scientist can discern stadial differences determined by underlying causes in human nature.

The stadial analysis had a further important function. It presupposed no particular contingent historical narrative such as "the Goths invaded," "Watt discovered the steam engine." Consequently, the "Age of Hunters" was not a particular time or place but rather a social arrangement built around a mode of subsistence that had existed, and perhaps would exist,

---

of "slavery and confinement" as well. For parallel criticisms, see Adam Smith, *Theory of Moral Sentiments,* ed. D. D. Raphael and A. L. Macfie (Oxford: Clarendon, 1976), III.iii; and *An Inquiry into the Nature and Causes of the Wealth of Nations,* ed. R. H. Campbell, A. S. Skinner, and W. B. Todd (Oxford: Oxford University Press, 1976), II.iii. Millar's main objection seems to have been that "the chief effect of debauchery . . . has been to turn the attention, from the pursuits of business or ambition, to the amusements of gallantry" (<108>). Although Millar did not mention the impartial spectator, given Smith's influence it seems that the criticism of prior stages of society was made with reference to an impartial spectator who approves and recognizes useful and agreeable qualities in the Age of Commerce, and criticizes their neglect or destruction in prior stages.

13. See pp. 85–86 below.

in many times and places. Thus the divide between "ancients and moderns" that fascinated thinkers like Hume in the first half of the eighteenth century and continued to interest many thinkers who promoted comparative stadial history—such as Kames, Monboddo, and Gilbert Stuart—was moot. Instead, history has a scientifically accessible structure with identifiable moral causes.

This does not mean that stages necessarily follow one another like clockwork. Rome declined because of excess luxury and the accidental cause of the barbarian invasions (< 218–19 >). Accidents enter into the forms of particular governments as well. For example, Solon's and Lycurgus's idiosyncrasies were partially responsible for the very different manners of Athens and Sparta. But for laws to have influence with the people whom they are to govern, they must harmonize with and speak to existing regularities. The scientist of human nature should discover these empirical regularities yet not dismiss the role of accident (< 7 >).[14]

So far this is of a piece with Hume and Smith. But Millar's *Ranks* goes beyond them in providing a stadial genealogy of particular rights and showing that rights should be understood as evolving responses to human needs. By focusing on familial rights Millar brought the problem of natural rights into sharp focus. If the most basic social rights are mutable and artificial, and if man is social, what is one to make of natural rights at all? Hume had pointed the way in his analyses of property in the *Treatise* and of the history of love by implying that all rights are to some degree adventitious, and natural rights of the Lockean sort are highly questionable. Millar's contribution was to push this analysis in a single-minded way within a well-worked-out historical theory.[15]

A comparison with Smith's discussion of the rights of husband over wife shows Millar's novelty. Smith taught jurisprudence through the framework of his predecessor and teacher Francis Hutcheson, building the discussion of the first of the rights "which belong to a man as a member of a family" around three aspects of marriage: "1st, the manner in which this union is

---

14. Cf. Millar's discussion of polygynous and matrifocal societies as a variant on the normal patriarchal structure of the first stage of society (< 53–54 >).

15. See Knud Haakonssen, *Natural Law and Moral Philosophy,* chap. 5.

entered into and the origin of it; 2dly, the obligation or rights that are thereby acquired and the injuries corresponding to these; and 3dly, the manner in which it is dissolved" (LJ (A), iii.2). Smith treated these rights historically, but the discussion was always structured by background issues in natural law: the standing of polygamy, the perpetuity of marriage, the reasons for dissolving a marriage. The primary purpose of Smith's lectures was to elucidate marriage; the historical evolution of marital rights was auxiliary. Similarly, Smith's very brief discussion of the right of father over children centered on the issue of greatest interest to natural lawyers: *patria potestas*.

Smith's discussions of the rights of the master and, most notably, the rights of the community member or citizen involve much more extensive stadial comparison. He used comparisons between societal stages to make a normative claim, "that the state of slavery is a much more tolerable one in a poor and barbarous people than in a rich and polished one" (LJ (A), iii.105), and he developed a complex stadial history of governments as well (iii.105–v. 43), both of which influenced the *Ranks*. Unlike Smith, however, Millar treated each of the rights directly through the stadial theory and showed how changes in the scope of the right arose from changing needs. We have seen this with the right of husband over wife; Millar made parallel arguments for the other three rights under consideration. Furthermore, he attempted to draw normative consequences about authority itself. Slavery and brutality toward inferiors have no place in progressive societies because authority has legitimacy when it is used to efficiently satisfy needs. The authority appropriate to an adventitious right in a particular historical stage ought to be limited by the useful and agreeable ends that the rights allow human groups to fulfill. Once a right gets in the way of the satisfaction of these needs, for example, by stopping useful and agreeable talents of women from being recognized, it is no longer legitimate. With this insight Millar had created a fully empirical moral theory centered on adventitious rights and allowing for normative criticisms.

John Craig's "Account of the Life and Writings of the Author"

Ranks is an important work of empirical moral philosophy, and the fourth, posthumous edition is further enhanced by John Craig's "Account of the

Life and Writings of the Author."[16] Craig's fascinating portrait details the
intellectual milieu of Glasgow, the teaching of law at the university, the
great regard in which Millar was held, and his rare personal qualities. John
Craig (1766–1840) was Millar's nephew, and he studied under him at Glasgow in the late 1770s, acquiring a firsthand acquaintance with his uncle's
teaching methods. He was, along with Millar's son-in-law James Mylne,
the literary executor of Millar's estate. The two also made a posthumous
edition of the *Historical View,* which added two volumes of manuscripts
(1803). Craig, a notable political theorist himself, wrote two works: *Elements
of Political Science* (1814), in which he drew out further consequences of
Smith's and Millar's political philosophy, and *Remarks on Some Fundamental Doctrines in Political Economy* (1821). Consequently, Craig was in a
unique position to understand Millar's life, his influences, and his doctrines
and should be the first stopping point for Millar's readers.[17]

Sources Used by Millar

Millar used a wide range of sources to make his stadial argument in the
Ranks. I will briefly consider four of the types of sources on which he drew.

1. Because of the comparative historical nature of Millar's project, travel
narratives were important sources. He kept up with this expanding literature and added footnotes to the second and third editions as evidence became available from newly published reports. Many of the travel writers he
drew on are now obscure, but by examining a few we can get a sense of the
breadth of Millar's reading.

Millar made extensive use of the Abbé Prevost's enormous collection of
travel reports, the *Histoire Générale.* Each volume of the *Histoire Générale*
includes a number of different "books"; hence Millar's citation procedure
refers to the volume, the book within the volume, and normally a chapter
within the book. He also made repeated use of another massive, popular
work, the *Modern Universal History,* which collects ancient sources, histories, and travel narratives in its forty-plus volumes.

---

16. Millar has had important if scant admirers since his death, including James Mill,
John Stuart Mill, and Werner Sombart. See Lehman, *John Millar of Glasgow,* chap. 14.
    17. Thanks to Knud Haakonssen for supplying me with information on Craig.

One of the best-known travel reports Millar drew on was William Dampier's *New Voyage* (1697). Dampier is now primarily remembered for a 1703 expedition in which Alexander Selkirk found Dampier so unbearable as a captain that he asked to be marooned on Juan Fernández rather than stay onboard the ship. He lived on Juan Fernández until 1709 and became the model for Defoe's Robinson Crusoe. Another important seventeenth-century source was Jean Chardin's *Journal du voyage du Chevalier Chardin en Perse et aux Indes Orientales* (1686), the most authoritative account of the Maghreb in the period and the basis for Gibbon's discussions of North Africa.

Millar made numerous references to similarly credible eighteenth-century sources covering disparate parts of the world: Peter Kolb's descriptions of southern Africa, the botanist Johann Georg Gmelin's account of his scientific expedition to Siberia, and the widely read works of Charlevoix and Lafitau on America. Not all of Millar's sources were so legitimate. Millar used the plagiarized edition of De Brosses's *Histoire des navigations aux Terres Australes* (1756) (consulted by Bougainville and Cook on their voyages to the South Seas) that was translated and published by John Callendar under his own name in Edinburgh (1766–68). Millar also accepted such unauthorized or slimly authorized sources as the journalist John Hawkesworth's compendium from the journals of various expeditions, including Cook's first voyage (1773).

2. Like Smith, Millar drew on ancient ethnographies—above all, Tacitus's *Germania* and Caesar's *De Bello Gallico*—and Roman legal works. In good eighteenth-century fashion he illustrated his arguments with passages from classical literature to strengthen his point and show off his erudition. Millar also used the Hebrew bible as an ethnographic source for the early history of nomadic and pastoral law in a strikingly detached and "scientific" manner. He cast the comparative net even wider with *Ossian*, James Macpherson's series of poems putatively translated from early Gaelic sources (but in fact only inspired by them). Millar seemed much less skeptical than Hume about the authenticity of Ossian.[18]

18. David Hume, "Letter 176," in J. Y. T. Greig, *The Letters of David Hume* (Oxford: Clarendon Press, 1932), I:328–31. Hume's argument is in part stadial: barbarians of the

3. Millar drew on natural lawyers and legal historians—Heineccius, de Noodt, Bynkershoek—but more for their interpretation of Roman law than for their own substantial doctrines. He did not cite the natural lawyers commonly discussed in jurisprudence or moral philosophy: Pufendorf, Barbeyrac, and so on.

4. Millar cited many French authors—Montaigne, Mably, Fontenelle, and Du Bos among them—but, with the exception of Montaigne, for their history, not their philosophy. Throughout the *Ranks* he also made erudite use of French histories of medieval chivalry. Like many Enlightenment thinkers, he was clearly as comfortable with French as with British sources.

In the first and second editions Millar cited his illustrious Scottish contemporaries—Hume, Robertson, and Smith—but it is notable that the reference to Robertson and those to Hume's *History* were eliminated from the third edition. This suggests that Millar had become more confident in his own interpretation of historical sources through teaching the historical sections of his "Government" course. Millar may also have developed a sense of himself as (along with Smith) belonging to the next generation of more rigorous "Scientific Whig" students of man. In keeping with the more sober tone of the preface to the third edition, a reference to Montesquieu's *Considerations sur les causes de la grandeur des Romains* was deleted.

One further striking change that concerns Hume lies behind the reference "See Dr. Wallace, on the numbers of mankind" (note, <267>). The note in the first and second editions read "See Essay on the populousness of ancient nations, by Mr. Hume." Hume and Wallace were involved in an amicable controversy concerning whether the ancient world was more or less populous than the modern world. Millar seems to have changed sides on this point by the time the third edition was published. This does not diminish Millar's lifelong admiration of Hume and advocacy of the "true old Humean philosophy";[19] in fact, it reflects a Humean belief in changing standards of empirical adequacy of research.

---

type Macpherson described would be incapable of this sort of poetry. In the letter Hume also implied that Smith accepted the authenticity of the first volumes of the Ossianic poems (which were, in fact, the most authentic).

19. "Millar to David Douglas 10 August 1790," in Millar, *Letters and Occasional Writings,* ed. Cairns and Garrett (Indianapolis, Ind.: Liberty Fund, forthcoming).

A NOTE ON THE TEXT

This edition reproduces the fourth edition of Millar's *Ranks*. A discussion of changes in the various editions can be found in appendix 1. Although the fourth edition was posthumous, it is in fact identical to the third edition, the final lifetime edition, except for the addition of Craig's Preface.

Millar documented his arguments in the *Ranks* and provided many footnotes, whose contents range from accurate titles and page numbers to far more elusive references. I have tried to fill in the references wherever possible and provide notes wherever necessary. I have for the most part erred on the side of parsimony, adding notes to Millar's text only when required for the ease of the reader. My additions to Millar's notes are enclosed in a double set of square brackets.

The text has been corrected only when there are clear typographical errors or spelling mistakes, and all such errors have been corrected without comment. Page breaks in the fourth edition are indicated here by the use of angle brackets. For example, page 112 begins after <112>. In addition, the errata from the third edition have been incorporated and flagged with footnotes.

ACKNOWLEDGMENTS

Thanks to Knud Haakonssen for answering many questions and helping to solve many puzzles in the notes; Wolfgang Haase for help with Millar's references to ancient texts; Charles Wolfe for a great deal of research assistance and French translation help; Steve Scully, Joel Berson, and Theo Korzukhin for assistance with Latin translations; Charles Griswold and the philosophy department at Boston University; the staff at the Houghton Library at Harvard University; and the staff at Liberty Fund.

THE ORIGIN OF
THE DISTINCTION OF RANKS

THE

ORIGIN

OF THE

DISTINCTION OF RANKS:

OR,

AN INQUIRY INTO THE CIRCUMSTANCES

WHICH GIVE RISE TO

INFLUENCE AND AUTHORITY,

IN THE

DIFFERENT MEMBERS OF SOCIETY.

BY JOHN MILLAR, ESQ.

PROFESSOR OF LAW IN THE UNIVERSITY OF GLASGOW.

THE FOURTH EDITION, CORRECTED.

TO WHICH IS PREFIXED,

AN ACCOUNT OF THE LIFE AND WRITINGS
OF THE AUTHOR,

BY JOHN CRAIG, ESQ.

EDINBURGH:

PRINTED FOR WILLIAM BLACKWOOD, SOUTH-BRIDGE STREET;

AND

LONGMAN, HURST, REES, & ORME, PATERNOSTER-ROW,

LONDON.

1806.

G. CAW, PRINTER, EDINBURGH.

TO
JOHN YOUNG, ESQUIRE,[1]
PROFESSOR OF GREEK IN THE UNIVERSITY OF GLASGOW.

MY DEAR SIR,

In presenting you with a Memoir on the Life of our late excellent Friend, Mr. Millar, I submit it to the person who, from long and familiar intercourse with him, will most readily perceive any misconceptions of his real character, or inaccuracies in the representation of his opinions.

I am fully aware of the difficulty of delineating a character such as Mr. Millar's, and I am not insensible of the danger of failing in a species of composition in which some late writings have accustomed the Public to the union, in an uncommon degree, of Philosophy and Taste; but I could <iv> not be deterred by any selfish regard to my own reputation, from making that attempt, for which, in the opinion of our mutual friends, my intimacy with Mr. Millar, begun by our near connection, and continued by his kind indulgence, had afforded me peculiar advantages.

I am, with the greatest regard,

MY DEAR SIR,

Your most obedient Servant,

JOHN CRAIG.

GLASGOW, *February,* 1806. <v>

1. Young (d. 1820) was one of Millar's closest friends and a student of Adam Smith's.

CONTENTS[2]

2. The page numbers used here are those from the fourth edition of 1806.

ACCOUNT
OF THE
LIFE AND WRITINGS
OF
JOHN MILLAR, ESQ.

John Millar, late Professor of Law in the University of Glasgow, was born on the 22d June, 1735, in the parish of Shotts, twenty-four miles west from Edinbugh. His father, Mr. James Millar,[3] a man much respected for his abilities, learning, and purity of manners, was then minister of that parish; but, two years afterwards, he was translated to Hamilton, where he spent the rest of his life. His mother[4] was a daughter of Mr. Hamilton of West-burn, a gentleman of considerable estate in the county of Lanark.

When the family removed to Hamilton, Mr. Millar went to reside at Milheugh, in the parish of <ii> Blantyre, about eight miles from Glasgow, with his uncle Mr. John Millar, who had been educated in Edinburgh as a writer to the signet, but, from bad health, had given up that profession, and retired to a small estate which had been long in his family. Here Mr. Millar, being taught to read by his uncle, continued to reside, till he was of the proper age to go to the Latin school. In 1742 he was brought to Hamilton to learn Latin and Greek, under Mr. Pillans, who taught the Grammar School of that town with considerable reputation.

In 1746, he went to Glasgow College, where he distinguished himself as an attentive and intelligent student. During one or two winters, he boarded in the same house with Mr. Morehead, afterwards of Herbertshire, with whom he formed an early friendship, which their very different pursuits in

3. James Millar (1701–85).
4. Ann.

7

after life never obliterated. When he was a few years older, he lived in College Chambers, and usually dined with the celebrated Dr. Cullen,[5] then Lecturer in Chemistry, whose wife was cousin-german to his mother. Those who have been so happy as to be acquainted with Dr. and Mrs. Cullen will recollect, with delight, the elegance which distinguished their conversation, and will easily be able to appreciate the advantages of this connection, to a <iii> young man, in forming his manners, and improving his taste.

In the evenings, as a relaxation from study, Mr. Millar used frequently to pass an hour or two at the house of Mrs. Craig, whose eldest son possessed a taste for literary conversation and philosophical experiment, not at that time very common among merchants. Here he met with several young men, intended for different professions, but almost all fond of literary inquiries; in particular, it was here that he formed an acquaintance with Mr. Watt,[6] now of Birmingham, whose discoveries have entitled him to the gratitude of his country, and the admiration of the world. At this time, Mr. Millar was remarkable among his companions for the vivacity of his conversation, as well as the extent of his knowledge, and his powers of argument. "In our meetings," says Mr. Watt, (in a letter with which he honoured me relative to this memoir) "the conversation, besides the usual subjects with young men, turned principally on literature, religion, morality, history; and to these conversations my mind owed its first bias to such subjects. Mr. Millar was always looked up to as the oracle of the company; his attainments were greater than those of the others; he had more <iv> wit, and much greater argumentative powers." He adds, with that modesty which ever accompanies real genius, "He was a man when I was a boy, though in years little my senior. The diversity of our pursuits made me know less of him afterwards than I should otherwise have done; but we always continued attached friends, and I consider myself as indebted to him for much useful knowledge."

It was also during Mr. Millar's studies at Glasgow, that he formed an

5. William Cullen (1710–90), first a professor of medicine at Glasgow then professor of chemistry at Edinburgh, was the main reforming influence on the teaching of medicine in Scottish universities as well as a celebrated medical researcher.

6. James Watt (1736–1819) was the discoverer of the steam engine and instrument maker to the University of Glasgow.

acquaintance and friendship with Dr. Adam Smith. He had attended the Logic and Moral Philosophy Classes before Dr. Smith was appointed to these Chairs; but, having come to the University for instruction, not merely to go through a common routine, he eagerly seized the opportunity of hearing Lectures which excited, and fully gratified, the public expectation. His intelligence and ardour soon attracted Dr. Smith's notice, and at this time was laid the foundation of that mutual esteem, which, during the few years they were afterwards Professors in the same University, produced lasting intimacy and friendship. It is probable that Mr. Millar's attention was first directed to that particular line of research, in which he afterwards became so eminent, by Dr. Smith's Lectures and conversa-<v>tion; and it was with much pleasure, that he afterwards seized every opportunity of acknowledging his obligations to the instructions he at this time enjoyed.* The very gratifying proof of Dr. Smith's esteem, which he received long afterwards, in being intrusted by him with the education of his relation, Mr. Douglas, (at a time when he himself could ill spare the pleasure of his society) has been noticed by the elegant biographer of that celebrated philosopher.†

Mr. Millar's friends intended him for the church, and it was with this view that he began his studies at Glasgow. In a young man ardent in inquiry, there must always, however, be some disinclination to fetter himself by established articles of belief; and the Church of Scotland holds out few inducements to the ambition of him who is conscious of superior talents: Mr. Millar, accordingly, soon betrayed a desire to adopt a different profession, and to this he was probably still farther induced, by his occasional residences, during the summer, at Milheugh. His uncle, though much re-

---

* See Historical view of the English Government, Book ii. Chap. 10. Note. [["I am happy to acknowledge the obligations I feel myself under to this illustrious philosopher, by having, at an early period of life, had the benefit of hearing his lectures on the History of Civil Society, and of enjoying his unreserved conversation on the same subject.— The great Montesquieu pointed out the road. He was the Lord Bacon in this branch of philosophy. Dr. Smith is the Newton."]]

† See Mr. Stewart's Life of Dr. Smith, at the conclusion. [[David Douglas (1769–1819), later Lord Reston as a senator of the College of Justice (i.e., judge in the Court of Session), was Smith's heir. See Dugald Stewart, "Account of the Life and Writings of Adam Smith, LL.D." included in Adam Smith, *Essays on Philosophical Subjects,* ed. L. D. Wightman (Oxford: Oxford University Press, 1980), 331–32.]]

tired from the world, and naturally diffident and reserved, was a man of
excellent understanding and most amiable <vi> manners. He had read,
with much attention, whatever related to the history of his own country,
and had observed, with much acuteness, the various struggles of parties
during his own times. An ardent friend of civil and religious liberty, zealously attached to the Revolution settlement, and to the party of the Whigs,
his early instructions probably contributed to form, in his nephew's mind,
those sentiments of independence, which, through his whole life, he himself had steadily maintained. Next to history and politics, his favourite subject of reading and conversation was Scotch Law, for which he always retained a fondness, derived from his early education, and perhaps increased
by the consequence it gave him as a Justice of Peace among his country
neighbours. It was natural that Mr. Millar, in choosing a profession, should
be influenced by the taste of his uncle, with whom he had passed the early
period of his life, who had instructed him by his conversation, and whom
he saw respected for his understanding and legal knowledge. Fortunately
Mr. Millar's father, though much attached to his own profession, and desirous that his son should succeed him in those duties, from the regular
and able discharge of which he had derived much happiness and great
respectabi-<vii>lity, was not inflexible in his determination; so that, with
little opposition from his friends, Mr. Millar was allowed to turn his attention from the Pulpit to the Bar.

About the time that Mr. Millar had finished his studies at Glasgow, he
received an invitation from Lord Kames to reside in his family, and superintend the education of his son. It would be superfluous to dwell on the
advantages he must have derived from the society of a man, so remarkable
for the variety of his knowledge, the ardour of his literary curiosity, and
his talent in communicating information in its most pleasing form. Considering Mr. Millar as a young man of superior abilities and attainments,
Lord Kames had much pleasure in solving any difficulties that occurred to
him on subjects of law, and few days passed without some improving conversations on various topics of philosophical research.* In this society he

---

* I am indebted for this information to Lord Kames' son, G. Drummond Home,
Esq.

spent about two years; during which time, that attachment to the study of the history of mankind and of political institutions, which Dr. Smith's lectures had excited, could not fail to be strengthened by the <viii> communications of a philosopher engaged in nearly similar pursuits.

It was chiefly at this period, also, that Mr. Millar had an opportunity of cultivating an acquaintance with Mr. Hume. The urbanity of this illustrious author never failed to conciliate the friendship even of those who viewed his political opinions with dislike, and his metaphysical tenets with abhorrence. Mr. Millar had few prejudices of this kind to conquer. Though a steady and zealous Whig himself, he had no enmity to speculative Tories; and, convinced of the truth of Mr. Hume's metaphysical opinions, he was not of a temper to abandon a system, which appeared to him to afford a satisfactory explanation of many of the phenomena of the human mind, because it had been attacked by ignorant and illiberal abuse. Mr. Hume's visit to the Continent, which took place a few years after this, together with Mr. Millar's change of residence and numerous avocations, prevented this acquaintance from being improved into that intimacy, which their mutual respect would, in other circumstances, have produced; but they never failed to seize such opportunities of enjoying each other's society, as afterwards occurred. From Mr. Hume, Mr. Millar received the same flattering mark of confidence as <ix> from Dr. Smith, having been entrusted with the education of his nephew, the present very eminent Professor of Scotch Law in the University of Edinburgh.[7]

In 1760, Mr. Millar was called to the Bar; or, according to the Scotch technical phraseology, he *passed advocate.* He was fortunate enough, during the very short time he practised as a lawyer, to have some opportunities of appearing before the *Inner House,* * and, on these occasions, he received very flattering compliments from several of the Judges. He was indeed universally considered as a very rising young lawyer; and it was not without surprise that his friends learned his intention, on the death of Mr. Hercules

---

* The supreme Civil Court, composed of all the fifteen Judges. A lawyer is often many years at the Bar before he has an opportunity of speaking, except in the *Outer House* where all causes are tried in the first instance, by a single Judge, without a jury.

7. Baron David Hume (1757–1838), author of *Commentaries on the Laws of Scotland* (1797).

Lindsay, of applying for the Law Professorship at Glasgow.[8] It seemed to them an extraordinary want of ambition in a young man, whose talents entitled him to look forward to the highest honours of his profession, at once to abandon all these hopes, and sit down contented with the moderate revenue, and the less brilliant reputa-<x>tion, of a Teacher of Law. They knew that he could not be prompted to such a step by timidity, for his temper was uncommonly sanguine; nor by indolence, for never was a mind more active. He was induced, however, to take this resolution, by his having, about this time, married Miss Margaret Craig, a lady nearly of his own age, to whom, while visiting on a familiar footing at her mother's, he had become strongly attached.

He saw that it was impossible for a young lawyer, whatever his abilities and diligence might be, to maintain a family, even with the most rigid oeconomy; and he was unwilling to risk the becoming a burden on his father and uncle. The emoluments of a Professor of Law were not, indeed, very great; but they were much superior to what, for many years, he could expect to reach at the bar; they were sufficient to enable him to maintain a family in a respectable manner; and, by his own exertions, he hoped to increase the number of students, on which, at Glasgow, the emolument of a Professor chiefly depends. The situation, too, if not brilliant, was highly respectable; and he was happy to think, that those speculations on law and government, which had always been his favourite studies, were now to become the business of his life, the <xi> source of his income, and the foundation of his future reputation.

With such views, he applied for the vacant Chair; and, through the interest of the guardians of the Duke of Hamilton, then a minor, and at the recommendation of Lord Kames and Dr. Smith, he was appointed Professor of Law in the University of Glasgow, in 1761, about sixteen months after he had been called to the bar.

From the absence of the higher Courts of Justice, Glasgow lies under many obvious disadvantages, as a school of law; and, accordingly, the students of Law in that University, previously to Mr. Millar's appointment, seldom exceeded four or five, and sometimes fell short even of that number.

8. Hercules Lindesay (d. 1761).

From the first moment of his appointment, there was a very general expectation that Mr. Millar would greatly improve, in this branch of education, the character of the University,[9] but I believe his most sanguine friends never entertained the idea, that he could possibly raise it to that degree of celebrity, which it soon attained. The improvement, in a few years, became rapid: he had, frequently, about forty students of Civil Law; while those who attended his Lectures on Government, often amounted to a much greater number. To establish and maintain the reputation <xii> of his classes, became with him the principal object of his life; and never, perhaps, was any object followed out with more ardour or perseverance. He was not merely desirous to convey to his students just views and accurate information; but he was anxious to convey them in the manner most likely to seize the attention, and to produce habits of original thought and philosophical investigation; thus rendering Lectures, formerly considered as useful only to lawyers, the most important schools of general education.

From the first establishment of the University, it had been the custom to employ the Latin language in all academical prelections; a custom originating in the exclusive admiration entertained of ancient literature, during the dark ages, and continued to later times, by the blind attachment of all public seminaries to old and antiquated forms. By degrees, it was discovered that every man will express his ideas with the greatest clearness and force in that language in which he is accustomed to think; and that an audience must lose much of the substance of a lecture, when part of the attention is necessarily occupied in estimating the exact import of the words. Such truths, obvious as they now appear, were but slowly received; but, at last, the practice of lecturing in English had been intro-<xiii>duced into the philosophical classes at Glasgow, and this alteration rendered it still more difficult for the students, now unaccustomed to follow the complicated arrangement of a Latin period, to comprehend, with facility and accuracy, the lectures on Roman Law, which still continued to be delivered in Latin. The old custom was however retained in those classes, after it had been laid aside in others, very possibly from some fancied propriety in lecturing on the Laws of Rome, in the language in which they had been promulgated

9. "(as a place for legal study);" appeared here in the third edition.

and compiled; and so wedded were the older members of the profession to this practice, that, when Mr. Lindsay (Mr. Millar's immediate predecessor) began to deliver lectures on the Institutes of Justinian, in English, the Faculty of Advocates made formal application to the University, requesting that the practice of teaching the Civil Law in Latin might be restored. Mr. Lindsay, with a steadiness which did him honour, refused to yield to this interference; and Mr. Millar, from the moment he was appointed to the Chair, adopted the English language in all the courses of lectures which he delivered. But, as Latin is still used in the customary trials, preparatory to a young man's being called to the Bar, he thought it proper to employ it in the daily <xiv> *examination* of the Civil Law classes, that his students might not be under the disadvantage of being altogether unaccustomed to the language in which the Faculty of Advocates still conduct their examinations.

Perhaps it is in some measure to the adoption of the English language in his several classes, that Mr. Millar owed part of his success. Had the same improvement been introduced at Edinburgh, it may, I think, be doubted whether his talents and utmost exertions could have raised the Law Classes of Glasgow from the low state to which they had fallen, and in which, from the absence of the Courts, they seemed destined to remain. But the Law Professors of Edinburgh, for a long time, continued to read their lectures in Latin, and, before they thought proper to abandon this custom, Mr. Millar's fame was too well established, and too widely diffused, to admit of any competition.

Mr. Millar never wrote his Lectures; but was accustomed to speak from notes, containing his arrangement, his chief topics, and some of his principal facts and illustrations. For the transitions from one part of his subject to another, the occasional allusions, the smaller embellishments, and the whole of the expression, he trusted to that extemporane-<xv>ous eloquence, which seldom fails a speaker deeply interested in his subject. In some branches of science, where the utmost precision of language is requisite to avoid obscurity or error, such a mode of lecturing may be attended with much difficulty, and several disadvantages: But in Morals, in Jurisprudence, in Law, and in Politics, if the Professor make himself completely master of the different topics he is to illustrate, if he possess ideas clear and defined, with tolerable facility in expressing them, the little inelegancies into which he may occasionally be betrayed, the slight hesitation which he may not always escape, will be much more than compensated by the fulness of his illustrations, the energy of his manner, and that interest which is excited, both in the hearer and speaker, by extemporaneous eloquence.

Lecturing is obviously more connected with public speaking than with writing. In a finished composition, we expect to find the author's arrangement accurate, his language correct and elegant, his ideas clearly and concisely expressed. Prolixity we regard as a fault both disagreeable and inexcusable; because, having his book before us, we can easily refer to any passage which we have forgotten or imperfectly comprehended, and thus <xvi> supply the defects of our memory or attention. In lecturing, the same rules will by no means apply. An idea must be turned on every side, that all its various connections may be perceived; it must be presented in a variety of lights, and a variety of forms, that, in some of them, it may be so fully impressed on the mind, as readily to recur when afterwards alluded to. For these purposes, it must be repeatedly urged with that earnestness of manner, which can seldom be commanded, in reading over, year after year, what was written at a distant period, and, probably, in a very different frame of mind. Those who were so fortunate as to witness the animation with which Mr. Millar delivered his Lectures, the delicacy with which he seemed to perceive when his audience fully understood his doctrines, the interest which he gave to subjects sometimes in themselves not very inviting, the clear conceptions that he conveyed, and the ardour of inquiry which he excited, will never hesitate to pronounce, that written lectures could not possibly have been so fascinating, or so instructive.

It is also a most important advantage attending extemporary lectures, that the Professor can, with ease to himself, follow the general progress of science, or insert the occasional results of his own <xvii> private investigations. The trouble of making alterations on written lectures is apt, on the contrary, to deter from future inquiry, and even to prevent the correction of acknowledged error. He who has, with much labour, transcribed a system of lectures sufficient for his regular course, can neither omit nor insert a topic, without extending or condensing some other department of his subject; he can change none of his principles, without altering his inferences, and expunging many allusions that may occur in other parts of his course; he can neither adopt new opinions, nor admit new facts, without inserting new conclusions, and new modifications of his other doctrines. Such a revision of written opinions will usually be found too great a task for human exertion; and the lectures will continue to be delivered with all their original imperfections. In the mean time, some of the students, more industrious than the rest, will perceive that the professor seems ignorant of what has been published on the science which he pretends to teach; the secret will soon be whispered round the class; and all respect for his talents and information will be irrecoverably gone. But an extemporaneous lecturer can alter, modify, and improve his system, with little comparative trouble. The addition of a few lines, <xviii> the expunging of a few words, even a particular mark upon the margin of his note book, will enable him to correct any errors into which he may have fallen, and to add whatever important discoveries have been made by himself or others. Accordingly, in Mr. Millar's notes, now before me, I find some pages effaced, many references, and many leaves inserted; and, from a distinct recollection of particular conversations, I can decidedly assert, that, although he delivered the same courses of Lectures for forty years, many improvements were made, many important disquisitions were introduced, within a very short period of his death.

Not satisfied with explaining his opinions in the most perspicuous manner in his Lecture, Mr. Millar encouraged such of the students as had not fully comprehended his doctrines, or conceived that there was some error in his reasonings, to state to him their difficulties and objections. With this view, at the conclusion of the Lecture, a little circle of his most attentive pupils was formed around him, when the doctrines which had been delivered were canvassed with the most perfect freedom. Before a professor can admit of such a practice, he must be completely master of his subject, and have acquired some confidence in his own quickness at refuting objections, and detecting sophistry. A few instan-<xix>ces of defeat might be injurious to his reputation, and to the discipline of the class. But, should he possess a clear comprehension of all the bearings of his system, joined to quickness of understanding and tolerable ease of expression, he will derive the most important advantages from the unrestrained communications of his pupils.

He will learn where he has failed to convey his ideas with accuracy, where he has been too concise, or where imperfect analogies have led him into slight mistakes; and he will easily find a future opportunity to introduce new illustrations, to explain what has been misapprehended, or correct what was really an error. To the students, such a practice insures accurate knowledge; it teaches the important lesson of considering opinions before adopting them, and gives an additional incitement to strict and vigilant attention. Accordingly, to be able to state difficulties with propriety, was justly looked upon by the more ingenious and attentive students as no slight proof of proficiency; and to be an active and intelligent member of the fire-side committee, never failed to give a young man some consideration among his companions.

The proper business of the Professorship to which Mr. Millar was appointed, is to deliver Lectures on the Institutions and Pandects of Justinian. <xx> But the employment of a whole winter in tracing, with the utmost accuracy and tedious erudition, the exact line of Roman Law, seemed to him a mere waste of time and study. Whatever it was useful to know of the Institutes, he thought might be sufficiently taught in the half of the session, or term; and he wished to devote the rest of it to a course of Lectures on Jurisprudence. After, therefore, going over the Institutes, according to the arrangement of Heineccius,[10] and explaining the nature and origin of each particular right as it occurred, he began a new course of Lectures, in which he treated of such general principles of Law as pervade the codes of all nations, and have their origin in those sentiments of justice which are imprinted on the human heart.

The multifarious doctrines to be explained in the Pandects prevented him from shortening the time allotted for that branch of legal study; but, aware that the ordinary arrangement is confused, and almost unintelligible, he soon published a new syllabus, following very nearly the order of the Institutes, according to which he discussed the various and sometimes discordant laws of Rome, and the still more discordant opinions of Roman lawyers. In these two courses, he gave every information that could be desired on Civil Law, <xxi> whether considered as merely an object of literary

10. See the introduction.

curiosity, or as the basis of modern Law, and consequently a most useful commentary on the municipal systems of the greater part of Europe.

These Lectures, which most men would have found sufficient to engross all their time, and occupy all their attention, still left Mr. Millar some leisure, which he thought he could not employ more usefully, than in giving a course of Lectures on Government.[11] As this class occupied an hour only three times a week, he was afterwards induced to appropriate the same hour, on two other days, to the teaching of Scotch Law, a branch of study useful to every Scotchman, and particularly necessary to a number of young men, who had no other opportunity of becoming acquainted with the principles of that profession, which they were afterwards to exercise. The class of Scotch Law he thought it sufficient to teach every second year.

A few years before his death, Mr. Millar was led, by the attention he always paid to the advantage of his pupils, to prepare and deliver a course of Lectures on English Law. In this course it could not be expected that he should convey more information than is contained in the best authors; but he greatly simplified and improved the arrange-<xxii>ment, and accounted for the various rules and even fictions of English Law, in a manner more satisfactory, than by vague analogies, or that last resource of ignorance, an unmeaning reference to the pretended wisdom of our ancestors.

It would be uninteresting to many of my readers, were I to enter into details respecting the Lectures on Roman, Scotch, or English Law; but Jurisprudence and Politics are sciences so important to all, and so instructive in the views they exhibit of human nature, that a slight sketch of Mr. Millar's manner of treating these subjects may not, perhaps, be unacceptable. Some view of these Lectures seems indeed the more requisite, as they were, in a great measure, the foundation of his high reputation; and, having never been committed to writing, they cannot now, in any perfect form, be submitted to the public. In attempting this sketch, I shall merely give an idea of the general principles and order, according to which he proceeded to investigate these most important sciences, passing slightly over the numerous and very ingenious disquisitions to which they naturally led, and omitting many important doctrines which he established on the firm basis

11. For a partial listing of the contents of the course, see appendix 3.

of justice, and the public good. To enter fully into the subject, would not be so much to give an account of Mr. Millar's <xxiii> life, as to write a number of treatises on what are at once the most abstruse, and most useful, branches of Law, Government, and Political economy.

The Ancients seem never to have thought of delineating a general system of laws founded on the principles of justice, independent of such modifications as have been produced, in each particular country, by circumstances not universally applicable to mankind. This important branch of science was reserved for the moderns, among whom Grotius is the first and most eminent author, who took a view of the subject so general and extended. He has been succeeded by a multitude of later writers, most of whom, however, may be considered rather as his commentators than as original authors. A science, promising such benefits to mankind, required only to be pointed out in order to excite the attention of the learned; it spread rapidly over the whole of Europe, and soon became an established branch of education in many Universities.

It was, indeed, a most important step in the advancement of legal study. By displaying to mankind an ideal perfection of Law, which, if attained, must have secured their prosperity and happi-<xxiv>ness, it furnished them with a standard by which the particular institutions of each country might be examined and corrected; and, by exhibiting the frequent deviations of municipal law from such a standard, it weakened that blind admiration of old and local usages, which is the great sanctifier of abuses, the most dangerous enemy of truth. The systems of Universal Law, however, which at different times have been given to the world, seem liable to several objections. They could be illustrated in no other way than by reference to particular laws, so intimately blended with other regulations, and with peculiar customs and manners, that the reasoning lost much of its universal character, and often assumed the appearance of dissertation on the institutions of an individual nation. For the most part, the writers on Jurisprudence followed too closely the system of Roman Law, even where that system is defective; but sometimes, also, in endeavouring to avoid this error, they entered so imperfectly into legal details, that their conclusions appeared vague and inaccurate.

It may farther be objected to almost all the writers on jurisprudence, that they have insisted too much on what a man, in a particular situation, *ought* to do, rather than on what he can justly be *compelled* to do; thus confounding the important distinction <xxv> between Ethics and Law, and forgetting that, though the one be a branch of the other, it is necessary to keep their respective limits strictly in view, if we would establish any system of rules for the conduct of individuals which society has a title to enforce. From the disregard of this distinction, systems of jurisprudence came to resemble systems of morals in almost every thing, except their being treated in a more formal, and far less interesting manner.

A new branch of study displayed itself to the capacious mind of Montesquieu. By considering the various and important deviations from the standards of jurisprudence observable in the laws of every state, he was led to compare together the different nations among whom similar deviations may be discerned; to contrast their situation with that of other countries where the laws have an opposite bias; and thus, from an extended view of human nature, to deduce the causes of those differences in laws, customs, and institutions, which, previously, had been remarked merely as isolated and uninstructive facts. In this inquiry he had been followed by many philosophers, in different parts of Europe, and by none more successfully than our countrymen, Lord Kames and Dr. Smith, the former in tracing the history of manners and <xxvi> of private law, the latter in delineating the progress of public institutions.

Mr. Millar, in his Lectures, conjoined those separate views of jurisprudence. He began by investigating the origin and foundation of each right in the natural principles of justice; and afterwards traced its progress through the different conditions of mankind; marking such deviations from the general rule as the known circumstances of particular nations might be expected to occasion, and accounting, in the most satisfactory manner, for those diversities in laws, which must otherwise have appeared irreconcilable with the idea that there is any thing stable or precise in the moral sentiments of mankind.

As a preparation for this course of inquiry, it was obviously necessary to investigate the principles of Moral Approbation. On this subject, Mr. Hume and Dr. Smith have written treatises, equally eloquent and ingenious; and, to Mr. Millar, little appeared to be wanting, but to combine their systems.

Both of these philosophers have shewn, by a very extensive induction, that whatever is considered as useful, to ourselves or others, gives us pleasure; whatever is thought detrimental, gives us pain. This is the case, whether the good or evil be produced <xxvii> by inanimate objects, or by sentient beings; but when by the latter, the pleasure, excited by the perception of increased happiness, is connected with a feeling of good-will towards the agent; and the pain, arising from the perception of hurt or injury, is attended with a sentiment of dislike. Whether the good or evil may affect ourselves or others, we never fail to experience such sentiments; where our own good is promoted, we feel direct pleasure and gratitude; where the good of others is increased, we experience a reflected or sympathetic pleasure and gratitude, exactly the same in their nature, though always weaker in degree.

The direct good, or evil, proceeding from an action, is often of less real importance to general happiness than such remote consequences as are neither intended by the agent, nor directly observable by the spectator. Every breach of duty, besides occasioning immediate evil, weakens the influence of those general rules, by which, while exposed to temptations, the virtuous regulate their conduct; and every crime that is unpunished tends to destroy the strongest barrier which human society can oppose to vice. But such remote and contingent results of actions, though they exert a powerful influence on our moral sentiments, do <xxviii> not affect us equally with their more direct and obvious effects. We enter more readily into what is immediately present to us, than into general and distant consequences, which it requires much experience and attention to discover, and some effort of imagination to delineate. Existing and present happiness makes a lively impression; future and contingent utility is more faintly and obscurely felt.

Although the system of utility thus accounts for much of our moral sentiments, Mr. Millar was convinced, that, by itself, it could afford no satisfactory solution of many difficulties suggested by the experience of mankind. The sentiment of approbation arising from utility seems cold and languid, when compared with the warm burst of applause sometimes excited by a virtuous action; an applause, too, which bears no proportion to that experience and knowledge, which might enable the spectator to grasp all the distant consequences of the action, but frequently is most enthusiastic in the young and ignorant. Nor does the degree, in which we approve of the different classes of virtues,[12] correspond to the respective degrees of utility; Prudence is, in most situations, a more useful, though certainly a less admired quality, than Courage; and Justice, the most essential of all the vir-<xxix>tues to human welfare, meets with less rapturous applause than irregular, and perhaps thoughtless, Generosity.

What was thus defective in the theory of utility seemed to Mr. Millar, in a great measure, to be supplied, by the systems which found our approbation of virtue on the sentiment of Propriety. We approve of such actions as we are led to expect from the particular circumstances in which the agent is placed, of such as appear to us agreeable to the general standard of human nature; and, as any remarkable deviation from the ordinary figure of the human body is disgusting, so are we displeased with any remarkable deviation from the constitution of the human mind. These sentiments of approbation and dislike have, by some authors, been referred to the influence of Custom; but they seem too steady and regular in their operations, to be the offspring of what is so very capricious. It is true that custom may bestow a higher applause on particular classes of virtues than, in themselves, they deserve; that it may diminish the abhorrence of certain vices, by rendering them objects of more cursory observation; that it may even reconcile us to flagitious crimes, which, from particular circumstances, we have associated with some of the higher <xxx> virtues; but all such effects of custom are merely to modify, and that in a smaller degree than is usually apprehended, the other sentiments of moral approbation springing from more regular sources.

Dr. Smith has given a most ingenious and eloquent account of our sentiments of propriety, which he derives from the pleasure of Sympathy with the feelings of the agent.[13] He has shewn, in the most satisfactory manner, that the perception of the coincidence of our own sentiments with those of others, is always attended with an exquisite enjoyment; and that the

---

12. Appeared as "different classes of their virtues" in the third edition.
13. Cf. Adam Smith, *Theory of Moral Sentiments,* vol. 1.

appearance of any repugnance between our feelings and those of our fellow-men is productive of disgust. Not only is this true with regard to moral sentiment, but in every taste, opinion, and emotion. Hence the charms of pure and disinterested friendship, and the difficulty of continuing an intimate intercourse with those who, on subjects of much interest and frequent occurrence, think very differently from ourselves. It is in judging of human conduct, however, that this principle acts its most important part. When our attention is called to the behaviour of another, we immediately conceive how we should have acted in similar circumstances; and, according as our sentiments do, or do not, correspond to those he <xxxi> has discovered, we feel pleasure and approbation, or pain and dislike. Nor are these moral feelings liable to any important irregularities. When removed from temptation, and free from the influence of passion, all men are brave, temperate, just, and generous; consequently, these virtues must always appear proper, and the opposite vices improper, to the unconcerned spectator.

Mr. Millar fully adopted this opinion of Dr. Smith; but still he thought the system would prove defective, unless more weight were given to an observation which had been stated, rather in a cursory manner, both by that author and Mr. Hume. The degree of applause excited by virtue is not dependent solely on the propriety and utility of the action, but also on the difficulty which we know the agent must have overcome, and the mental energy which he has displayed, in reducing his feelings to the level of those of the unconcerned spectator. The passions, in many cases, being slightly affected, a small exertion is sufficient; in other situations, the utmost effort of self-command is indispensible: The one we simply approve; the other we applaud and admire. In this view, our moral sentiments bear a striking analogy to the principles of taste; and, though Mr. Millar did not admit that intimate and necessary connection between them which has <xxxii> been asserted by an eminent author,* he traced, with much ingenuity, and much felicity of illustration, the likeness which exists, both between the

---

* Lord Kames, in the Introduction to the Elements of Criticism. [["[A] taste in fine arts goes hand in hand with the moral sense" (Henry Home, Lord Kames, *Elements of Criticism*, 3rd ed. [Edinburgh, 1765], 5).]]

sentiments themselves, and the means by which they are excited. That virtue which is new or extraordinary in its nature, which breaks forth when we expect and dread the opposite vice, which exhibits high powers of self-control, and produces some great and striking benefit to man, raises our admiration to sublimity and rapture; while a life spent in acts of beneficence and kindness, like a rich and beautiful landscape, excites the more gentle emotions of complacence and delight.

Such are the outlines of the analysis of our moral sentiments, according to which Mr. Millar accounted for the various rights acknowledged and protected by society. In doing this, he was careful to separate and distinguish Justice from the other virtues. The rules of Justice,[14] he observed, are satisfied, when a man abstains from injuring others, although he should make no addition whatever to general or particular happiness. He who fails in prudence, in temperance, in courage, or beneficence, may become an object of dislike; he may destroy his own happiness, and disregard many <xxxiii> opportunities of promoting that of others; but, having done no direct injury, he can scarcely become the object of general indignation. The infringement of the rules of Justice, on the other hand, never fails to excite resentment in the breast of the person injured, and indignation in that of the spectators;—an indignation, sometimes satisfied with the redress of the wrong, sometimes demanding the infliction of farther pain or mortification on the delinquent. At the same time, he who has thus subjected himself to merited punishment, can never complain of a sentence, which his own conscience must approve, or pretend that he was not aware of the natural consequence of his crimes. The rules of conduct prescribed by Justice, unlike the dictates of the other virtues, are always clear and precise. Frequently it may be a matter of some difficulty to determine what measure, in the particular circumstances of the case, may be most prudent or most beneficent; but never can any person be at a loss to know, when he deliberately diminishes the comforts or enjoyments of others, or be unconscious, that by so doing, he renders himself the object of merited punishment. For these reasons, it is on the virtue of Justice, and on that virtue alone, that

14. Appeared as "The rules of virtue" in the third edition.

Laws, the object of which is to maintain <xxxiv> rights and repress injuries, must be altogether founded.

General systems of Law have rarely, if ever, been formed by the prospective wisdom of legislators, but have arisen gradually, and almost insensibly, from the slow progress of human experience. When a dispute has taken place between two individuals, the spectators will naturally assist him, with whose motives they sympathize; who seeks no undue advantage, but merely wishes to retain what, without loss to others, is already in his possession. They will disapprove of the conduct and motives of that person, who, disregarding the good of his fellow-men, seeks his own advantage by the direct injury of another, and they will perceive that, by preventing his intentions, they take nothing from those comforts, which, with innocence, he can command. Between two such competitors for the possession of any object, there being no room for hesitation, the spectators are led immediately to interfere, and prevent injustice. Being also sensible that they themselves are liable to similar wrongs, against which a general combination is the only effectual protection, they are farther prompted to such an interference, by a species of self-interest. Such simple and obvious considerations must occur to <xxxv> men even in the rudest state of society; and, in Mr. Millar's opinion, they sufficiently account for that general resemblance, which may be discovered in the laws of all countries, however different in their circumstances, or remote in their situations. It was therefore to such simple ideas, not to great and extended views of policy, that he traced the origin of the different recognised rights of individuals, and on such universal feelings, that he established their justice.

But, when we examine more particularly the laws and customs of different countries, we are struck with a diversity, and even opposition, among their regulations, which might almost lead us to suspect, that different nations, had been influenced, by opposite, and inconsistent, principles of Morals.

A nearer inspection, however, will convince us, that these diversities, important as they certainly are, may frequently arise from diversities no less striking in the conditions of different nations. Some tribes, drawing a precarious subsistence from hunting and fishing, and improvident for futurity, seem scarcely raised above the rank of irrational beings: Others, having learned to domesticate particular animals, are exempted from the danger of immediate want, yet forced to wander from place to place, in search of the spontaneous productions <xxxvi> of the earth: Those who inhabit a country of greater fertility, or who have discovered the means of improving fertility by labour, relinquishing their wandering habits, trust for their subsistence to the more certain resources of agriculture: From particular situation, or gradual discovery, some nations are led to meliorate, by human art, the rude produce of the soil, or to exchange their superfluous commodities for other, and to them more desirable, means of enjoyment: Distinctions of professions, and of ranks, are introduced; new sources of gratification are discovered; new wants excite to new exertions; the human mind is cultivated and expanded; and man rises to the highest pitch of civilization and refinement.

It were surely unreasonable to expect that, during all these successive changes, the laws should remain the same. Rules are gradually multiplied, as inconveniencies are felt, as new modes of injustice are detected; and such rules, simple and inartificial at first, are gradually modified and rendered more complex, by the subterfuges and evasions of fraud, as well as by the more general views of utility suggested by extensive experience and improved habits of reasoning.

These observations, however, Mr. Millar considered as but one step in his proposed inquiry; for among <xxxvii> nations advanced very nearly to the same degree of civilization, very opposite laws often prevail. This may frequently be accounted for by accurate observation of the real line of progress, which these different nations have described. All have not passed through exactly the same stages of improvement; all have not advanced with equal rapidity; some have remained long stationary at an early period of their course; while others, hurrying on with rapid strides at first, have appeared to repose for a while at a more advanced station, from which they have again proceeded with increased celerity and vigour. From whatever circumstances of soil, climate, or situation, such differences may have arisen, they must be attended with corresponding differences in the rules of law. The powerful effect of custom is discernible in all the institutions of man. Those views to which he has long been habituated he does not easily relinquish; those laws from which he has long derived protection he does not easily perceive to be defective. The rude institutions of a nation, which has remained stationary at any particular stage of improvement, become so rooted in the habits of the people, and in the opinions even of legislators, that it is long before a change of circumstances can produce any correspondent <xxxviii> change upon the laws. It was thus that the Patria Potestas, originating in very rude ideas, maintained its ground even during the most civilized times of Rome:* and thus the Feudal law, adapted to a state of society which has long ceased to exist, still continues to regulate the landed property of Scotland.

But besides the direct tendency of the progress of civilization to alter and modify the Laws, it has an indirect influence, still more important. In another course of Lectures (which I shall soon have occasion to mention more particularly), Mr. Millar had traced the natural progress of Government, as arising from the most obvious views of utility, as improved and varied by the advancement of a community, from the state of a rude horde to that of a civilized nation, and as influenced by many circumstances both of general and of particular application. He had, at the same time, pointed out the various distributions of Property that took place; the various distinctions of Ranks; the innumerable diversities of Public Opinion, of Public Institutions, and of National Character. All these varieties, from whatever circumstances they proceed, cannot fail to oc-<xxxix>casion endless diversities in systems of Law. But, by an attentive inquirer the causes of such diversities may usually be discovered; and thus all anomalies of Law will be explained, and the uniformity of our moral principles established, by an examination of what, at first view, has the appearance of irreconcileable contradiction.

It was on these principles, that Mr. Millar proceeded in the investigation of the Origin and History of private Rights. He rejected, as fabulous, the great and sudden alterations said to have been introduced by particular legislators, or at least he reduced such interpositions to a mere modification of what must have been occasioned by the circumstances of the times; and he doubted, if he did not altogether discredit, those wonderful effects that have been ascribed to the *direct* operation of climate on the human mind.

* See the Origin of the Distinction of Ranks, Chap. II. Sect. II.

I shall only add to the reasons he himself has assigned for these opinions,*
that, by accounting from moral causes for the varieties which occur between
the codes of different nations, he rendered unnecessary and unphilosoph-
ical, all historical assertions resting on <xl> questionable authority, and all
assumed physical affections of the human mind, from their own nature,
incapable of proof; substituting for such gratuitous hypothesis, a simple
and universal theory, founded on the acknowledged nature of man, and
capable of receiving confirmation from the whole history of the human
race.

A system of Jurisprudence, embracing so many and such important disquisitions, reducing such apparently discordant facts in human nature to a
few simple principles, and exemplifying the operation of our moral sentiments in such a variety of situations and circumstances, is surely one of
the noblest efforts of the mind of man: Nor can any branch of education
be considered as more important. While, by the richness of its illustrations,
the variety of its facts, and the unexpected simplicity of its results, it fixes
the attention, and delights the imagination; it accustoms the student to an
accuracy of discrimination, and a generalisation of ideas, which are the
surest characteristics of a philosophic mind. But, unconfined in their operations to a few individuals, the effects of studies so conducted may often be
extended to the welfare of nations. By proving that no institutions, however
just in themselves, can be either expedient or permanent, if inconsistent
with established ranks, <xli> manners, and opinions, a system of Jurisprudence checks inconsiderate innovation, and indiscriminate reform; while,
on the other hand, it points out, to the enlightened Legislator, such parts
of the municipal code, as, introduced during ruder times, have remained
in force, long after the circumstances from which they arose have ceased to
exist, and directs him in the noble, but arduous, attempt, to purify and
improve the laws of his country.

---

* In the Introduction to the Origin of the Distinction of Ranks. With regard to the
direct effects of climate on the human mind, see Hume's Essays, Moral, Political, and
Literary, Part I. Essay XXI. [["Of National Characters," in David Hume, *Essays, Moral,
Political, and Literary,* rev. ed., ed. Eugene V. Miller (Indianapolis: Liberty Fund, 1985),
197–215. Passages from Hume's *Essays* are cited by essay number and paragraph number
as well as page number.]]

The investigation of the Nature and History of the several rights, subsisting between Individuals, called Mr. Millar's attention to another species of rights, those subsisting between different Orders, and Classes, of the community. The former are so remarkably modified by the latter, that, in his Lectures on Jurisprudence, he had very frequently found it necessary, to give some explanation of the principles, according to which, distinguished powers and privileges are committed to particular persons: but this he had always done in as concise a manner as was consistent with perspicuity. The origin and progress of authority seemed to demand a more detailed investigation, than could <xlii> be introduced into his other Lectures, and promised to open up both an amusing and very useful field of inquiry.

To many of his students, indeed, who, without any intention of becoming practical lawyers, had been sent to the University, as to a seminary of liberal education, a course of Lectures on Public Law seemed more important than on almost any other science. In a free country, every man may be said to be born a politician; and the higher classes of society, those who chiefly resort to Universities as general students, are frequently obliged, by their situation in life, to give opinions on various subjects of Government, which may have considerable influence on the welfare of their country. To them a knowledge of Public Law must be an object of the first importance, whether they look forward to the degree of estimation in which they would wish to be held in their respective counties, or listen to the voice of honourable ambition, which calls them to add lustre to their names, by defending the rights and augmenting the happiness of their fellow-men. With the view of being serviceable to this class of Students, and, at the same time, with the conviction that a knowledge of Public Law is essential to a just and liberal conception <xliii> of the rules of the Municipal Code, Mr. Millar paid very particular attention to the course of Lectures on Government; introducing whatever disquisitions, connected with his subject, he thought likely to awaken curiosity, or illustrate the general principles of his theory. Hence he indulged himself in many speculations on Manners, on National Character, Literature, and the Fine Arts, which, though arising naturally from his subject, and intimately related to it, both by their influence on the theory of Government, and their tendency to illustrate the general progress of improvement in man, might, in some points of view, be considered as digressions.

The order which Mr. Millar had followed in his Lectures on Jurisprudence was not, in its full extent, applicable to the subject of Government. In private rights, a very considerable uniformity may be traced in the regulations of all countries, arrived at the same stage of improvement. The same associations, and the same obvious views of utility, suggest to all very similar laws; and though, indeed, many diversities, and some contrarieties may be observed, yet the general rule is always apparent, and the exceptions may usually be traced, by a short investigation, to a few circumstances peculiar to those countries in which they have occurred. <xliv>

But, in looking to the governments that have existed in the world, little of a similar uniformity appears. So many circumstances, besides the gradual improvement of mankind, have influenced the distribution of political power, and these circumstances are so various in their nature, so complicated in their mutual relations, that, on a cursory view, every thing seems irregular and anomalous; and it is only by a careful survey of the history of each nation, that the causes of its particular institutions can be discovered.

In treating of Jurisprudence, the most convenient and most philosophical arrangement was, to state the origin and history of each several right, explaining, as they occurred, the most remarkable deviations from the general rules. But, had the same method been followed in the Lectures on Government, the digressions to the circumstances, and institutions, of particular nations, must have been so frequent, and so minute, that, all traces of uniform principle being lost, the course would have appeared a series of partial and unconnected disquisitions.

Influenced, as is probable, by such considerations, Mr. Millar divided the course of Lectures on Government into three parts. <xlv>

I. He began with what Mr. Stewart has called a *theoretical or conjectural history* of government,* tracing its natural progress, according to the gradual civilization of mankind. In this part of his course, he noticed the modifications arising from circumstances of extensive influence; from the fertility of the soil; the extent and population of the state; the condition of surrounding nations; the exposure to attack; the facility of making great or

* Life of Dr. Smith, page 34. [[*Essays on Philosophical Subjects,* 293.]]

permanent conquests: But he treated the subject generally, without any farther reference to the history of particular nations than was necessary to
explain and illustrate his system.

The different conditions in which mankind have been discovered, Mr.
Millar, with other authors, divided into four; the state of Hunters and Fishers; the Pastoral state; the Agricultural; and the Commercial.[15] He was far
from meaning to assert, that every nation, which has arrived at a high state
of improvement, must have passed, successively, through all these conditions. He knew well that narrowness of territory might prevent even an
inconsiderable tribe from existing by hunting, and force them to have recourse to the rearing of cattle; that a mild and fertile region, by the abundance of <xlvi> its spontaneous productions, might induce a preference of
grain and roots to animal food, which must be acquired by exertion, and
preserved by care; that an ungrateful soil might very early turn the attention
of a people inhabiting an island or bay to piracy or commerce; that, above
all, great and extensive conquests sometimes made the most rapid change
on the condition of the conquerors, and of the conquered. But he adopted
the ordinary division as the most convenient for suggesting and introducing
the various changes recorded on human institutions and manners; and,
while the progress which it assumed had the advantage of leading from the
simple to the more complex views of human society, he considered it,
though not universal, as probably the most general course of improvement
which could be traced in history.

In each of those stages of society, he examined the powers which were
likely to be placed in the hands of the Sovereign, and in those of the Nobility; the privileges which might probably be asserted by the People; and
the Judicial establishments naturally resulting from the distinction of ranks,
and distribution of property and power. He was particularly careful to mark
the variations which occurred, when a nation passed from one of those
conditions to another; and he noticed the various modifica-<xlvii>tions
arising from circumstances of such extensive operation, as to be reducible
to general rules.

Mr. Millar was well aware that, in the early part of the progress of man-

15. Adam Smith and Lord Kames. See the introduction.

kind, he could find few authentic materials for his theoretical history; but this defect was in some measure compensated, by the similarity of the public institutions of savage nations, in different parts of the world, and by the general agreement of travellers in describing the very few features which form their characters. As he proceeded, his authorities became more full, and more precise; while the discordances between the manners and institutions of different countries becoming also more important, made it necessary for him to enter more minutely into details, and to point out many distinctions, and many modifications of his general doctrines. In the commercial state, in particular, it was requisite to enumerate very fully the circumstances, which, on the one hand, exalted the power of the sovereign, and, on the other, raised up a spirit of independence among the people; as it depended altogether on the early prevalence of the one or the other, whether a despotical or free Government should be established or maintained.

Having followed the progress of civilization and government, till they reached the greatest perfec-<xlviii>tion of which we have experience, Mr. Millar examined, at some length, the question, whether this advancement can be continued without end, or whether, from the nature of human affairs, it be not subjected to certain limitations. Of those nations, which have sunk from riches and power to poverty and insignificance, the downfall has been occasioned, either by despotical government, a casual effect of opulence which may probably be corrected by the greater diffusion of knowledge, or by the inroads of barbarians now guarded against by the balance of power, and the improvements of modern tactics. Neither did Mr. Millar conceive that the high wages of labour, arising from the general diffusion of wealth, could so far counterbalance the advantages resulting from superior capital, from improved machinery, and from the division of labour, as to enable a poor nation to outstrip a richer, in the commercial competition. In none of those causes usually assigned for the decay of opulent states, did he see any reason for believing that there are fixed impassable limits to the improvement of man. But, in examining the changes produced by wealth on the national character, he was struck with that sordid love of gain, that exclusive attention to individual interests, which debase the character of man, and under-<xlix>mine the generous enthusiasm for the public welfare, on which alone Public Liberty can securely rest. Even without Patriotism, he did not deny that, by wise institutions, a semblance of Freedom might long be preserved; but this he considered as a mere phantom, always liable to disappear, through the arts of the court, or the blind fury of the populace. Nor did it escape his observation, that a very great diffusion of wealth has a tendency to impair those habits of active industry, on which the successful cultivation of the ordinary arts of life altogether depends. Should any such relaxation of industry take place, a relaxation which the influence of imitation and fashion may extend from the higher to the lower orders of society, it cannot fail very speedily to be followed by poverty and vice, with their usual concomitants, servility and oppression: neither can this deterioration be checked, while the profligate habits, occasioned by the former affluence of the country, continue to prevail.

This part of the course Mr. Millar concluded with a detailed examination of the principles which produce the idea of obligation in submitting to Government. He dismissed, as scarcely worthy of refutation, the doctrines of Divine Right; but he was at some pains to enforce Mr. Hume's objections <l> to the fiction of an Original Compact, long the favourite opinion of English Whigs.* He referred the origin of the Rights of Government, partly to the natural deference for abilities, birth, and wealth, which he denominated the principle of authority; partly to obvious and powerful considerations of utility. His opinions on this subject are very distinctly stated in a posthumous publication, to which I shall refer the reader.†

II. This theoretical history of Mankind was followed by a survey of the particular forms of Government, established in the principal countries, of ancient and modern times; which, while it illustrated the principles that had been explained, pointed out many causes of deviation from the general system. Of the constitutional history of each of those nations, Mr. Millar gave a rapid sketch, in which, without omitting any thing material or fundamental, he passed slightly over the less important, or what may be con-

---

* See Hume's Essays, Part I. Essay 5. [["Of the Original Contract," in Hume, *Essays, Moral, Political, and Literary,* 465–87.]]

† See the Historical View of the English Government, Vol. IV. chap. 7.

sidered as the technical, forms of their several Governments. His object
was to delineate the successive changes that took place in each of these
States; to shew how their Governments had arisen; what altera-<li>tions
they had undergone during the progress of improvement; and in what manner these alterations had been produced by the peculiar circumstances in
which they were respectively placed.

In this Review, the Athenian Government naturally attracted his attention, by its admirable effects in exalting the powers of Intellect, and in
refining, to a degree hitherto unexampled, those of Taste. In another respect, also, it merited particular examination. From the barrenness of Attica, and the convenience of its harbours, the inhabitants, even before making any considerable advances in agriculture, had become first pirates, and
afterwards merchants. A similar progress might probably have occurred in
several other states of antiquity; but the memorials of such nations are few
and mutilated, while the history of Athens has been transmitted to our
times with uncommon accuracy and fulness. That country, therefore, he
considered as one of the few instances in which the influence of early commerce on national character, and on the structure and genius of the government, may be duly appreciated.

In treating of Sparta, Mr. Millar examined, in detail, those regulations
which are commonly ascribed to Lycurgus;[16] proving them to have been
such as would naturally prevail in a country which <lii> had long remained
in a rude condition, and indeed very similar to customs and institutions
which may be found in other parts of the world. He was ready to allow
that Lycurgus might, in some respects, improve the Laws, and perhaps, by
his personal influence, give superior stability to the Institutions of his country; but he ascribed their duration chiefly to particular circumstances, such
as constant wars, and inattention to commerce, which, keeping Sparta poor
and barbarous, confirmed her early customs, by the force of habit.

The Roman Government Mr. Millar considered at greater length, on
account, both of the superior importance of that state, and of the more
accurate information which has come down to us respecting its Laws and
Institutions. That Government, too, seemed particularly deserving of at-

16. Semimythical founder of the Spartan legal code.

tention, because the Roman Law has been the foundation of almost all the modern Codes, and is still appealed to, as decisive authority, in the silence of the municipal regulations of modern Europe.

To these Lectures may be applied Mr. Millar's own remark, on what might have been expected from the Treatises Dr. Smith once proposed to write on the Greek and Roman Republics. "After all that has been published on that subject, his <liii> observations suggested many new and important views, concerning the internal and domestic circumstances of those nations, which displayed their several systems of policy, in a light much less artificial, than that in which they have hitherto appeared."*

In the institutions of Modern Europe, a much greater similarity may be traced, than in the Governments of ancient states. All the kingdoms of the south of Europe, were founded by rude shepherds, overrunning extensive tracts of cultivated country, and incorporating with the civilized inhabitants of the Roman Provinces. All those barbarians, bringing with them similar institutions, and making similar conquests, established political systems, in their principal features, very nearly alike. Previously, therefore, to delineating any of the Governments of modern Europe, Mr. Millar thought it useful, to give a general picture of the whole; and, in doing so, he found it convenient to separate the Civil from the Ecclesiastical Jurisdiction; a distinction unnecessary in treating of the ancient Governments, but important respecting those of modern times.

It would carry me too far, were I to attempt to <liv> give any account of Mr. Millar's original and ingenious speculations, respecting the Feudal system: I shall merely remark, that he steered a middle course between the older Antiquarians, who conceived that the system of Tenures was completed soon after the settlement of the barbarians, and the partizans of the more modern opinion, that the whole lands were originally held allodially, and that Fiefs were introduced entirely by subsequent resignations.† Nor

---

* See Mr. Stewart's Life of Dr. Smith, page 36. [[*Essays on Philosophical Subjects,* 295.]]
    † Some account of Mr. Millar's views of the feudal system may be found in the Origin of the Distinction of Ranks, chap. IV. and V. They are much more fully illustrated in the Historical view of the English Government, where his opinions, respecting the progress of Ecclesiastical Jurisdiction, are also detailed. [[See *An Historical View,* II:4.]]

shall I attempt to follow him in his very masterly sketch of the rise, elevation, and decline, of Ecclesiastical Power.

Having taken a general survey of the constitutional history of Modern Europe, both in Church and State, Mr. Millar entered upon a particular examination of the Governments of France, Germany, and England; concluding this part of his course with a rapid view of the Histories of Scotland, and of Ireland. Here, it is unnecessary for me to attempt to follow him; as he has laid before the public the historical view of the English Government, which will sufficiently evince the saga-<lv>city of research, and the comprehensiveness of view, which so eminently characterised these Disquisitions.

III. The History of the British Government led, by a very natural transition, to an account of the Constitution, as settled at the Revolution in 1688, which formed the third branch of these Lectures. To this, indeed, the other parts of the course might be considered as in some degree subordinate. However curious and instructive speculations on the progress of Government may be, their chief use is to suggest different views, and various comparisons, by which we may estimate the advantages of our present institutions, and thence be led to venerate and support what is excellent, to correct and improve whatever may be defective.

In this important part of the Lectures, Mr. Millar entered with a minuteness, which renders it impossible for me, in this short essay, to give even an outline of his opinions, into the consideration of all the parts of the British Government; occasionally relieving the dryness of detail, by remarks, and even discussions, on the advantages of the present system; on the dangers to which it is exposed; and on such means of improvement as are consistent with the present state of manners and opinions, and with those established distinc-<lvi>tions of Rank which it is often unjust, and always hazardous, to abolish. Animated by the love of his country, he delivered his opinions openly and explicitly; opinions equally removed, on the one hand, from courtly servility, and on the other, from unbending republicanism. After discussing the constitution and rights of Parliament, the privileges of the several branches of the legislature, and the ministerial or executive powers of the Crown, he entered, at considerable length, into the detail of the Judicial establishments in England and in Scotland; concluding with a short comparison between them, in which, with what by many will be thought a Scottish prejudice, he, upon the whole, seemed to give the preference to those of his own country.

From the very slight sketch which I have now given of these Lectures, their high importance will be sufficiently apparent. Though nothing un-interesting was introduced, they comprehended a greater variety of topics than almost any other subject could have afforded; and gave occasion to very numerous disquisitions, having an immediate reference to the public welfare. The general student was delighted with the acuteness of the ob-servations, the sagacity of the antiquarian researches; the number and el-egance of the analo-<lvii>gies, the comprehensiveness and consistency of the doctrines: The young Lawyer, by tracing the progress and views of the Government, was instructed in the spirit and real intention of the Laws: But, to the future statesman, were opened up views of human society, of the nature and ends of Government, and of the influence of Public Insti-tutions on the prosperity, morals, and happiness of states; views which could hardly fail to impress a veneration for liberty on his heart, and which, through his exertions, might essentially promote the welfare of his country.

When Mr. Millar was appointed Professor of Law, the University of Glas-gow enjoyed that very high reputation for philosophical inquiry, which, by the continued exertions of its professors, it still maintains. Dr. Hutchison laid the foundation of this fame, by his very amiable and ingenious system of Morals, and, under his successors, Dr. Smith and Dr. Reid, the character which the Moral Philosophy Class then acquired has been both established and extended. The originality of the speculations of these Philosophers has given a de-<lviii>cided bias, at Glasgow, to moral and metaphysical re-search; a bias in some degree unfavourable to the study of the ancient lan-guages, and even to the important sciences of Physics and Mathematics. Yet, in these departments, also, the University can boast of professors of no common reputation. Dr. Moor and Mr. Muirhead, joined to an intimate acquaintance with the stores of ancient literature, much critical knowledge and acuteness: Dr. Wilson distinguished himself by several astronomical discoveries of considerable moment: The writings of Dr. Simson are known and admired by every mathematician in Europe; and Dr. Cullen and Dr. Black, did more than perhaps any other English philosophers, in extending and improving the sciences of medicine and chemistry.*

In a university, where so many learned men had excited a general spirit of inquiry, and where so many original investigations were going forward, it was a natural wish, that there should be some established mode of mutual communication by which new ideas might be elicited, and error, ever prone <lix> to insinuate itself among new discoveries, might speedily be detected. Such were the views with which THE LITERARY SOCIETY, consisting chiefly of Professors, together with some Clergymen of the city and neighbourhood, had been instituted in 1752.[17]

On Mr. Millar's coming to Glasgow, he found this society in a very flourishing state, and, from a conviction of the advantages attending such an institution, both to its particular members, and to the general interests of science, he immediately became a very active and zealous promoter of its views. Till his death, he continued to attend the meetings with a punctuality of which I believe there are few examples. So far as I can learn, he never once failed, in the course of forty years, to read a discourse in his turn; and it was very seldom indeed that he allowed any other engagement to interfere with his attendance. The society became a kind of weekly habit to him;

---

* For obvious reasons, I have avoided mentioning the names of any professors still alive, otherwise I should have had much pleasure in bearing testimony to the distinguished abilities of some gentlemen whom I have the honour to rank among my personal friends. [[Francis Hutcheson (1694–1746), Smith (1723–90), and Thomas Reid (1710–96) were the three most famous holders of the Chair of Moral Philosophy at Glasgow and three of the most eminent philosophers of the eighteenth century. James Moor (1712–79), the professor of Greek at Glasgow, and George Muirhead (1715–73), the professor of Oriental languages at Glasgow, together produced the renowned Foulis edition of Homer (1747). Alexander Wilson was the type-founder of the Foulis press and later professor of practical astronomy and observer. Craig is likely referring to Wilson's discoveries of sunspots. Robert Simson (1687–1768) was a professor of mathematics at Glasgow and a geometer (much admired by Adam Smith) who produced an important edition of Euclid's *Elements,* also with the Foulis press (1756). Joseph Black, one of Smith's closest friends (1728–99), was among the most celebrated chemists of the eighteenth century; his discoveries in thermal chemistry led to Watts's steam engine. All of these professors and intellectuals socialized together in Glasgow's clubs and intellectual societies.]]

17. The Literary Society was one of the main meeting places for Glasgow intellectuals. Black, Smith, Watt, and others initially presented some of their most influential research to the society.

and he seemed to feel considerable disappointment and uneasiness, when any circumstance prevented its regular meeting.

The members of the Literary Society are accustomed to read papers on those subjects of science or taste, with which they are most conversant; each professor usually making choice of some to-<lx>pic connected with the particular business of his class, or taking the opinion of his colleagues on such speculations as he may be preparing for the press. The reading of the essay is followed by a conversation, sometimes by a debate, on the opinions that have been maintained; strictures are made on the arrangement, illustrations, or language; new ideas are occasionally started by the speakers; various improvements are suggested; and not unfrequently the whole foundations of the system are unreservedly attacked. The author is thus made sensible of any obscurity that may have pervaded his statements, or of any sophistry that may have insinuated itself into his arguments; he is led to revise his positions, to re-examine his authorities, and sometimes to perceive new views and new combinations, productive of the most important discoveries. To the other members, much useful knowledge is conveyed, on subjects often remote from their ordinary studies; and, by the diffusion of a general curiosity respecting all branches of science, that narrow exclusive attention to one particular study, which is so apt to proceed from the division of intellectual labour, is, in some measure, corrected.

Mr. Millar usually took a leading part in these discussions. Few subjects could be proposed on <lxi> which he had not, in some degree, reflected; and, though occasionally the essays entered so minutely into abstract science, that a person possessed only of general knowledge could not deliver a profound opinion; yet, even in such cases, his natural acuteness, and scientific habits, frequently enabled him to detect any inaccuracy in the arrangement, or inconsistent opinions in different parts of the discourse. His favourite subjects, however, those which he always canvassed with new interest and delight, were the sciences connected with the study of the human mind. A zealous admirer of Mr. Hume's philosophical opinions, which he had early adopted, and of the truth of which, after inquiries increased his conviction,* he was necessarily engaged in frequent debate with Dr. Reid.

* In saying that Mr. Millar adopted Mr. Hume's metaphysical opinions, I chiefly allude to those contained in his Essays. It is not a little surprising, that, even after this

Each, firmly persuaded that he maintained the cause of truth, used every exertion to support his own opinions and overthrow those of his opponent. No <lxii> weapon was rejected. To the utmost subtility of argument, to the most acute detection of sophistry, were sometimes joined the powers of ridicule; and occasionally, when arguments, conceived to be refuted in former debates, were again, on either side, introduced, some impatience might appear, some expressions might be used which seemed to convey the idea of contempt. But such feelings never, for a moment, survived the debate; and it is honourable to both, that frequent, and even acrimonious disputation never weakened their sentiments of friendship, nor impaired that mutual esteem which their worth, their talents, and their unwearied ardour in the investigation of truth, were calculated to inspire.

On several evenings, each winter, in place of a regular essay being read, a member of the society is appointed to open a debate on a given subject; and, on such evenings, the speeches assume more of the character of public harangues. Mr. Millar's elocution when he became a member of the Literary Society, has been described to me as, in some degree, embarrassed, cold, and constrained. To him, who was resolved to deliver extemporary Lectures, nothing could be more important than to conquer such defects; nor could there be any more certain means of accomplishing this object, <lxiii> than were furnished by the meetings of the society. A flow of ideas and expression, can be acquired only by practice, and by that self-possession and confidence which spring from repeated attempts, and repeated success. In the Society, too, Mr. Millar had frequent opportunities of comparing very different styles of oratory, and, in particular, of listening to the elegant

---

author had expressly stated his desire that these writings alone should be considered as containing his philosophical opinions, his opponents should still continue to refer to the Treatise of Human Nature; a work of equal or perhaps still greater ingenuity, but wanting the elegance, and accuracy of expression, which distinguish Mr. Hume's later publications. [[See David Hume, "Advertisement," *Essays and Treatises on Several Subjects* (London, 1777), II:2. By "opponents," Millar seemed to have James Beattie, John Oswald, and, perhaps, Thomas Reid in mind. As the volume of the *Essays* to which the "Advertisement" was appended included the *Enquiries,* Hume was suggesting that his opponents read the *Enquiries* as opposed to the *Treatise* for his most current views. It is notable that Craig remarks that the *Treatise* is of "greater ingenuity," showing, *pace* common opinion, that the *Treatise* did not go completely unappreciated by Hume's readers.]]

and pleasing eloquence of his friend Dr. Wight, who, by the liveliness of his manner, and brilliancy of his imagination, often foiled the superior information and strength of argument by which he was assailed.* By seizing every opportunity of improvement, Mr. Millar soon overcame any disadvantages under which he at first might labour, and placed himself, as a speaker, decidedly at the head of the Society. Feeling a lively interest in most of the questions proposed, he never failed to communicate something of this interest to his hearers; following the most natural order of ideas, he took a firm and steady hold of his subject; possessed of extensive knowledge, and a very lively imagination, he drew illustrations from a vast variety of topics; fond of wit, and not averse to ridicule, he enlivened the discussion with <lxiv> fanciful allusions, with delicate irony, and pointed satire; and, sometimes, rising with his subject, his eye on fire, his action strong and energetic, his tones impressive, his language bold and figurative, he astonished by the force of his declamation, and reached the highest pitch of impassioned eloquence.

After the business of the society was concluded, such of the members, as happened to have no other engagements, frequently adjourned, for a few hours, to a tavern in the neighbourhood. Here the discussion was sometimes continued, but with more sudden transitions, greater play of imagination, and all those sallies and deviations which are the charm of unrestrained conversation. In this part of the evening's amusement, Mr. Millar was as conspicuous, as in the previous discussions. His convivial talents, his unfailing vivacity and good humour, called out the powers of many, who would otherwise have remained silent and reserved; the liveliness of his fancy suggested infinite topics of conversation or of mirth; and his rich stores of information enabled him to supply endless sources of knowledge and amusement.

In most men, distinguished powers of conversation are merely an agreeable talent, the source of pleasure to their friends, and of affection to-<lxv>wards themselves; but, in Mr. Millar's particular situation, they were

---

* Dr. Wight, a man of most engaging manners and amiable character, was first Professor of Church History, and afterwards of Divinity. [[William Wight (1730–82), professor of church history, later of divinity, at Glasgow.]]

of higher importance; enabling him, with the most distinguished success, to discharge the duties of an instructor of youth. It has long been the custom at Glasgow, for several of the professors to admit into their houses young gentlemen, of whose education they take a general superintendence. While, by this means, they derive a considerable addition to their moderate incomes, they hold out a new inducement to men of fortune to send their sons to a University, where their conduct and manners, as well as their studies, will be under the watchful eye of a man of established reputation. For some years, Mr. Millar's time was too much occupied, in collecting materials for his Lectures, to allow him to receive domestic pupils; but, when this part of his labour was nearly completed, he found that, notwithstanding his public duties as a professor, it was in his power to do full justice to such young men as, with the views above alluded to, might be entrusted to his care. To their instruction he devoted a very considerable part of his time; he had much delight in conversing with them on their several studies, in leading them to inquire and to reflect, and, particularly, in encouraging such talents as promised future discoveries in science, or future eminence in the state. <lxvi>

Perhaps nothing contributed so much to the improvement of his pupils, as the art with which he contrived to make them lay aside all timidity in his presence, and speak their sentiments without constraint. While he was thus enabled to judge of their abilities and attainments, he acquired, in addition to the respect due to his talents, that confidence and friendship which ensure the attention of young men, and render the office of a teacher not undelightful. This easy and liberal communication of sentiments extended equally to every subject; to the doctrines taught in his own classes; to criticism; to contested points of History; and to the political struggles of the day. Whatever Mr. Millar's own opinions were on these subjects, he never wished to impose them on his pupils. In those discussions, which his conversation often introduced, and which, as a most useful exercise to their minds, he was always ready to encourage, he was pleased with ingenious argument, even when he did not adopt the conclusion; and he exposed sophistry, even when exerted in defence of his favourite opinions. In consequence of his own command of temper, he could at once repress any improper warmth that might appear; and, when the debate seemed to lead to unpleasing wrangling, he was always ready, with some whim-<lxvii>sical allusion, to restore good humour, or, by the introduction of some collateral topic, to change the subject of discourse. Wherever he discovered uncommon literary talents, his conversation called them into exertion, his warm applause produced that degree of self-confidence which is almost necessary to excellence, and his good humoured raillery, or serious remonstrances, reclaimed from indolence and deterred from dissipation.

In his domestic intercourse, he encouraged, at times, the detail of the juvenile pursuits and amusements of the young men, both from indulgence to their inclinations, and from a desire of tracing, in such unreserved communications, the temper and dispositions of his pupils; but he instantly repressed all trivial details, and all insignificant or gossiping anecdotes of individuals. Even in doing so, he avoided, as much as possible, every appearance of restraint or severity; and the ease and affability of his manners contributed more, perhaps, than even his talents, to produce that affectionate attachment, with which almost all his pupils were inspired. This attachment he had great pleasure in cultivating, as the most gratifying reward for his labours, and the most effectual control on young men, more apt to be influenced in their behaviour by their affections, than by stern, <lxviii> and what often appears to them, capricious, authority. While under Mr. Millar's care, all his pupils were treated alike; or rather the differences which might be remarked in his attentions, were the consequence of superior talents or application, never of superior rank. When they left his house, his connection with most of them necessarily ceased. He was always delighted, indeed, to hear of their success or eminence; but his regular occupations rendered it impossible for him to continue an epistolary correspondence; and his proud independence of mind made him rather decline, than cultivate, the friendship of those who succeeded to honours, or rose to power.

Such were his regular and stated occupations, during the winter. For some years after he was settled in Glasgow, he was in the habit of spending great part of the summer with his father at Hamilton; but, as his family increased, this became more inconvenient; and his uncle, ever attentive to his comfort, gave him a small farm near the village of Kilbride, about seven miles from Glasgow.

The farm of Whitemoss consisted of about thirty acres of very indifferent land, lying in a climate no way genial. Such circumstances, however,
did not prevent him from feeling all the ardour of an improver. Many a
scheme did he devise for rais-<lxix>ing crops, and clothing his fields with
verdure; and, though these schemes were never very successful, they were
carried on at little expence, served to amuse his leisure, and, to a certain
degree, diminished the natural bleakness immediately round his house.

His life at Whitemoss was very uniform; but, occupied with the cultivation of his little farm, interested in his studies, and surrounded by his
family, he felt no languor, and desired no variety. He had few neighbours,
and visited them very seldom. With Sir William Maxwell of Calderwood,[18]
to whose lady Mrs. Millar was distantly related, he always lived on terms
of friendship; and with Dr. and Mrs. Baillie, on a footing of intimacy. Dr.
Baillie,[19] after being elected Professor of Divinity, resided, during the summer, at Long Calderwood, about a mile from Whitemoss; and, after his
death, his widow and daughters made it their abode for several years. Their
society added much to Mr. Millar's enjoyments and to those of his family;
the young people were together almost every day; their time of life and
amusements were the same; and the celebrity which Dr. Baillie of London
afterwards acquired in his profession, the universal admiration which his
sister has secured by her <lxx> Dramatic Compositions, have been sources
of the purest pleasure to their early friends.[20]

In the year 1784, Mr. Millar's uncle, who had ever been most kind and
attentive to him, from unwillingness to prevent improvements of which
Milheugh was very capable, but which he was much too old either to direct
or even altogether to approve, went to reside with his brother at Hamilton;
where he remained till his death, which happened in the following year.
The two old men had, during the whole of their lives, been very strongly
attached to each other, and had often been heard to wish that the fate of

18. The 5th Baronet of Caldwell (d. 1789).
19. James (d. 1778) and Dorothea Baillie (the sister of William and John Hunter).
James was elected professor of divinity at Glasgow in 1775.
20. Their son, Matthew Baillie (1761–1823), was the author of the first work on mor-
bid anatomy and later physician extraordinary to George III. Joanna Baillie (1762–1851)
was a well-known playwright and poet.

two brothers who had died in Hamilton, within a few days of each other, might also be theirs. In this wish they were not disappointed. The old clergyman, after his brother's death, became uneasy and restless, but could not be prevented from attending the funeral. Being so near Milheugh, he took a last view of the scenes of his infancy, and, with singular liberality of mind, gave his approbation to alterations which had swept away many objects of his early partiality. The agitation of his mind, the want of sleep, and the heat of the weather overpowered him. By the time he returned to Hamilton, symptoms of an inflammatory fever had appear-<lxxi>ed, and, in a few days, he followed his beloved brother to the grave.

Milheugh possesses many natural beauties. It consists of several small meadows, separated from each other by the Calder, a little stream which winds among them, sometimes skirting, at other times intersecting, the valley. The bushes which fringe the edges of the rivulet, and a number of large trees standing near the house, and shading several of the principal walks, give great richness to the scene, while the steep banks, which rise from each side of the valley, suggest ideas of retirement and seclusion. But, when Mr. Millar came to Milheugh, there was much to alter and improve. He removed many formal hedges, which subdivided the little meadows, or, by stiff unbending lines, marked too distinctly the course of the rivulet. He formed the old orchard into pleasing group of trees around the house; left bushes irregularly scattered on the banks of the stream; and carried plantations along the top of the banks. Every thing throve in this sheltered situation, and Milheugh is now one of the sweetest little retirements that could be desired. Its beauties are elegant and simple, and perhaps it would be difficult to point out any farther embellishments that would accord with the character of the place. <lxxii>

For some time, Mr. Millar's summers were altogether devoted to his improvements. Every tree that was planted, still more every bush that was cut down, was the subject of many consultations with his family: The direction of a path, the opening up of a new view, or the discovery of a new object in one of his prospects, engrossed the whole of his mind: and, when he could not enjoy these higher pleasures, he watched, with delight, the progress of his young plantations, and enjoyed, by anticipation, the future beauties of his plans. By degrees, as his improvements were completed,

Milheugh occupied less of his attention; but it never ceased to interest and delight him. It was endeared to him by no common ties; it had been the scene of his early years, and was now embellished by his mature taste: in one view, it was associated with his most pleasing recollections; in another, it might almost be considered as the production of his own mind.

Mr. Millar's intercourse with his neighbours was scarcely more frequent at Milheugh, than it had been at Whitemoss. He was, indeed, no way dependent on society; but he was fond of the occasional visits of his acquaintances, and of the variety arising from the addition of a few strangers to the family circle. He was therefore much gratified, <lxxiii> soon after he went to Milheugh, by the establishment, in his near neighbourhood, of Mr. Jardine,* one of his most respected friends, who, induced chiefly by the desire of enjoying his society during the summer, purchased a small estate, not above two miles distant. Their frequent intercourse was to both a source of much enjoyment.

When in the country, Mr. Millar employed a great part of his leisure in perusing such books as his other avocations in winter had prevented him from reading, and in preparing his own works for the press. The *Origin of the Distinction of Ranks,* was written chiefly at Hamilton, and Glasgow; The *Historical View of the English Government,* altogether at Whitemoss and Milheugh. While carrying on this last work, it very frequently became the subject of conversation in the family, and all the opinions and speculations it contains were freely canvassed. He had long been in the habit of consulting Mrs. Millar with regard to his literary works, and some of his children being, by this time, competent judges of composition, he oc-<lxxiv>casionally read over to his family the most amusing or interesting passages, and listened with much attention to their various criticisms. By this means, besides increasing that mutual confidence which ever subsisted

---

* Professor of Logic. To this Gentleman I am indebted for many particulars of Mr. Millar's life, and for the free use of a memoir which he read in the Literary society, at the first meeting after Mr. Millar's death; a memoir, which, had it not been composed with a particular view to the society, might have rendered this essay unnecessary. [[George Jardine (1742–1827) was a younger colleague of Millar's. He moved the Glasgow logic curriculum away from traditional formal logic and toward the modern subject of the mental faculties for language and taste.]]

between him and his family, he had the means of detecting any little errors which had escaped his own observation, and he formed the taste, while he improved the judgment of his children.

Of the subjects which Mr. Millar had occasion to discuss in his Lectures on Jurisprudence and Government, none seemed more interesting in themselves, or so capable of being detached from his other disquisitions, as that of the various Ranks which are established in society, the various degrees of authority and power which are distributed among the several members of a community. In so far as such differences of rank and power are founded on fixed and universal relations, they may be traced to four distinct sources. The difference of sex has, in every country, occasioned remarkable differences between the habits, occupations, acquirements, and authority of men and women: The helplessness of infancy, and the habits at that time contracted, have produced a dependence, more or less complete, of children on their parents: Various circumstances have subjected some men to <lxxv> others as servants or slaves: And the wants of society, the necessity of a warlike leader for each tribe, the natural authority of strength, courage, wisdom, and riches, have raised particular members of the community to political power. The three first of these sources of the distinction of Ranks are the foundation of what, in the Civil Law, are called the Rights of Persons, the last is the basis of the rights of Government; consequently they had all been the subjects of inquiry, in the several courses of Lectures delivered by Mr. Millar in the University.

Believing that some account of the origin and progress of those distinctions of Ranks might be generally interesting, Mr. Millar was induced, in 1771, to publish a short treatise on this subject, which was very favourably received. Even to cursory readers, it was calculated to afford amusement, by the various views of human nature which it exhibited, and by the singularity of many of the traits of manners, as well as of national characters and institutions, which it traced to their sources. To the philosopher, it delineated a general but instructive view of the changes consequent on the progress of improvement; accounting, in a satisfactory manner, for the introduction of many of the most singular institutions described in history; and, by the explanation it afforded of the causes of <lxxvi> what has existed, directing his speculations, and giving a reasonable degree of certainty to his conclusions respecting the future destinies of mankind. From its first publication, this work attracted considerable attention, and several successive editions have been called for by the public. It also became known and esteemed on the Continent, through a translation, executed, I believe, by Garat, who afterwards, at a most eventful period of the French Revolution,* was, little to his own honour or the public advantage, appointed Minister of Justice.

The subjects of this publication were part of those which had been treated of in the Lectures on Jurisprudence and Government; but the point of view in which they were considered was, in some respects, different. Mr. Millar, in this treatise, proposed to confine himself altogether to the changes produced on the several relations of society, by the gradual progress of civilization and improvement. He neither intended to give any account of the laws and institutions springing from these relations, except when necessary for illustration, nor to investigate, in a detailed manner, the effects produced upon them by particular systems of Government <lxxvii> or Religion. Thus, in tracing the condition of the female sex, he abstained from a detailed inquiry into the subjects of Marriage and Divorce, and took only a very cursory view of the effects of particular systems of Government or Religion on the condition of women, or of the comparative advantages attending the different degrees of consideration, which, at different periods, they have acquired. All these subjects, he had treated very fully in his Lectures on Jurisprudence; but, in this publication, his object was simply

---

* During the struggle between the Brissotines and Terrorists, 1792. [[The Brissotines, more commonly referred to as the Girondists, were a moderate revolutionary faction (associated with Jacques-Pierre Brissot) who struggled for control of the revolution with Robespierre and the "Mountain," in particular following the massacres of September 2–6, 1792. Many leading Brissotines were subsequently expelled from the Convention and fled to the provinces (their main base of support) or were guillotined (including Brissot himself). Dominique Joseph Garat was the minister of justice during this period—the period of the trial and execution of Louis XVI—and read the king his death verdict. He was not a member of the most radical faction of the revolution, and was imprisoned during the Terror. It appears that Jean-Baptiste-Antoine Suard, not Garat, translated the work. Garat and Suard were friends, and Garat later wrote a well-known work about his friend Suard, *Mémoires historiques sur la vie de M. Suard, sur ses écrits et sur le XVIIIe siècle* (1820). Whether true or not, the association of the work with a regicide would be embarrassing!]]

to exhibit a theoretical history of the condition of women, as affected by the gradual progress of refinement, and by that progress alone.

In those chapters which trace the progress of political power, Mr. Millar has bestowed much attention on the Feudal Governments of modern Europe. He has shewn how such institutions naturally arose from the condition of the German tribes, the extent of their conquests, and the reciprocal influence on each other of the manners of the old and new inhabitants; and he has detected many traces of similar institutions in the laws of other countries. This was indeed a very favourite subject with him, and his speculations respecting it were considerably different from those of other writers. They are marked by that simplicity and clearness of view <lxxviii> which characterise all his disquisitions, and they produce that conviction which never fails to attend a system, simple in its construction, consistent in itself, and satisfactory in accounting for a multitude of facts.

Of his opinions respecting the Feudal System, the changes on the state of servants in modern Europe, and the origin of that spirit of chivalry which has still left remarkable traces in modern manners, (subjects which are sketched in a very spirited manner in The Origin of the Distinction of Ranks) Mr. Millar had afterwards occasion to publish many additional illustrations, in his principal work, the Historical View of the English Government.

It has already been mentioned that, in his Lectures on Government, he paid particular attention to the constitution of his own country; tracing it through all its successive changes, and accounting for its several modifications, from the known state of manners, opinions, and property. On this subject, many rash and erroneous speculations have, at different times, been given to the world. Some authors have fondly traced the institutions of Britain to the woods of Germany, flattering the national vanity with the idea that our rude forefathers possessed juster views of Government, more liberal sen-<lxxix>timents, and better digested laws, than can be found among other barbarians.[21] The majority of writers, less prone to investigation, have satisfied themselves with ascribing whatever is remarkable in

---

21. This likely refers to Gilbert Stuart, *An Historical Dissertation Concerning the Antiquity of the English Constitution* (Edinburgh, 1768).

the constitution, to the general wisdom of our ancestors; meaning, if indeed they have had any accurate meaning, that it arose from such views of remote utility, as may be sufficiently obvious to us, but never have had any very perceptible influence on the public measures of an early age. Several authors, among whom is Mr. Hume, have conceived that, at the Norman Conquest, all traces of former liberty were abolished, and an absolute government established, on which various encroachments have successively been made, when the weakness of the monarch, or the embarrassment of public affairs, afforded a favourable opportunity, to the turbulence of the Barons, or seditions of the people. Such being the favourite creed of the Tories, it was encountered with more ardour than acuteness by the Whigs, who pretended that, at a time when vassals held their lands chiefly during the pleasure of their superiors, and the inhabitants of towns were universally slaves, the present fabric of our constitution was completed, and a fair representation of the Commons in Parliament fully established. <lxxx>

Mr. Millar saw that a connected view of the changes which have taken place in the English Government would completely overthrow such opinions, from which many dangerous inferences have often been drawn: and, besides being in this view highly important, he conceived that a detail of the various steps by which a constitution, uniting the advantages of monarchy to those of popular government, has gradually been brought to its present form, (steps, in many instances, productive of consequences very different from the considerations of temporary convenience in which they originated) could not fail to afford a most interesting and improving object of research. Animated by such expectations, he devoted the leisure of his summers to the arranging and extending of this branch of his Lectures, and, in 1787, he gave to the world *The Historical View of the English Government, from the settlement of the Saxons in Britain, to the accession of the house of Stewart.* This work, containing much inquiry into the remote periods of our Government, and many disquisitions which it demands some effort of attention fully to understand, could not be of a very popular nature: but it has been justly appreciated by those who were fitted, by their habits and previous studies, to take an interest in such researches, and, consider-<lxxxi>ing the nature of the subjects of which it treats, its having already reached a third edition is no slight proof of public approbation.

It is by no means my intention to attempt any analysis of the Historical View; nor, indeed, is it possible, by an analysis, to do justice to a work in which every opinion is already stated with all the conciseness consistent with perspicuity. To detach any one speculation from the rest, to sketch the progress of the kingly power, of the privileges of parliament, of the judicial establishments, or of the ecclesiastical jurisdiction, separately from each other, would be to deprive the whole of that evidence, (perhaps the most convincing to a philosopher), which results from the congruity of all its parts, from the connection of the several institutions with each other, and the dependence of the whole on the real and ascertained improvement in the condition of the people.

Indeed Mr. Millar is frequently obliged to rest the truth of his opinions on this internal proof. Ascending to a period of which the records are scanty, and disfigured with fable, he often, without reference to such uncertain authority, produces a conviction, stronger perhaps than can ever be derived from the testimony of an individual, always liable to be deceived. His argument, founded on <lxxxii> unconnected circumstances all tending to one effect; his successive positions, derived from the acknowledged condition of the several ranks of inhabitants, flowing naturally from the state of manners and property, and leading, by easy transition, to what we know was afterwards established; his frequent illustrations, by reference to similar institutions existing in other countries, and by a distinct enumeration of circumstances in some nations leading to opposite results: His disquisitions, so conducted, produce a confidence in his conclusions, to which the authority of rude and careless annalists can have no pretension.

Institutions familiar to early historians seldom appear to them objects of curiosity or research. Occupied in giving a bare narration of events, which have passed in their own times, or have been handed down by tradition, they may occasionally notice some existing institutions; but, with regard to their origin, the time of their introduction, or the successive steps which led to their improvement, they are usually extremely ignorant. Such objects of inquiry seem to them of no importance; what is familiar excites no curiosity; what has existed during the whole life of the author may have existed for ever. Long before the importance of any particular change in the manners, state of property, <lxxxiii> or government becomes apparent, the circumstances from which it arose are usually effaced; the want of information is supplied by the invention of some puerile story; or the fame of a particular prince, or the wisdom of our ancestors, are referred to as a satisfactory solution of all difficulties and doubts. Such vague accounts of the origin and progress of the most important Institutions, at first brought forward without authority, are afterwards repeated without examination, and are too frequently considered as the well authenticated facts of history.

From such authorities, Mr. Millar could derive little assistance. There was seldom any controversy respecting the existence of particular institutions, and it was in vain to seek, from such writers, any accurate information of their nature, or of the gradual and unobserved steps which led to their establishment. Nothing, indeed, could have been easier, than to have crowded his margin with references; but this show of erudition must have been altogether illusive, and such affectation he regarded with contempt. Where his opinion could derive real support from a reference, or quotation, he did not disregard it: where it could not, he never presumed on the ignorance or carelessness of his reader, but rested his doctrine, openly and fairly, on its intrinsic evidence. Yet, so much are we now accustomed to the cita-<lxxxiv>tion of numerous authorities even for what no man ever doubted, that, very possibly, Mr. Millar paid too little regard to the prevailing taste of antiquarians, and deprived his work too much of that kind of support, on which they are accustomed, almost exclusively, to depend.

It has been often remarked that the style of Mr. Millar's writings is very different from what the vivacity of his conversation, and the copious diction of his extemporary eloquence, gave reason to expect. When he sat down to compose, he seems to have discarded every idea not strictly connected with the subject of his inquiry, and to have guarded, with a vigilance very unfavourable to the lighter graces of composition, against all equivocal expressions, or fanciful allusions. His language, as has been well observed by one of his friends,* is the *expression* rather than the *ornament* of his thoughts. Clear, accurate, precise, it never fails to convey his ideas with a distinctness which precludes all misapprehension; but frequently it conveys them in a manner, neither the most striking, nor the most alluring, to the

---

* Mr. Jardine.

reader. The structure of his sentences is always extremely simple. Following the most obvious arrangement, and avoiding all such inversions, as, though delighting the ear, might occasion <lxxxv> some risk of mistake in the sense, he produces a degree of monotony in his pauses, and gives a severity, sometimes repulsive, to his writings. These were circumstances which Mr. Millar was accustomed to disregard. His object was to convey clear and accurate ideas; and that object he so fully accomplished, that perhaps it would be impossible to find a sentence in his book, which can require a second perusal to be distinctly understood.

Similar views seem to have restrained him from employing those figurative expressions and fanciful allusions, which an imagination such as his could not fail to suggest. Simple correctness and accuracy are so much the characteristics of his style, that, even when he rises from plain narration to warmth and energy, (and there are many such passages in his writings), the force is always in the principal idea, seldom in the accessories. Not unfrequently, we meet with a strong conception distinctly expressed, and affecting the reader by its native energy; seldom with a collection of associated ideas and sentiments hurrying on the mind by their accumulated force.

It can scarcely be doubted that this steady rejection of metaphor and allusion, as well as the particular construction of his period, was adopted, after due consideration, as the style best suited to a <lxxxvi> didactic subject. No man had more command of his ideas; none could combine them more readily, where his purpose was to address the imagination: But, in establishing a great and comprehensive system, he was anxious that the mind should not be diverted from the full consideration of all its parts, and of their several relations and dependencies. Perhaps he did not sufficiently consider, that many readers can be engaged in such disquisitions, only by the charms of style, and that, to those unaccustomed to severe investigation, some relief is necessary from continued exertion; some relaxation is required, that they may afterwards proceed with renovated ardour. By a person already interested in such inquiries, Mr. Millar's style may probably be preferred to one of greater variety and embellishment; but it may be doubted how far it is calculated to excite such interest, where it does not previously exist.

The Origin of the Distinction of Ranks, and the Historical View of the

English Government, are the only works to which Mr. Millar prefixed his name. Nor do I find that he published any other Tracts, except one or two anonymous pamphlets, on such political questions as he thought important to the public welfare, and a few articles in the Analytical Review. These Tracts I shall not par-<lxxxvii>ticularize, because what he never acknowledged, even to his acquaintances, I do not feel myself at liberty to divulge. The plan adopted in the Analytical Review, at its first establishment, was to give such an abstract of the different publications as might enable its readers to judge of their matter, and to insert such extracts as might give some idea of their style.[22] Mr. Millar, in the articles which he wrote, adhered very rigidly to this plan, stating, as shortly as possible, any observations that seemed necessary on the merits of the publications, and introducing very sparingly his own particular opinions. To review in this manner obviously requires a very accurate study of the several books; more study than is always convenient for Reviewers; and therefore it was gradually laid aside for that careless and rash Criticism, which are so conspicuous in most other publications of the same nature. No sooner did this change of system appear, than Mr. Millar thought it advisable to withdraw his assistance.

Mr. Millar, notwithstanding all these occupations, still found time for limited practice as a lawyer, a profession which he had not altogether abandoned, in undertaking the duties of a Public Teacher. He was very frequently consulted, as Counsel, previously to the commencement of a law suit, or <lxxxviii> when any difficulty occurred in conveyancing; and the time he could spare from his other employments was occupied in determining causes referred to his arbitration. The delay and expence of lawsuits, partly unavoidable in a commercial country, but partly also owing to the constitution of the Court of Session, has rendered it extremely common for parties, when both are convinced of the justice of their claims, to refer their disputes to private arbitration. For the office of Arbiter, Mr. Millar was singularly qualified. While, from his residence in a mercantile town, he could easily be informed of the usages of merchants, he was led, by his

---

22. "The true design of a Literary Journal is, in our opinion, to give such an account of new publications, as may enable the reader to judge of them for himself" (*Prospectus of the Analytical Review* [London, 1788], i).

professional habits, to pay that attention to strict law, which is requisite to substantial justice, in a country where all agreements are entered into with the knowledge that they may become the subject of legal interpretation. His natural acuteness, too, led him to seize very readily the important circumstances of a case, and to detach them from such collateral topics, as might have bewildered the judgment, and certainly must have protracted the investigation. His decisions were consequently prompt, but they never were inconsiderate. As the surest guard against error, he was in the habit, before pronouncing his awards, of submitting his opinion, with a short statement of <lxxxix> the principles on which it rested, to the parties; and, not unfrequently, these statements were drawn up in a manner so clear and satisfactory, as to convince even the party against whose claims he intended to decide.

At the circuits, Mr. Millar was in the habit, for many years, of appearing as counsel for those unfortunate men who are brought to the bar to answer for their crimes. Thinking, with other philosophers, that the criminal laws of this country are, in many instances, unnecessarily and unjustly severe, he entered with warmth into the defence of those who, however profligate in their morals, were in danger of being subjected to punishments more than adequate to their offences. In the examination of witnesses, he showed uncommon skill and penetration; and his addresses to the Juries,* besides containing a most acute and severe examination of such part of the evidence as seemed unfavourable to the prisoner, exhibited a clear view of whatever tended to establish his innocence, and, not unfrequently, were terminated by a most powerful appeal to the feelings of his audience. Before I was old enough to attend to criminal <xc> trials, Mr. Millar had declined appearing at the Circuits, that he might not deprive younger lawyers of an opportunity of displaying their talents; but I have been assured by many gentlemen, on whose opinions I can rely, that his addresses to the Jury were very brilliant and successful exertions of forensic eloquence.

Fully occupied, in the winter, with the duties of his office, and engaged, during the summer, in improving his Lectures, or preparing his works for

---

* In Scotland, the counsel for the prisoner is allowed to address the jury upon the whole evidence, as well as to state the nature of the defence in an opening speech.

the press, Mr. Millar went seldom from home: sometimes, however, he made a short excursion to different parts of Scotland, or the north of England, occasionally he passed a few days with his friends in Edinburgh, and, for several summers, he paid an annual visit to his favourite pupil, Lord Maitland, now the Earl of Lauderdale. With none of his pupils did Mr. Millar continue on a footing of so much intimacy and friendship as with Lord Lauderdale; and it is to their frequent and unreserved communication of sentiment, that a similarity, observable between their opinions of the nature of the profit of stock, may be ascribed.* Which of them first suggested this ingenious idea, it would probably have been difficult, even for <xci> themselves, to determine: it is likely to have occurred in some of their conversations on political oeconomy, and, having been afterwards developed and improved by both, it naturally conducted them to similar results.

Mr. Millar paid two visits to London; the first was in 1774. Having remained in the capital about two months, and having seen the principal objects of curiosity, he made a short excursion to Cambridge, and stopped for three weeks at Oxford, on his return; partly with the view of making himself acquainted with the present state of these celebrated Universities, and partly for the purpose of consulting several authors on the early history of Modern Europe, whose works he had not an opportunity of perusing at home.

His second visit to London he made in 1792, accompanied by Mrs. Millar and his eldest daughter. Having set off in the beginning of May, immediately after the conclusion of his Lectures, he arrived in London in sufficient time to be present at several very important debates, in both houses of Parliament, and he enjoyed the satisfaction of becoming ac-

---

* See the Historical View, vol. iv. chap. 3. and Lord Lauderdale on Public Wealth, chap. 3. [[James Maitland, 8th Earl of Lauderdale, *An Inquiry into the Nature and Origin of Public Wealth* (Edinburgh, 1804). Smith had argued (*Wealth of Nations,* I.vi.9) that profit derived from stock was actually derived from the labor added by the workman to the raw materials. Lauderdale argued, against Smith and Turgot, that "in every instance where capital is so employed as to produce a profit, it uniformly arises, either—*from its supplanting a portion of labour, which would otherwise be performed by the hand of man; or—from its performing a portion of labour, which is beyond the reach of the personal exertion of man to accomplish*" (161).]]

quainted with Mr. Fox and the other leaders of opposition, whose talents he admired, whose steady patriotism, unshaken by obloquy, and superior to popular cen-<xcii>sure or applause, was the object of his highest veneration. The chief part of his time, however, that from which he probably derived the greatest enjoyment, was passed in the society of his former pupils, Lord Lauderdale, and Mr. Adam, now one of the King's Counsel, and Attorney General to the Prince of Wales, and in the family of his old friend, Dr. Moore, the celebrated author of Zeluco and Edward.[23]

The greatest intimacy had subsisted between Dr. Moore and Mr. Millar, from the time they were young men; an intimacy which had been farther promoted by their marrying ladies who were companions and friends. While Dr. Moore was on the continent, with the Duke of Hamilton, engaged in those travels, with an account of which he afterwards delighted the world, Mrs. Moore was a frequent visiter at the college, and Mr. Millar took a general superintendence of the education of her sons. During the short stay the Doctor made in Glasgow, after his return, he spent a great deal of his time with Mr. Millar, and, on his going to reside in London, they began a correspondence, some part of which might not have been uninteresting to the public, had they thought it proper to preserve letters written merely for each other's <xciii> perusal.* Their talents were calculated to produce mutual esteem, and their powers of conversation to contribute very highly to each other's amusement.

Mr. Millar had the art, in a most uncommon degree, of adapting his conversation to those around him. Even to children, he could make himself a most amusing companion; and no young person ever left his company without being charmed with his vivacity. His countenance was uncommonly animated and expressive; his stature about the middle size; his person strong, active, and athletic, rather than elegant. When he first entered a

---

* This was almost the only regular correspondence in which Mr. Millar ever engaged. When absent from his family, he indeed wrote letters calculated for their amusement, and remarkable for the same playfulness which distinguished his conversation; but he was very averse to the preservation of any of his letters. His numerous avocations rendered it impossible for him to correspond with his friends, except when some kind of business required it.

23. John Moore (1729–1802).

room, his manner was not altogether free from formality and constraint; but this continued only for a moment. The first subject that was started kindled animation in his eye, and seemed entirely to engross his mind. Never did he show the slightest absence, nor allow any carelessness, or con-temptuous indif-<xciv>ference, to escape him. Never, indeed, did he feel that languor from which they most commonly proceed. However trifling the subject might be, he was always lively and animated; his constant flow of spirits enabled him to extract some amusement from every topic, and every character; and his repartees, though not rising to that high species of wit, which can delight on repetition, flowed so naturally from the conver-sation, and were accompanied with so much gaiety, playfulness, and good humour, that, perhaps, no company ever was dull or languid in his presence.

His conversation was equally agreeable to those who preferred subjects of a graver or more improving kind. His information reached to almost every subject which was likely to occur in conversation. He was completely master of whatever had been written on the sciences connected with the study of mind, and had added many new opinions and combinations to the discoveries of others. The whole range of history was familiar to him, and there was little in the manners or customs of any nation, which he could not state with accuracy, and account for with surprising quickness and ingenuity. Nor was he ignorant of the physical sciences, although his knowledge of them rather embraced the different theories by which the facts are <xcv> explained, than showed any very intimate acquaintance with the facts themselves. To the task of minute observation, or the drudgery of accurate experiment, he could not submit: but, wherever there was an ap-pearance of system, his attention was roused so fully, that, for a time, it almost engrossed his mind. It was thus, that, after Lavoisier[24] published his aston-ishing experiments, and no less astonishing system built on these experi-ments, Mr. Millar, for a whole winter, thought of nothing but chemistry; and so great was his veneration for that philosopher, that no circumstance in the French Revolution struck him with so much horror, as the murder of the man whom he considered as the brightest ornament of the age.

24. Antoine-Laurent Lavoisier (1743–94), discoverer of oxygen, executed in the Terror.

In Literature and Belles Lettres, perhaps the most delightful of all subjects for conversation, Mr. Millar was completely conversant. In his youth, he had read all the classics with such pleasure and discrimination, that, although his line of study was afterwards extremely different, he could always refer to the most impressive passages, and discuss, with much intelligence, their relative beauties and defects. His acquaintance with English Poetry was also very general, though his taste might be considered as somewhat fastidious. Mediocrity, in every thing, but particularly in verse, he was <xcvi> accustomed to treat with marked contempt; and the frequent recurrence of such expressions in his conversation, joined to the ridicule with which, in a sportive humour, he sometimes treated even compositions of considerable merit, gave those not intimately acquainted with him, an idea that he had little relish for poetry. Perhaps the severity in which he indulged rather arose from a taste too delicate and refined. Seldom have I known any person more alive to the higher kinds of poetry; to those striking and sublime allusions, that rich and varied imagery, that loftiness of thought, and dignity of expression, which delight the imagination and elevate the mind. Nor did he confine his admiration to poets of the highest order; to Milton, Akenside, and Gray: He was highly delighted with the fancy, the elegance, and varied talents of Pope, the natural and impressive descriptions of Thomson, and that charming blending of melancholy with ideas of pleasure, which a great critic has failed to discover, in the little poems of Prior.*
He was also well acquainted with the best French <xcvii> and Italian Poets; but, while he was obliged to admit the more refined eloquence, and superior conduct of the French Drama, he always contended for the superiority of the English, in delineating the simple and genuine feelings of the human

---

* It is surprising that Dr. Johnson seems never to have perceived this beauty in Prior. The same blending of ideas of pleasure and of melancholy constitutes the greatest charm in the writings of Horace and in the beautiful little odes of Cheaulieu. [[Mark Akenside (1721–70) was a celebrated poet and doctor best known for the "Pleasures of Imagination"; James Thomson (1700–1748) was a Scottish poet best known for *The Seasons* and probably the author of "Rule Britannia"; Guillaume Amfrye de Chaulieu (1639–1720) was a well-known French poet. Johnson said of Matthew Prior (1664–1721): "Whatever Prior obtains above mediocrity seems the effort of struggle and of toil" (Samuel Johnson, *Lives of the English Poets*, ed. George Birkbeck Hill [New York: Octagon Books, 1967; reprint of the 1905 Clarendon Press edition], II:209.)]]

heart, and in using a measure of versification which is at once capable of approaching the looseness and facility of prose, and of being adapted to the expression of exalted and heroic sentiment.

Nor was Mr. Millar averse to argument; or to the display of his ingenuity in supporting paradoxes, often the children of the moment. He was indeed so complete a master of debate, that it was unsafe to attack him, even when he occupied most disadvantageous ground. Ever acute and collected, he was apt, by slight sarcasms, to put his antagonist off his guard, and to surprise him by unexpected inferences from whatever was unadvisedly admitted. He overpowered his opponent by innumerable analogies, drawn from the most remote quarters, and presented in the most forcible points of view. He covered, with infinite art, the weaker parts of his own argument, and exposed, with much ingenuity, any mistakes or fallacies by which he was assailed. When fairly driven from all his positions, he often became most formidable: seiz-<xcviii>ing some unguarded expression, or some unfortunate illustration, he held it up to ridicule, with a degree of vivacity and humour, which carried off the attention from the previous subject of debate, and secured him the honours of a triumph, when he had really suffered a defeat. On the subject of Politics he argued always with zeal; and, towards the end of his life, with a considerable degree of keenness. He, who had refused the offer of a lucrative place, which might have introduced him to higher honours, because he feared that his acceptance might be construed into an engagement to support an administration whose measures he condemned,* had little allowance to make for those who sacrificed their principles to their interest. Ever steady and consistent himself, he was apt to suspect the purity of the motives from which all violent or sudden changes in political opinion arose; without perhaps making a due degree of allowance for that alarm, which, however hurtful in its consequences, was the natural result of the blind fanaticism of several popular societies. On a subject, too, which he had studied with the utmost care, he naturally, might be rather impatient <xcix> of ignorant and presumptuous contradiction; nor could his mind brook the imputations, which, at a season of

---

* I am not at liberty to give the particulars of this transaction, but I pledge myself to its truth.

political intolerance, were so liberally passed on all the opposers of Ministerial power. Arguing, frequently, under considerable irritation of mind,
perhaps unavoidable in his particular circumstances, it is not impossible
that expressions may have escaped him which might afford room for mistake, or misrepresentation; and, on this account, it is but justice to his memory, to give an impartial detail of his real opinions and political conduct.

Occupied in the examination of different systems of Government, and in
tracing their several effects on the morals, prosperity, and happiness of nations, it was scarcely possible that Mr. Millar should not take a lively interest
in the political transactions of his own country, and of his own times. Even
a general view of history is sufficient to prove the intimate connection between liberty and the improvement of man. Wherever the laws are dictated
by the will of a few, wherever they can be altered or modified according to
the caprice or <c> convenience of the rulers; there we shall find them ill
digested and worse administered; there we shall find the people borne down
by insolence, dispirited by oppression, indolent, ignorant, and profligate.
On the other hand, the never failing results of free government are that
justice in the laws, that fairness in their execution, which, by giving every
man a certainty of enjoying the full produce of his labour, incite to industry
and exertion, the only secure foundations of general prosperity and happiness. It is thus, that the particular distribution of Political Privileges exerts
its powerful influence on the civil rights enjoyed by the inhabitants, on their
morals, and their general welfare.

Political power, indeed, ought not to be distributed, in the same manner
in all nations. Where the people are extremely ignorant and debased, from
whatever circumstances this may have proceeded, it is obviously for their
own advantage, that they should be excluded from all share in the government, and directed, even at the risk of being occasionally oppressed, by
those of higher rank and more liberal education. But, as a nation improves
in knowledge, as the manners become more civilized, as industry produces
a more obvious interest in the peace and good order of the state, <ci> there
comes to be not only less inconvenience, but the most important public
advantage, in a more wide diffusion of political power.

Unhappily, the history of mankind very seldom displays this gradual and beneficial progress towards liberty. There seems a constant and incorrigible tendency in governors of all descriptions to extend their own powers, and abridge those of the people. This desire, which usually springs from the most despicable personal motives, may sometimes arise even from virtuous feelings, from an honest conviction of the beneficial tendency of many measures liable to be thwarted by public ignorance or private interests.* To whichever source we may be disposed to ascribe the spirit of encroachment, the whole history of mankind will prove that it never for an instant is asleep; that even when veiled under apparent moderation, it watches the most favourable opportunity; and that its prevalence is, either immediately or more remotely, destructive of patriotism, and of the prosperity of the state. A strong view of this almost universal tendency of <cii> government, and of the calamities inseparable from the loss of freedom, rendered Mr. Millar a strenuous opposer of the power of the Crown, whether in the undisguised shape of prerogative, or the more insidious, and perhaps more dangerous, form of secret influence.

He, accordingly, attached himself zealously to the party of the Whigs; and, in particular, to that branch of the Whigs, who acknowledged the Marquis of Rockingham, and afterwards Mr. Fox, as their leaders.[25] From the opinions of these illustrious statesmen, he seldom had occasion to dissent; and, even when he could not altogether approve of their measures, he was led to acquiesce in their decisions, by his great deference for their authority, his full confidence in their uprightness, and, above all, his steady conviction, that no effectual barrier could be raised against the increasing influence of the Crown, without a regular and vigorous co-operation of all who agreed in the general principles of their political conduct. The necessity of a union of talents and rank, to limit the growing influence of the

* It was in this view, that the French Economists favoured despotical government. They thought it easier to convince a monarch, than a whole nation, of the truth of those abstract principles, on which they had founded their system. [[Craig is describing the doctrine of legal despotism as exemplified in François Quesnay's *Despotisme de la Chine* (1767).]]

25. Charles Watson-Wentworth, Marquess of Rockingham (1730–82), and Charles James Fox (1749–1806) were leaders of the Whig faction successively named after them. Rockingham and Fox vigorously opposed the war against America and attempted to constrain the authority of George III. Fox strongly supported the French Revolution.

Court, might be considered as the leading article of Mr. Millar's political creed; and it was only when he found this combination entirely broken by recent events, that he became fully convinced of the necessity of henceforward founding <ciii> National Liberty on a much more general diffusion of political power.

He has himself stated the grounds of his conviction, "That the power of the Crown has, since the Revolution, made the most rapid and alarming advances." He has, distinctly and fairly, enumerated the various sources of a most extensive influence; and he has justly remarked, that such an influence "is apt to be the greater, as it operates upon the manners and habits of a mercantile people: a people engrossed by lucrative trades and professions, whose great object is gain, and whose ruling principle is avarice."* Even to such elevated rank as might be thought most likely to exclude the operation of this mercantile spirit, the national character must always, in some measure, extend; and it is too obvious to be denied, that the general luxury of the times has introduced such a degree of extravagance, that the expences, even of the most opulent families, are apt to exceed their incomes, and to render ministerial dependence their only resource against what to them is really indigence. In such circumstances, he almost despaired of again witnessing so great a co-operation of leading families, of patriotism, and <civ> of talents, as might effectually check that increasing influence which seemed firmly erected on the immense patronage of the Minister, and the present manners and character of the nation. A change of circumstances implied a change in the mode of resisting the progress of power; and, no longer expecting to find this important object accomplished by the great families of England, Mr. Millar was led to consider more attentively the condition of the people.

Here he found some grounds for reasonable hope. The diffusion of riches has produced a general spirit of independence, and a very wide diffusion of knowledge. The simpler principles of politics, and even of political economy, are more universally studied, more frequently the ordinary topics of conversation, than at any former period; and it may safely be asserted, that the great majority of the middling ranks have now much more

---

* See Hist. View of the English Gov. vol. iv. chap. ii.

information, on such subjects, than was enjoyed by the highest orders of
the community, before the Revolution. The great body of the nation, those
who may justly be styled the People, attentive to the conduct of public
men, and capable of estimating public measures, might now be entrusted
with the power of choosing Representatives, without much risk of their
choice being very inconsiderate, <cv> and without much disadvantage resulting from occasional errors or delusions affecting the public opinion.
But, whenever such an extension of the elective suffrage has become safe,
it must, of necessity, be highly beneficial. It prevents the enactment of laws
favourable to private views or private interests; it gives the people a new
motive of attachment to their country, a new incitement to virtuous and
patriotic exertion; and, if any barrier can be effectual against the tide of
corruption, it must be found in a body so large as to be independent of
Court favour, and in some degree exempt from secret intrigue. At all times
had Mr. Millar viewed the inequality of Representation as a defect in the
Government; but, while there was a powerful union of great families to
repress encroachment, he had considered it rather as a blemish, than a very
important practical evil. Now, when all appearance of effective control has
vanished before the luxury of the age, and the immense revenue and patronage of the Crown, he thought it essential to the existence of freedom
that such a reform should take place, as might interest the great body of
the people in public measures, and enable them, in a constitutional manner,
to withstand the encroachment of the Executive Power. <cvi>

But, while he became more and more favourable to a wider extension
of the elective franchise, Mr. Millar was ever decidedly hostile to the system
of *universal suffrage,* conceiving it altogether impossible that the lowest of
the people can ever be independent in their circumstances, or so enlightened as to prefer the public good to their immediate pecuniary interest.
Universal suffrage, far from raising an effectual barrier against the influence
of the Crown, could only, he thought, spread wider the evils of corruption,
and more completely annihilate the control of the wiser part of the nation.
It would, in ordinary cases, confirm the dominion of the Minister, whose
means of corruption are almost inexhaustible; sometimes it might occasion
disorderly tumult, or enable the poor to dictate laws equally unjust and
destructive; never, in his opinion, could it tend to just equality of rights,
or vindicate the cause of rational liberty.

Even a just and prudent reform of Parliament seemed to Mr. Millar no adequate defence, in itself, against an influence founded on so immense a revenue as that of Britain: But he trusted in the intelligence and virtue of a House of Commons, freely chosen by the people, for the adoption of other measures, imperiously demanded by every consideration of policy and justice. Of this nature he <cvii> deemed the abolition of all sinecure places, the diminution of the national expenditure, and the strict appropriation of the revenue to the several heads of the public service. He also considered it as most important, that the appointment to all offices, wherever such a regulation was consistent with the nature of the duty, should be vested in the freeholders of the several counties, or in some description of persons altogether unconnected with Administration. By such changes he hoped that the influence of the Crown might be checked, and the approach of what Mr. Hume has denominated the true Euthanasia of the British Constitution at least retarded.*

Mr. Millar's opinions and conduct, respecting the principal events of the present reign, were in strict conformity to these principles. He openly disapproved of the attempt to tax America, as equally unjust and impolitic; and, when that country, by a series of ill digested measures was driven to the declaration of Independence, he explicitly avowed his wishes for a total separation, rather than a conquest. In the one, there was undoubtedly a humiliation of Great Britain, and some diminution of her power; though, as he suspected, and as the <cviii> event has shewn, none of her commerce: But the subjugation of America would have been the triumph of injustice, and was likely, by increasing the ministerial influence, and putting under the command of the crown a large army accustomed to act against the people, to be as fatal to the liberties of the conquerors, as to those of the conquered. In a town, such as Glasgow, depending wholly, at that time, on the American trade, it will easily be believed that those opinions were extremely unpopular, though now their truth is very generally admitted.

The much lamented death of the Marquis of Rockingham blasted the hopes raised by the dissolution of Lord North's administration, and the

---

* Hume's Essays, Part I. Essay 7. [["Whether the British Monarchy Inclines More to Absolute Monarchy, or to a Republic," in Hume, *Essays, Moral, Political, and Literary*, p. 53 (I.vii.7).]]

triumph of the Coalition over a party, composed of the friends of Prerogative joined to some of those who had formerly supported the rights of the People, was incomplete and transient. Of the Coalition between Lord North and Mr. Fox, many defences have been made, not only as natural, when the grounds of their former differences no longer existed, but also as necessary, on the part of the Whigs, to prevent that uncontrollable influence which must have arisen from a coalition between Lord North and Lord Shelburne.[26] Mr. Millar entered warmly into all these views, but the event <cix> has shown, that the nation considered it as a measure, by which principle was sacrificed to the love of power; and, however erroneous this opinion may be, its consequences have been very fatal to the cause of Liberty.

Soon after this occurred the important struggle between the Crown and

26. Craig describes one of the most heated dramas in late-eighteenth-century British politics. Frederick, Lord North (1732–92), was prime minister of England between 1770 and 1782, including the years of Britain's disastrous defeat by the colonies. North resigned after Cornwallis's surrender at Yorktown and was followed in short order by Rockingham and a coalition of Fox and North. The king loathed Fox, and so took Rockingham's death in 1782 as the chance to make Shelburne prime minister and to bring William Pitt into the government. Fox went into opposition but then in 1783, following upon Shelburne's unpopular negotiations with the colonies, formed a government with his erstwhile opponent Lord North. The cohabitation was necessary as neither North nor Fox had enough votes to form a government on his own, but it was shocking to important parts of the Whig constituency and abhorred by George III. The defeat of Edmund Burke's reform bill for India in 1783 gave Pitt and George III the upper hand in the 1784 elections and for many years after. Craig intimates that had Fox not cohabited with North, a Shelburne-North government dominated by George III would have resulted. It is notable that in spite of Craig's comments Shelburne was a complete, confirmed Smithian: "I owe a Journey I made with Mr. Smith from Edinburgh to London, the difference between light and darkness through the best part of my life. The novelty of principles, added to my youth and prejudice, made me unable to comprehend them at the time, but he urged them with so much benevolence, as well as eloquence, that they took a certain hold, which, though it did not develop itself so as to arrive at full conviction for some few years after, I can fairly say, has constituted, ever since, the happiness of my life, as well as any consideration I may have enjoyed in it" (Dugald Stewart, "Account of the Life and Writings of Adam Smith, LL.D.," in *Adam Smith, Essays on Philosophical Subjects,* ed. W. L. D. Wightman [Oxford: Oxford University Press, 1992], 347). Shelburne's attempt to resume trade relations quickly with the colonies after the British surrender, and his antimercantilist, antimonopolist rhetoric, were fully Smithian. Cf. "Speech on Preliminary Articles of Peace," in *On the Wealth of Nations: Contemporary Responses to Adam Smith,* ed. Ian S. Ross (Bristol: Thoemmes, 1998), 149–51.

the House of Commons, in 1784, which, terminating in the triumph of the former, gave, in Mr. Millar's opinion, a fatal blow to the British Constitution. The right of the king to avail himself of his negative against any bill, which has passed through both Houses of Parliament, cannot be contested, though that negative seems nearly to have fallen into disuse; but in this case, it was almost admitted that an indirect interposition took place at a more early stage of Mr. Fox's India Bill, and such an interposition has always been considered as highly illegal. Soon, however, a still more important question occurred. The House of Commons petitioned for the removal of Ministers; and his majesty was advised not only to refuse their desire, but to dissolve Parliament, for the avowed purpose of acquiring a majority in a new House of Commons. Mr. Millar did not deny that, according to the letter of the Constitution, such prerogatives are vested in the crown; but he contended for its being essential to all idea <cx> of free Government, that the Representatives of the people should have an effective control over the appointment of Ministers; and he maintained that the circumstances of England and of Europe, have rendered the old constitutional checks, by the withholding of the supplies, or the reduction of the army, altogether inapplicable. He held it to be the duty of the king to exercise all his prerogatives for the good of his people, and according to the advice of his Parliament: He, in an especial manner, considered it as important that he should act by such advice, in dismissing Ministers who had rendered themselves obnoxious or suspected, and he viewed a dissolution on account of a petition for the removal of Ministers, as an attempt not only to evade all practicable control, but to influence and overawe future Parliaments. He observed, that, if all the Prerogatives of the Crown are to be exercised in their full extent, after so great an influence, quite unknown at the Revolution, has been created, then has the Government of this country undergone a most material alteration; and he considered a threat of Dissolution as likely, in future, to establish a most pernicious influence over the members of the House of Commons, whose returns have usually been procured with much trouble and at great expence. <cxi>

But however highly Mr. Millar valued Civil Liberty, he considered Personal Freedom as infinitely more important; and had Mr. Pitt vigorously prosecuted the abolition of the Slave Trade, he might have been brought to overlook the mode in which his power was acquired, in consideration of its beneficial exertion. Domestic slavery he viewed as equally unjust and impolitic; as ruinous to the morals both of the masters and of the slaves; and as detrimental even to that industry, and that accumulation of riches, for which alone it is avowedly continued. Without pretending that West India planters are more cruel than others would be in their situation, he contended that absolute power is ever liable to abuse; that the habitual indulgence of every passion must engender cruelty; and that, where there is no restraint, there must frequently be vexatious caprice. The nominal interference of laws executed by the masters, in the very few cases capable of proof, must of necessity, be but a small and rare palliation of the evil.* But the abolition of the Slave Trade would have recommended humanity by the powerful motive of interest; and such are the laws of the Universe, that to assert the impossibility of keeping up the stock of slaves <cxii> without importation, is fully to acknowledge the misery of their condition, and to establish, in a manner more convincing than a thousand facts, the cruelty and oppression of their Masters. Mr. Millar accordingly took a most active part in favour of the abolition of the Slave Trade, by attending all the meetings held at Glasgow for that purpose, by drawing up the Petition to the House of Commons, and using every exertion to interest his Towns-men in the cause of humanity and justice.

The French Revolution, from its first appearance, rivetted Mr. Millar's attention, and, in its early progress excited his fondest hopes. Doubtful, at first, of France being in a condition effectually to oppose the will of the king, and the joint power of the nobility and the church, he feared that the splendid attempt might end in the ruin of the friends of liberty, and the aggravation of the public wrongs. But Mr. Millar was not of a temper to despond after the will of the nation was distinctly pronounced; and, though he lamented, and sometimes ridiculed the precipitation with which the Constituent Assembly swept away all former institutions, he admitted that this, in some instances, might be unavoidable from the inveteracy of abuses, or useful in supporting the enthusiasm of the peo-<cxiii>ple. The confis-

---

* If this required any proof, it has been abundantly furnished by the official documents lately published.

cation of Church property, without an equivalent provision for the present incumbents, he never failed to reprobate, as an act of flagrant injustice; nor could he be brought to excuse the Assembly for rashly and presumptuously abolishing all those distinctions of ranks to which the people had been habituated, and by the influence of which they might have been restrained from many excesses. It was only in smaller deviations from rectitude, and in less hazardous experiments, that he thought allowance should be made for the inexperience of unpractised legislators, and the impatience of a nation new to liberty.

Similar considerations diminished his apprehensions from the few, and not very sanguinary, tumults, which occurred in the more early stages of the Revolution. No man could deplore such excesses more than Mr. Millar; none could be more convinced of their tendency to excite terror, and diffuse general misery; none could be more fully aware of the odium they must bring on the cause of freedom over the whole of Europe, and of their powerful influence in supporting ancient abuses: But, while he abhorred all instances of popular rage or revenge, he knew that, in so unexampled a change from slavery to freedom, some excesses <cxiv> were unavoidable; and in the temporary commotions which took place, he was more frequently struck with the generous patriotism of the people, than surprised at the occasional acts of cruelty, into which they were betrayed. When a nation, depraved by previous servitude, rises to assert privileges long trodden under foot, it were vain to expect regularity of proceedings, or even constant justice of intention: Yet for a considerable time, the conduct of the Assembly and that of the nation, with occasional exceptions, was firm, resolute, and temperate.

The spirit of freedom seemed to be aroused in this country, by the force of example, and, as might be expected, it was, by some, carried to the most extravagant lengths. Mr. Millar, who had always considered government as instituted for the good of the people, and who had been accustomed to examine all political institutions by this criterion alone, treated with the utmost contempt all assertion of metaphysical Rights, inconsistent with practical utility: But, while he ridiculed the idea of imprescriptible, indefeasible, right in the people, to conduct the affairs of Government, he was aware that the doctrines then afloat were of a popular nature, and he thought the best and only solid refutation of them, was such a reform of par-<cxv>liament, as, in itself highly desirable, had now become almost necessary, to rally the great body of the nation around the constitution. Actuated by such motives, he became a zealous member of the society of the Friends of the People, and, with those great characters whom he venerated, willingly exposed himself to obloquy in performing what he considered as an important duty to his country.

The inconsiderate violence of the Republicans of France, on the one hand, and the obvious determination of the Court, on the other, to obey the forms and evade the spirit of the new constitution, soon hurled the benevolent, but misguided, Monarch from his throne, and exposed the country to the most imminent danger of subjugation by a foreign power. Feeling every respect for the motives and characters of the Brissotine party, Mr. Millar regretted deeply that want of energy, of combination, and of resource, which unfitted them to contend either with their foreign or domestic foes. He was no way surprised to see the people, jealous after having been repeatedly betrayed, when struggling for the existence of their country, at last throw themselves into the arms of a faction, odious from its ferocity, but, able, prompt, and energetic. No person could lament more sincerely the disgusting and atrocious scenes which marked <cxvi> the administration of Robespierre in characters of blood; but his horror for such atrocities was always accompanied with the most lively indignation at that combination of the Princes of Europe, to which alone he ascribed the continental war, the destruction of the Brissotines, and the acquiescence of the nation in a system, which, however horrible in itself, was represented as the only means of opposing the dismemberment, or total conquest, of the state.

The imbecility and rapacity of the Directory excited the most sovereign contempt;[27] and Mr. Millar, though he was far from approving of the means by which Buonaparte rose to supreme power, and still farther from approving of the constitution he established, acknowledged that this new rev-

---

27. The French instituted the Directory in 1795, following the fall of Robespierre and the end of the Terror in 1794; it lasted until Bonaparte's coup in 1799. It was widely, if not entirely fairly, reviled for incompetence and corruption.

olution had been rendered almost unavoidable by previous misconduct, and trusted to the melioration of the Government, at the period of a general peace.

Before this event took place, Mr. Millar was no more. Had he lived to witness the servility of France, under the present system, he would have been grieved by so melancholy an illustration of his own remark. "Even in countries," says he, "where the people have made vigorous efforts to meliorate their government, how often has the collision of parties, the opposite attractions of public and private interest, the fermentation of numberless discordant ele-<cxvii>ments, produced nothing at last, but a residue of despotism."* But Mr. Millar's sanguine disposition, even under all these disappointments, would have found reason still to hope for a final result less fatal to the future destinies of man. He would have remembered that England, after a noble and successful struggle against regal tyranny, sunk for a time under the arts of a hypocrite, the corruption of a profligate, and the sanguinary violence of a bigot: but that she roused herself at last, shook off her fetters, and established a constitution which has been the admiration of the world. So would he have expected France to rise from her depression, when the minds of men, no longer appalled by recent horrors, should return to reason, and again feel the salutary influences of patriotism and hope.

It must be sufficiently obvious that, to a man of Mr. Millar's way of thinking, the whole conduct of the British Ministry towards France must have appeared highly reprehensible. Having seen them remain quiet spectators, and even refuse their mediation, when that country was threatened with subjugation, he could not easily credit that solicitude which they afterwards expressed for the ba-<cxviii>lance of power: Finding that Holland made no requisition for our protection, and recollecting that the same Ministers had taken no steps whatever, when the Emperor, some years before, had threatened to open the Scheldt by force, he could scarcely ascribe their interference at this juncture to a pure love of justice, or a scrupulous adherence to treaties: Being well convinced that their real intention was to force a Monarchical Government on France, he paid little regard to the

* Hist. View of the English Gov. Vol. IV. Chap. 7.

abhorrence they expressed at that decree of the Convention, which, until explained, and restricted, threatened the most unjustifiable interference in the internal policy of independent states. Looking on all these as mere pretences, he was well convinced that the war originated in a determination to prevent the reforms meditated at home, to re-establish the ancient despotism in France, and to rivet the fetters of the rest of Europe. He rejoiced that the defeat of a combination, formed on such principles, though for the present unfavourable to the balance of power, rendered abortive the project of shackling, by open force, the spirit of Freedom, and cramping for ever the improvement of man: and he deeply lamented that the atrocities of the French insured complete success to one of the objects of the war, <cxix> by checking the progress of reform in Britain, and injuring the cause of liberty over the world.

So soon after the awful events to which we have been witnesses, it would be presumptuous to say that Mr. Millar's views on this subject were always wise; that he never was deceived by his own passions, nor hurried away by those of others. In considering a situation of affairs, so new, so interesting, and so complicated, he might, occasionally, be misled by hasty or partial views, his hopes might be excited by his wishes, and his expectations might often be disappointed by the event. In the heat of debate, too, he might sometimes be hurried into assertions or illustrations, which his cooler judgment would have disowned; and, at a time when political rancour rose to an unexampled height, it is no way surprising, that the open and manly avowal of his sentiments should have exposed him to much calumny and misrepresentation. But those who knew his worth always did justice to the purity of his motives: and it is with much pleasure I quote the testimony of one of his Friends, who entertained opinions of the French Revolution and the late war, directly opposite to his. "However much," says Mr. Jardine, "we may have differed from him on these subjects, respecting his zeal and good intentions, there can be, as I con-<cxx>ceive, but one opinion. No little ideas of private interest, no narrow views of advantage or emolument, sunk him to the level of party politicians; but firm, resolute, and decided, he was, from first to last, the enlightened and manly defender of what he conceived to be, The Rights and Liberties of Mankind."

Mr. Millar's virtues were the spontaneous growth of an understanding strong, enlightened, and capacious; of a heart overflowing with benevolence and sensibility. Of these, his uncommon candour in judging of his own claims, and those of others, was one of the most conspicuous. Never was his opinion warped by his private interest, never did he palliate or excuse that in himself, which he would have blamed in his friend. His conduct was uniformly guided by the most delicate attention to the rights, claims, and expectations of others, by the strictest sense of honour. Always aware of the tendency of a man's interest, and desires, to pervert his judgment, against such partiality and self-deception, he guarded with the most vigilant care; anxious not only to abstain from all injustice, but to avoid every suspicion, in his own mind, of his <cxxi> having done what any person informed of the circumstances, could possibly disapprove.

This delicate purity of conduct is the more remarkable, as Mr. Millar's temper was uncommonly sanguine. What he wished he always convinced himself was probable; what he dreaded he seldom allowed himself to think could take place. His ingenuity in deceiving himself was sometimes most surprising. The slightest favourable circumstances were so combined as to seem a solid foundation for confidence; the smallest doubt of the truth of unwelcome intelligence was strengthened and corroborated, till it lulled, if it could not entirely overcome, apprehension. Even when there was an end of hope and of fear; when a disagreeable or distressing event had actually occurred, he could turn his mind, with surprising facility, to new views, and new circumstances, from which he still expected favourable results. Such a temper, to a man engaged in active life, must be the source of many precipitate measures, of much disappointment and distress; not unfrequently of absolute ruin. But to him, who was rather a spectator than an actor in the scene, it could occasion no very serious calamity, and was often the cause of real happiness. <cxxii>

That sensibility, which was in some measure the source of this sanguineness of temper, made Mr. Millar enter, with the greatest warmth, into the feelings of every person around him. It was this sensibility, this delicacy of attention to the habits, wishes, and feelings of others, which rendered his conversation so generally agreeable, and gained him the affections of those friends to whom he was ever warmly and steadily attached. To all of them, when an opportunity offered, he was always ready to do every act of kindness, and to do it in that delicate manner which produces a more lasting gratitude than any favour; and from all of them, he experienced the most cordial affection and respect.

He was, indeed, always disposed to do good, whether to a friend or to a stranger. So far was he from being actuated by selfish considerations, that his generosity sometimes exceeded what his limited fortune might altogether warrant. Nothing was so despicable in his mind, as any sordid attention to money; and, while he knew that he could place his family in independent circumstances, he was less anxious about farther accumulation. The liberality of his disposition made him equally ready to contribute to every useful institution, and to relieve private distress; and in his charities, in his good offices, he was always attentive to save the feelings <cxxiii> of the person whom he relieved, from that sense of degradation which, to many, is more intolerable than want.

The same warmth of feeling which displayed itself in Mr. Millar's services to strangers, and still more amiably in the kindness with which he treated every member of his family, and every person whom he called his friend, made him feel with the greatest poignancy, those more intimate distresses, from which no man can be exempt. Afraid, however, of intruding his grief on others less nearly interested, or less violently affected, he was at the utmost pains to repress every exterior mark of affliction, every thing which might appear a demand on the sympathy of his friends. So far did he carry this command over his own mind, that a stranger might have mistaken his character, and supposed him perfectly tranquil, at the very time when he was in the deepest affliction. No man could more completely bring his behaviour to a tone in unison with the feelings of those around him: But in his anxiety to accomplish this, and his unwillingness to be any restraint on society, he sometimes perhaps went beyond the exact line of propriety, and gave an impression of severity and unconcern, which were far from belonging to his character. In the astonishing exertions of self- <cxxiv>command he often displayed, it was scarcely possible that he should not occasionally be carried too far by the violence of the effort over his own feelings, and the want of confidence in his own strength of mind. Those who enjoyed his friendship were never deceived by such appearances of tranquillity. They saw them not as proofs of real ease, far less as proofs of indifference; but as the most unequivocal indications of an habitual attention to the feelings of others struggling against poignant distress.

For a long time, Mr. Millar, though exposed to many smaller misfortunes, was almost exempt from family affliction. He lost, indeed, two infants; but all his other children grew up around him, and repaid his cares by the most lively affection. It was not till 1791 that he had occasion to support their mother, under what might almost be considered as the first breach in the family. During that summer, their second daughter died of consumption. Mrs. Millar's health, not long after, began to decline; and, in summer 1795, a long and painful illness, which she bore with admirable constancy and even cheerfulness, was terminated by her death. The first burst of Mr. Millar's grief was such as might be expected in a man of the deepest sensibility, deprived of the companion of his life, the <cxxv> woman who, for 34 years, had enjoyed his fullest confidence, and possessed his fondest affections. On visiting him, the day after this melancholy event, I found that he had resumed his accustomed control over his own mind. He spoke to me of his loss with feeling, but without weakness; like a man deprived of much happiness, but not abandoning himself to affliction; neither priding himself in stoical indifference, nor undervaluing the comforts he still enjoyed in the affections of his family and of his friends.

It was not long till he was again called upon for a new exertion of his self-command. His eldest son, on whose education he had bestowed uncommon attention, who was respected for his literary talents, and endeared to all his friends by the singular excellence and amiableness of his dispositions, met, for some time, with a success at the Bar equal to his most sanguine hopes. With very flattering prospects of rising in his profession, he married the youngest daughter of Dr. Cullen, a lady of most fascinating manners and uncommon talents and acquirements. He was, however, soon after seized with an indisposition, which lasted for a considerable time; and, though he recovered from it in a great degree, yet his professional labours continued to be too severe, and indeed very hurtful to his health. <cxxvi> At this period, the violence of political parties rose to an extreme height in Scotland, and it was impossible for the son of Mr. Millar, carrying his conviction of the necessity of reform in some degree farther than his father, and equally open and steady in maintaining his opinions, to escape that obloquy with which the violent and interested in political parties always attempt to overwhelm their opponents. Averse to contention, hopeless of a pacific change in the political institutions of his country, and finding himself in a state of health which rendered laborious application improper, he resolved, in spring 1795, to emigrate to America. Soon after his arrival there, he was offered an advantageous purchase of lands, and the management of an extensive settlement in the back country of Pennsylvania. This, as he was particularly fond of agricultural pursuits, he immediately accepted. On arriving at the settlement, he began to plan and execute improvements, with all the ardour natural to his temper; but having incautiously exposed himself, in a very hot day of summer, he was struck with a coup de soleil, of which he almost instantly expired.

I saw Mr. Millar a few hours after he had received intelligence of his death; and, though still there were faint hopes that the accounts might be untrue, seldom have I witnessed more deep distress. He <cxxvii> had opposed his son's quitting his profession and his country, in the full confidence that the political animosities could not be of long duration; already symptoms of the decline of party rancour were beginning to appear: and, perhaps, he had never relinquished the secret hope of again seeing him in the midst of those valued friends from whom he had parted with deep regret. The final disappointment of all these hopes Mr. Millar felt most acutely; but, after the first shock, he resumed his self-possession; and, even at the very time that he was most strongly agitated, I am convinced that the presence of a stranger would have recalled him to himself, and that he would have conversed with firmness and apparent ease.*

---

* The rest of his family, three sons and six daughters, survived him. His eldest son [[James Millar (1762–1832)]] is Professor of Mathematics in the University of Glasgow; the second [[William Millar]] is a Major of Artillery, and the third [[Archibald Millar]] a writer to the signet in Edinburgh: one of his daughters [[Agnes]] is married to Mr. [[James]] Mylne [[(1757–1839)]], Professor of Moral Philosophy in Glasgow; and another [[Margaret]] to Mr. [[John]] Thomson [[(1765–1846)]], Professor of Surgery in Edinburgh. With that attention to the comfort of his family which ever guided his conduct, Mr. Millar directed by his will, that Milheugh, to which they were so fondly attached

Mr. Millar's athletic form, his agility, surprising in a man of his years, his temperance of every <cxxviii> kind, and his regular habits of exercise, gave his friends reason to expect that he would have enjoyed long life and continued health. He never was subject to those little temporary complaints, which spring from a weak constitution or indolent habits, and which, while they diminish the enjoyment of life, gradually bring on old age. Always vigorous and alert, his mind was free from languor, his appearance youthful, and his strength unimpaired. But, in the end of 1799, he was seized with a very dangerous inflammatory complaint, from which, after a few weeks of severe illness, he seemed perfectly recovered; and, although those who paid anxious attention to his appearance saw that he had lost something of the youthful spring of his step, and was less able to endure any violent exertion, to others he seemed as healthful and vigorous as ever.

In May 1801, when he was in perfect health he incautiously exposed himself to a hot sun for several hours, fearing no bad effect from changes of weather to which he had always accustomed himself. That very night he was taken ill; and his complaint soon put on the appearance of the most dangerous pleurisy. I happened to be at a distance from Glasgow, when I should have wished most to be near him. The instant I heard of his danger, <cxxix> I hurried to Milheugh; but, on the 30th of May, the day before my arrival, I had lost that Friend, whose continued kindness will always live in my remembrance. Of Mr. Millar's behaviour during his last illness, his son-in-law, Mr. Mylne, who was present during the distressing scene, has given the following short, but interesting account:

"In the midst of his family, he encountered the severe trial presented by the sufferings and prospects of a death-bed. That trial he nobly sustained. His last scene was altogether worthy of the part he had uniformly maintained on the stage of life. Soon after the very unexpected attack of the disease which brought him to the grave, he foresaw the issue, and awaited it with the most perfect composure. No symptom of impatience or of alarm

---

should continue to be the place of residence of his unmarried daughters. [[There was a son older than James, John (1760–96), who wrote *Elements of the Law Relating to Insurances* (1787). Craig left him off the list of Millar's children because he did not survive his father.]]

ever escaped him: and no thought gave him pain but the thought of being separated from his family, with whom he had long enjoyed the purest happiness, and to whose happiness his life was so important."

On his death-bed, Mr. Millar committed the care of his manuscripts to his son the Professor of Mathematics, his son-in-law Mr. Mylne, and myself. As he had at one time given orders to destroy his whole manuscripts, a resolution from which he was <cxxx> with difficulty diverted, we considered ourselves as particularly called upon, in executing the trust reposed in us, to publish only what seemed to have been carefully revised, and written out for the press. The Historical View of the English Government, we found in a state less complete than we had expected. For several years, the public attention had been so fully engrossed by the important events passing on the theatre of Europe, that there remained little curiosity respecting those steps by which the British Constitution had reached its present state. The minds of men were more intent on discovering what is best, than what has actually taken place; and perhaps even the author was, for some time, less interested in his usual speculations, while every appearance indicated that a new era had commenced, and that the future Governments of Europe were likely to have little dependence on former institutions. But, though these considerations might, for a time, diminish Mr. Millar's ardour in this particular study, he never for a moment abandoned his intention of completing the Historical View of the English Government, and of presenting to the Public a detailed account of the various branches of the British Constitution.

In pursuance of this intention, he had completed <cxxxi> his account of the period from the accession of the House of Stewart, to the Revolution, in a manner which cannot fail to add to his reputation. Here he appears more openly in opposition to Mr. Hume, than in the earlier part of the History; pointing out, with clearness and precision, the sources of that very eminent author's misapprehensions. Without directly misrepresenting, or even suppressing, any important fact, Mr. Hume has passed slightly over the ambitious designs, and profligate insincerity of Charles the First, dwelling frequently and fully on such irregularities as were probably unavoidable in the measures of the Commons, and on what, in a more enlightened age, appears the revolting bigotry of the times. What had occa-

sionally been done, when obviously useful and necessary, without exciting
the attention of a rude and simple age, even exercises of power which had
been declared illegal by statute, he represents as the ordinary rule of the
Constitution: what had become requisite to guard public liberty against the
future attempts of a king who, never yielding without mental reservations,
had stretched his prerogative far beyond its just bounds, and, aided by the
clergy, had well nigh put an end to all the liberties and privileges of the
Nation, he has ventured to re-<cxxxii>prehend as unwarrantable encroachments. In opposition to such representations, Mr. Millar, without a particular examination of every measure of the Crown or Parliament, has
given a very masterly sketch of the transactions of that important period,
characterising, in a just and striking manner, the views and motives of the
several parties, whose struggles and collisions prepared the Revolution settlement, by which the prerogatives of the Crown were defined, and the
Rights of the People finally ascertained.

Of the period since the Revolution, we found several chapters; but in a
state so incomplete, that we did not think it proper to give them to the
public. There were, however, several Dissertations, written with the intention of forming part of the History, or perhaps with the view of having the
substance of their speculations interwoven with it; and these treatises contained such ingenious disquisitions on the rise of the influence of the
Crown, and on the effects of extended commerce in giving birth to a spirit
of independence in the people; they exhibited so animated a sketch of the
changes produced by refinement on national character, and of the natural
progress of poetical composition; that we thought, we should be doing
injustice to the me-<cxxxiii>mory of our Friend, by withholding them
from the world.*

---

* Several circumstances prevented the publication of Mr. Millar's posthumous works
till late in spring, 1803; and then the distance we all were from London induced us to
trust the publication too much to others. In consequence of this, there are such blunders
in the edition, as, though they do not obscure the sense, require an apology to the public.
It was originally intended that the posthumous work should appear alone under the title
of A Historical View of the English Government from *the Accession of the House of
Stewart:* but afterwards it was thought better to give a uniform edition of the whole
work. The present title page was therefore sent up, with orders, which were neglected,

Among Mr. Millar's manuscripts, we found no others, which, consistently with the rule we had laid down for ourselves, we thought proper for publication. There were indeed many valuable chapters of *The Account of the Present State of the British Government,* and several ingenious treatises on various subjects, composed for the Literary Society; but some of them were imperfect, and none were written with that care which, without many alterations and corrections, would have justified us in sending them to the press. From what Mr. Millar had written of the delineation of the British <cxxxiv> Government, and from the very excellent Lectures he used to deliver on that subject, it is particularly to be regretted that he did not live to finish a work which must have added greatly to his reputation, and which might have been of the most important advantage to his country.

After all that has been published on the British Constitution, a work which should exhibit, not a fanciful theory, but the real practice of the Government, is still wanting;[28] and such a work, if executed with judgment and impartiality, would resolve the important questions, how far, in the course of the last century, the various branches of the Legislature have actually, though silently, encroached on the powers of each other, and what changes in the forms of Government have consequently become necessary, to restore it, in principles and spirit, to the Revolution settlement in 1688.

> That what is well may keep
> Its goodness permanent, and what requires
> Our healing hand, with mild severity
> May be corrected.[29]
>
> POTTER'S AESCHYLUS.

---

to entitle the third volume Book III. of the Historical View, and to publish the fourth volume as separate Dissertations. As to the verbal errors, they were occasioned by the absence of the Publisher from London, while the work was in the press.

28. Appeared as "still a wanting" in the third edition.

29. R. Potter, ed. and trans., *The Tragedies of Aeschylus* (Norwich, 1777), 262. [Translation of *Agamemnon* 846–50.]

THE
ORIGIN
OF THE
DISTINCTION OF RANKS.

Introduction

Those who have examined the manners and customs of nations have had chiefly two objects in view. By observing the systems of law established in different parts of the world, and by remarking the consequences with which they are attended, men have endeavoured to reap advantage from the experience of others, and to make a selection of such institutions and modes of government as appear most worthy of being adopted.

To investigate the causes of different usages has been likewise esteemed an useful as well as an entertaining speculation. When we contemplate the amazing diversity to be found in the laws of different countries, and even of the same country at different periods, our curiosity is naturally excited to enquire in what manner mankind have been led to embrace such different rules of conduct; and at the same it is evident, that, unless we are ac-<2>quainted with the circumstances which have recommended any set of regulations, we cannot form a just notion of their utility, or even determine, in any case, how far they are practicable.

In searching for the causes of those peculiar systems of law and government which have appeared in the world, we must undoubtedly resort, first of all, to the differences of situation, which have suggested different views and motives of action to the inhabitants of particular countries. Of this kind, are the fertility or barrenness of the soil, the nature of its productions, the species of labour requisite for procuring subsistence, the number of individuals collected together in one community, their proficiency in arts,

the advantages which they enjoy for entering into mutual transactions, and
for maintaining an intimate correspondence. The variety that frequently
occurs in these, and such other particulars, must have a prodigious influence
upon the great body of a people; as, by giving a peculiar direction to their
inclinations and pursuits, it must be productive of correspondent habits,
dispositions, and ways of thinking.

When we survey the present state of the globe, we find that, in many
parts of it, the inhabitants are so destitute of culture, as to appear little
above the condition of brute animals; and even when we peruse the remote
history of polished nations, we have seldom any difficulty in tracing them
to a state of the same rudeness and barbarism. There <3> is, however, in
man a disposition and capacity for improving his condition, by the exertion
of which, he is carried on from one degree of advancement to another; and
the similarity of his wants, as well as of the faculties by which those wants
are supplied, has every where produced a remarkable uniformity in the several steps of his progression. A nation of savages, who feel the want of
almost every thing requisite for the support of life, must have their attention
directed to a small number of objects, to the acquisition of food and clothing, or the procuring shelter from the inclemencies of the weather; and their
ideas and feelings, in conformity to their situation, must, of course, be
narrow and contracted. Their first efforts are naturally calculated to increase
the means of subsistence, by catching or ensnaring wild animals, or by
gathering the spontaneous fruits of the earth; and the experience, acquired
in the exercise of these employments, is apt, successively, to point out the
methods of taming and rearing cattle, and of cultivating the ground. According as men have been successful in these great improvements, and find
less difficulty in the attainment of bare necessaries, their prospects are gradually enlarged, their appetites and desires are more and more awakened and
called forth in pursuit of the several conveniencies of life; and the various
branches of manufacture, together with commerce, its inseparable attendant, and with science and literature, the natural off-<4>spring of ease and
affluence, are introduced, and brought to maturity. By such gradual advances in rendering their situation more comfortable, the most important
alterations are produced in the state and condition of a people: their numbers are increased; the connections of society are extended; and men, being

less oppressed with their own wants, are more at liberty to cultivate the feelings of humanity: property, the great source of distinction among individuals, is established; and the various rights of mankind, arising from their multiplied connections, are recognised and protected: the laws of a country are thereby rendered numerous; and a more complex form of government becomes necessary, for distributing justice, and for preventing the disorders which proceed from the jarring interests and passions of a large and opulent community. It is evident, at the same time, that these, and such other effects of improvement, which have so great a tendency to vary the state of mankind, and their manner of life, will be productive of suitable variations in their taste and sentiments, and in their general system of behaviour.

There is thus, in human society, a natural progress from ignorance to knowledge, and from rude to civilized manners, the several stages of which are usually accompanied with peculiar laws and customs. Various accidental causes, indeed, have contributed to accelerate, or to retard this advance-<5>ment in different countries. It has even happened that nations, being placed in such unfavourable circumstances as to render them long stationary at a particular period, have been so habituated to the peculiar manners of that age, as to retain a strong tincture of those peculiarities, through every subsequent revolution.[1] This appears to have occasioned some of the chief varieties which take place in the maxims and customs of nations equally civilized.

The character and genius of a nation may, perhaps, be considered as nearly the same with that of every other in similar circumstances; but the case is very different with respect to individuals, among whom there is often a great diversity, proceeding from no fixed causes that are capable of being ascertained. Thus, in a multitude of dice thrown together at random, the result, at different times, will be nearly equal; but in one or two throws of

---

1. "Whatever it be that forms the manners of one generation, the next must imbibe a deeper tincture of the same dye; men being more susceptible of all impressions during infancy, and retaining these impressions as long as they remain in the world" ("Of National Characters," I.XXI.9).

a single die,[2] very different numbers may often be produced. It is to be expected, therefore, that, though the greater part of the political system of any country be derived from the combined influence of the whole people, a variety of peculiar institutions will sometimes take their origin from the casual interposition of particular persons, who happen to be placed at the head of a community, and to be possessed of singular abilities, and views of policy. This has been regarded, by many writers, as the great source of those differences <6> which are to be found in the laws, and government of different nations. It is thus that Brama is supposed to have introduced the peculiar customs of Indostan; that Lycurgus is believed to have formed the singular character of the Lacedemonians; and that Solon is looked upon as the author of that very different style of manners which prevailed at Athens. It is thus, also, that the English constitution is understood to have arisen from the uncommon genius, and patriotic spirit, of King Alfred. In short, there is scarcely any people, ancient or modern, who do not boast of some early monarch, or statesman, to whom it is pretended they owe whatever is remarkable in their form of government.

But, notwithstanding the concurring testimony of historians, concerning the great political changes introduced by the lawgivers of a remote age, there may be reason to doubt, whether the effect of their interpositions has ever been so extensive as is generally supposed. Before an individual can be invested with so much authority, and possessed of such reflection and foresight as would induce him to act in the capacity of a legislator, he must, probably, have been educated and brought up in the knowledge of those natural manners and customs, which, for ages perhaps, have prevailed among his countrymen. Under the influence of all the prejudices derived from ancient usuage, he will commonly be disposed to prefer the system

---

2. *"First,* If you suppose a dye to have any biass, however small, to a particular side, this biass, though, perhaps, it may not appear in a few throws, will certainly prevail in a great number, and will cast the balance entirely to that side. In like manner, when any *causes* beget a particular inclination or passion, at a certain time, and among a certain people; though many individuals may escape the contagion, and be ruled by passions peculiar to themselves; yet the multitude will certainly be seized by the common affection, and be governed by it in all their actions" ("Of the Rise and Progress of the Arts and Sciences," I.XIV.3). Millar's Introduction is full of Humean language throughout.

already estab-<7>lished to any other, of which the effects have not been ascertained by experience; or if in any case he should venture to entertain a different opinion, he must be sensible that, from the general prepossession in favour of the ancient establishment, an attempt to overturn it, or to vary it in any considerable degree, would be a dangerous measure, extremely unpopular in itself, and likely to be attended with troublesome consequences.

As the greater part of those heroes and sages that are reputed to have been the founders and modellers of states, are only recorded by uncertain tradition, or by fabulous history, we may be allowed to suspect that, from the obscurity in which they are placed, or from the admiration of distant posterity, their labours have been exaggerated, and misrepresented. It is even extremely probable, that those patriotic statesmen, whose existence is well ascertained, and whose laws have been justly celebrated, were at great pains to accommodate their regulations to the situation of the people for whom they were intended; and that, instead of being actuated by a projecting spirit, or attempting, from visionary speculations of remote utility, to produce any violent reformation, they confined themselves to such moderate improvements as, by deviating little from the former usage, were in some measure supported by experience, and coincided with the prevailing opinions of the country. All the ancient systems of legislation that have <8> been handed down to us with any degree of authenticity, show evident marks of their having been framed with such reasonable views; and in none of them is this more remarkable than in the regulations of the Spartan Lawgiver, which appear, in every respect, agreeable to the primitive manners of that simple and barbarous people, for whose benefit they were promulgated.

Among the several circumstances which may affect the gradual improvements of society, the difference of climate is one of the most remarkable. In warm countries, the earth is often extremely fertile, and with little culture is capable of producing whatever is necessary for subsistence. To labour under the extreme heat of the sun is, at the same time, exceedingly troublesome and oppressive. The inhabitants, therefore, of such countries, while they enjoy a degree of affluence, and, while by the mildness of the climate they are exempted from many inconveniencies and wants, are sel-

dom disposed to any laborious exertion, and thus, acquiring habits of indolence, become addicted to sensual pleasure, and liable to all those infirmities which are nourished by idleness and sloth. The people who live in
a cold country find, on the contrary, that little or nothing is to be obtained
without labour; and being subjected to numberless hardships, while they
are forced to contend with the ruggedness of the soil, and the severity of
the seasons, in earning their scanty provision, they become <9> active and
industrious, and acquire those dispositions and talents which proceed from
the constant and vigorous exercise both of the mind and body.

Some philosophers are of opinion, that the difference of heat and cold,
of moisture and dryness, or other qualities of the climate, have a more
immediate influence upon the character and conduct of nations, by op-
erating insensibly upon the human body, and by effecting correspondent
alterations in the temper. It is pretended that great heat, by relaxing the
fibres, and by extending the surface of the skin, where the action of the
nerves is chiefly performed, occasions great sensibility to all external impressions; which is accompanied with proportionable vivacity of ideas and
feelings.[3] The inhabitants of a hot country are, upon this account, supposed
to be naturally deficient in courage, and in that steadiness of attention
which is necessary for the higher exertions of judgment; while they are no
less distinguished by their extreme delicacy of taste, and liveliness of imagination. The weakness, too, of their bodily organs prevents them from consuming a great quantity of food, though their excessive perspiration, the
effect of the climate, requires continual supplies of such thin liquors as are
proper to repair the waste of their fluids. In this situation, therefore, temperance in eating and drinking becomes a constitutional virtue.

The inhabitants of a cold region, are said, on the other hand, to acquire
an opposite complexion. <10> As cold tends to brace the fibres, and to
contract the operation of the nerves, it is held to produce a vigorous constitution of body, with little sensibility or vivacity; from which we may
expect activity, courage, and resolution, together with such calm and steady
views of objects, as are usually connected with a clear understanding. The

3. This refers to Montesquieu's doctrine that national character is partially formed
by physical causes (*The Spirit of the Laws,* XIV.2).

vigorous constitutions of men, in a cold climate, are also supposed to demand great supplies of strong food, and to create a particular inclination for intoxicating liquors.

In some such manner as this, it is imagined that the character of different nations arises, in a great measure, from the air which they breathe, and from the soil upon which they are maintained. How far these conjectures have any real foundation, it seems difficult to determine. We are too little acquainted with the structure of the human body, to discover how it is affected by such physical circumstances, or to discern the alterations in the state of the mind, which may possibly proceed from a different conformation of bodily organs; and in the history of the world, we see no regular marks of that secret influence which has been ascribed to the air and climate, but, on the contrary, may commonly explain the great differences in the manners and customs of mankind from other causes, the existence of which is capable of being more clearly ascertained. <11>

How many nations are to be found, whose situation in point of climate is apparently similar, and, yet, whose character and political institutions are entirely opposite? Compare, in this respect, the mildness and moderation of the Chinese, with the rough manners and intolerant principles of their neighbours in Japan. What a contrast is exhibited by people at no greater distance than were the ancient Athenians and Lacedemonians? Can it be conceived that the difference between the climate of France and that of Spain, or between that of Greece and of the neighbouring provinces of the Turkish empire, will account for the different usages and manners of the present inhabitants? How is it possible to explain those national peculiarities that have been remarked in the English, the Irish, and the Scotch, from the different temperature of the weather under which they have lived?

The different manners of people in the same country, at different periods, are no less remarkable, and afford evidence yet more satisfactory, that national character depends very little upon the immediate operation of climate. The inhabitants of Sparta are, at present, under the influence of the same physical circumstances as in the days of Leonidas. The modern Italians live in the country of the ancient Romans.

The following Inquiry is intended to illustrate the natural history of mankind in several import-<12>ant articles. This is attempted, by pointing out the more obvious and common improvements which gradually arise in the state of society, and by showing the influence of these upon the manners, the laws, and the government of a people.

With regard to the facts made use of in the following discourse, the reader, who is conversant in history, will readily perceive the difficulty of obtaining proper materials for speculations of this nature. Historians of reputation have commonly overlooked the transactions of early ages, as not deserving to be remembered; and even in the history of later and more cultivated periods, they have been more solicitous to give an exact account of battles, and public negociations, than of the interior police and government of a country. Our information, therefore, with regard to the state of mankind in the rude parts of the world, is chiefly derived from the relations of travellers, whose character and situation in life, neither set them above the suspicion of being easily deceived, nor of endeavouring to misrepresent the facts which they have related. From the number, however, and the variety of those relations, they acquire, in many cases, a degree of authority, upon which we may depend with security, and to which the narration of any single person, how respectable soever, can have no pretension. When illiterate men, ignorant of the writings of each other, and who, unless upon religious subjects, had no speculative <13> systems to warp their opinions, have, in distant ages and countries, described the manners of people in similar circumstances, the reader has an opportunity of comparing their several descriptions, and from their agreement or disagreement is enabled to ascertain the credit that is due to them. According to this method of judging, which throws the veracity of the relater very much out of the question, we may be convinced of the truth of extraordinary facts, as well as of those that are more agreeable to our own experience. It may even be remarked, that in proportion to the singularity of any event, it is the more improbable that different persons, who design to impose upon the world, but who have no concert with each other, should agree in relating it. When to all this, we are able to add the reasons of those particular customs which have been uniformly reported, the evidence becomes as complete as the nature of the thing will admit. We cannot refuse our assent to such evidence, without falling into a degree of scepticism by which the credibility of all historical testimony would be in a great measure destroyed. This observation, it is hoped, will serve as an apology for the multiplicity of facts that are sometimes stated in confirmation of the following remarks. At the same time, from an apprehension of being tedious, the author has on other occasions, selected only a few, from a greater number to the same purpose, that might easily have been procured. <14>

Of the Rank and Condition of Women in Different Ages

SECTION I

The effects of poverty and barbarism, with respect to the condition of women.

Of all our passions, it should seem that those which unite the sexes are most easily affected by the peculiar circumstances in which we are placed, and most liable to be influenced by the power of habit and education. Upon this account they exhibit the most wonderful variety of appearances, and, in different ages and countries, have produced the greatest diversity of manners and customs.

The state of mankind in the rudest period of society, is extremely unfavourable to the improvement of these passions. A savage who earns his food by hunting and fishing, or by gathering the spontaneous fruits of the earth, is incapable of attaining any considerable refinement in his pleasures. He finds so much difficulty, and is exposed to so many hardships in procuring mere necessaries, that he has no leisure or encouragement to aim at the luxuries and conveniencies of life. His wants are few, in proportion to the narrowness of his <15> circumstances. With him, the great object is to be able to satisfy his hunger, and, after the utmost exertions of labour and activity, to enjoy the relief of idleness and repose. He has no time for cultivating a correspondence with the other sex, nor for attending to those enjoyments which result from it; and his desires being neither cherished by affluence, nor inflamed by indulgence, are allowed to remain in that moderate state which renders them barely sufficient for the continuation of the species.

The facility with which he may commonly gratify these appetites, is another circumstance by which his situation is peculiarly distinguished. In the most rude and barbarous ages, little or no property can be acquired by particular persons; and, consequently, there are no differences of rank to interrupt the free intercourse of the sexes. The pride of family, as well as the insolence of wealth, is unknown; and there are no distinctions among individuals, but those which arise from their age and experience, from their strength, courage, and other personal qualities. The members of different families, being all nearly upon a level, maintain the most familiar intercourse with one another, and, when impelled by natural instinct, give way to their mutual desires without hesitation or reluctance. They are unacquainted with those refinements which create a strong preference of particular objects, and with those artificial rules of decency and < 16 > decorum which might lay a restraint upon their conduct.

It cannot be supposed, therefore, that the passions of sex will rise to any considerable height in the breast of a savage. He must have little regard for pleasures which he can purchase at so easy a rate. He meets with no difficulties nor disappointments to enhance the value of his enjoyment, or to rouse and animate him in the pursuit of it. He arrives at the end of his wishes, before they have sufficiently occupied his thoughts, or engaged him in those delightful anticipations of happiness which the imagination is apt to display in the most flattering colours. He is a stranger to that long continued solicitude, those alternate hopes and fears, which agitate and torment the lover, and which, by awakening the sensibility, while they relax the vigour of his mind, render his prevailing inclinations more irresistible.

The phlegmatic disposition of savages, in this particular, has accordingly been often remarked as a distinguishing part of their character. There is good reason to believe that, in the state of simplicity which precedes all cultivation and improvement, the intercourse of the sexes is chiefly regulated by the primary intention of nature; that it is of consequence totally interrupted by the periods of pregnancy; and that the same laws, with respect to the difference of seasons, which govern < 17 > the constitution of inferior animals, have also an influence upon the desires of the human species.*

It is true, that, even in early ages, some sort of marriage, or permanent union between persons of different sexes, has been almost universally established. But when we examine the nature of this <18> primitive alliance, it appears to have been derived from motives very little connected with those passions which we are at present considering. When a child has been produced by the accidental correspondence of his parents, it is to be expected that, from the influence of natural affection, they will be excited to assist one another in making some provision for his maintenance. For this purpose, they are led to take up their residence together, that they may act

---

* A late ingenious author imagines that this coldness of constitution is peculiar to the natives of America; and he accounts for it, in a most whimsical manner, from the moisture of the climate, by which the inhabitants of that country are, in his opinion, rendered inferior, both in mind and body, to those of the old world. [[Cornelius De Pauw.]] [Recherches philosophiques sur les Americains.] [[I:23]] [[De Pauw, a diplomat in the court of Frederick the Great, argued in this widely read work that America was an enervated and degenerate continent due to its climate.]] But though it must, perhaps, be admitted that particular climates have some influence upon the passions of sex, yet, in most parts of the world, the character of savages, in this respect, exhibits a remarkable uniformity. [See an account of the Samoiedes, histoire generale des voyages, tome 18. p. 509, 510.— Of the inhabitants of Kamtschatka, ibid. tome 19. liv. 2. chap. 4.]

Even among people somewhat advanced beyond the mere savage life, we frequently meet with traces of a similar temperament. "Sera juvenum Venus," says Tacitus of the Germans, "eoque inexhausta pubertas, nec virgines festinantur. Ergo septa pudicitia agunt, nullis spectaculorum illecebris, nullis conviviorum irrationibus corruptae." Tacit. de mor. Germ. §. 19, 20. [["Love comes late to the young men, and their virility is not drained thereby. Nor are maidens hurried along (§20). . . . Accordingly they lead lives of well-protected chastity, corrupted by none of the temptations of banquets (§19)." (J. B. Rives, trans.)]]

The same circumstance is mentioned by Caesar concerning the character of the ancient Gauls. "Qui diutissime impuberes permanserunt, maximam inter suos ferunt laudem: hoc ali staturam, ali vires, nervosque confirmari putant. Intra annum vero vicesimum feminae notitiam habuisse, in turpissimis habent rebus." Caes. de bell. Gall. lib. 6. §. 21. [["They who remain longest in chastity win greatest praise among their kindred; some think that stature, some that strength and sinew are fortified thereby. Furthermore, they deem it a most disgraceful thing to have had knowledge of a woman before the twentieth year." (H. J. Edwards, trans.) The passage actually describes the Germans, not the Gauls as Millar suggests.]]

in concert with each other, and unite their efforts in the preservation and care of their offspring.

Among inferior animals, we may discern the influence of the same principle in forming an association between individuals of different sexes. The connection indeed, in this case, is commonly of short duration; because the young animal is soon in a condition to provide for its own subsistence. In some of the species of birds, however, the young which are hatched at one time, are frequently incapable of procuring their own food before the mother begins to lay eggs a-new; and the male and female are, therefore, apt to contract a more permanent attachment. To this circumstance we may ascribe the imagined fidelity of the turtle, as well as the poetical honours that have been paid to the gentleness of the dove; an animal which, notwithstanding the character it has so universally acquired, appears remarkable for its peevish and quarrelsome temper. Among common poultry, <19> on the contrary, whose offspring is reared without much assistance even from the dam, the disposition to unite in pairs is scarcely observable.

But the long culture which is necessary in rearing the human species, will generally afford to the parents a second pledge of their commerce, before their assistance can be withdrawn from the former. Their attention, therefore, is extended from one object to another, as long as the mother is capable of child-bearing; and their union is thus continued by the same causes which first gave rise to it. Even after this period, they will naturally be disposed to remain in a society to which they have been so long accustomed: more especially, as by living at the head of a numerous family, they enjoy a degree of ease, respect, and security, of which they would otherwise be deprived, and have reason, in their old age, to expect the assistance and protection of their posterity, under all those diseases and infirmities by which they are rendered incapable of providing for themselves.*

These were in all probability the first inducements to marriage among the rude and barbarous <20> inhabitants of the earth. As it appears to have

---

* It seems unnecessary to observe, that what is here said with regard to marriage, together with many other Remarks which follow concerning the manners of early nations, can only be applied to those who had lost all knowledge of the original institutions, which, as the sacred scriptures inform us, were communicated to mankind by an extraordinary revelation from heaven.

taken its origin from the accidental and unforeseen exertions of parental affection, we may suppose that it would be commenced without any previous contract between the parties, concerning the terms or duration of their correspondence. Thus, among the Romans, it should seem that the most ancient marriage was formed merely *by use;* that is, by the parties living constantly together for the space of a year; a period which, in the ordinary course of things, was sufficient to involve them in the care of a family.* It is believed that the early Greeks were accustomed to marry in the same simple manner.† The Kalmuck Tartars have, at present, a similar practice. Among them, it is usual for a young pair to retire, and live together as man and wife for one year; and if, during this time, the woman has produced a child, their marriage is understood to be completed; but if not, they either separate at pleasure, or agree to make another year's trial.‡ Traces of this primitive custom may still be discovered in the law of Scotland; according to which, a marriage dissolved within a *year and day,* and without a child, has no legal consequences, but restores the property of either party to the same situation as if no such alliance had ever existed. <21>

Time and experience gradually improved this connection, and discovered the many advantages of which it is productive. The consideration of those advantages, together with the influence of fashion and example, contributed to promote its universal establishment. The anxiety of parties, or of their relations, to avoid those disputes and inconveniencies with which it was frequently attended, made them endeavour, by an express stipulation, to settle the conditions of their union, and produced a solemn and formal celebration of marriage. The utility of this contract, as it makes a regular provision for multiplying the inhabitants of a country, gave rise to a variety of public regulations for promoting the institution in general, for directing its particular forms, and for discouraging the vague and irregular commerce of the sexes.

---

* Cicero pro Flacco [[XXVII § 84]], Heinec. antiq. Roman. [[Johann Gottlieb Heineccius, *Antiquitatum Romanarum Jurisprudentiam,* I.X.14.]]

† See Brisson. de vet. rit. nuptiar. [[Barnábe Brisson, "De Veteri Ritu Nuptiarum et Jure Connubiorum," in *Opera Minorae Varii Argumenta,* 304.]]

‡ Travels through the Russian empire and Tartary, by John Cook, M. D. vol. I. chap. 56.

The marriages, however, of rude people, according to all accounts, are usually contracted without any previous attachment between the parties, and with little regard to the gratification of their mutual passions. A savage is seldom or never determined to marry from the particular inclinations of sex, but commonly enters into that connexion when he arrives at an age, and finds himself in circumstances, which render the acquisition of a family expedient or necessary to his comfortable subsistence. He discovers no preference of any particular woman, but leaves it to his parents, or other relations, to make choice of a person whom <22> it is thought proper that he should marry: He is not even at the trouble of paying her a visit, but allows them to begin and finish the bargain, without concerning himself at all in the matter: If his proposals are rejected, he hears it without the least disturbance; or if he meets with a favourable reception, he is equally unmoved; and the marriage is completed, on both sides, with the most perfect indifference.* <23>

---

* Lafitau, moeurs des sauvages Ameriquains, 4to. tom. 1. pag. 564. Histoire generale des voyages, tom. 3. liv. 7. cap. 13. §. 1. Ibid. tom. 6. liv. 14. cap. 3. §. 4. Travels of the Jesuits, vol. 2. p. 446.
Father Lafitau takes notice of a particular custom among the savages of America, which shows the indifference with which their marriages are usually contracted, and marks, at the same time, the inattention of that people to the gratification of their passions. "Il est de l'ancien usage, parmi la plûpart des nations sauvages, de passer la premiere année, aprés le mariage contracté, sans le consommer. La proposition avant ce tems-là, seroit une insulte faite à l'epouse, qui lui feroit comprendre, qu'on auroit recherché son alliance, moins par estime pour elle, que par brutalité. Et quoique les epoux passent la nuit ensemble, c'est sans prejudice de cet ancien usage; les parens de l'epouse y veillent attentivement de leur part, et ils ont soin d'entretenir un grand feu devant leur natte, qui éclaire continuellement leur conduite, et qui puisse servir de garand, qu'il ne se passe rien contre l'ordre prescrit." Moeurs des sauvages Amer. tom. 1. p. 564. [["The ancient custom, amongst most of the savage nations, is to spend the first year after the marriage has been contracted, without consummation. To attempt to consummate the marriage before that time would be an insult to the bride, leading her to believe that union with her was sought less out of esteem for her than out of animal considerations. Even though the wedded couple spend the night together, it is without contravening this ancient custom; the parents of the bride carefully keep watch, and maintain a great fire in front of the marriage bed, which sheds light on their conduct, and serves as a guarantee, that nothing takes place that goes against these rules."]] In some parts of Great Britain, the common people hold it a point of decorum, that, after the ceremony of marriage, the married persons should sleep together one night without consummation.

From the extreme insensibility, observable in the character of all savage nations, it is no wonder they should entertain very gross ideas concerning those female virtues which, in a polished nation, are supposed to constitute the honour and dignity of the sex.

The Indians of America think it no stain upon a woman's character, that she has violated the laws of chastity before marriage; nay, if we can give credit to travellers who have visited that country, a trespass of this kind is a circumstance by which a woman is recommended to a husband; who is apt to value her the more, from the consideration that she has been valued by others, and, on the other hand, thinks that he has sufficient ground for putting her away, when he has reason to suspect that she has been over-looked.*

Young women, among the Lydians, were not accustomed to marry, until they had earned their doweries by prostitution.†

The Babylonians had a public regulation, founded upon their religion, and probably handed down from very remote antiquity, that every woman, of whatever rank, should, once in her life, submit to a public prostitution in the temple of Venus.‡ A <24> religious ceremony of a like

---

* Ulloa's voyage to South America. [[George Juan and Antonio de Ulloa, *A Voyage to South America*, VI.v (I:429).]]

† Herodot. lib. 1. [[Herodotus *History* I.93.]]

‡ Strabo, lib. 16. [[*Geography* XVI.20.]]—See also Herodotus, lib. 1. who describes the form of this wonderful institution with his usual simplicity. [[I.199: "The ugliest of the customs among the Babylonians is this: every woman who lives in that country must once in her lifetime go to the temple of Aphrodite and sit there and be lain with by a strange man. Many of the women who are too proud to mix with the others—such, for instance, as are uplifted by the wealth they have—ride to the temple in covered carriages drawn by teams and stay there then with a great mass of attendants following them. But most of the women do thus: they sit in the sacred precinct of Aphrodite with a garland round their heads made of string. There is constant coming and going, and there are roped-off passages running through the crowds of women in every direction, through which the strangers walk and take their pick. When once a woman has taken her seat there, she may not go home again until one of the strangers throws a piece of silver into her lap and lies with her, outside the temple. As he throws a coin, the man says, 'I summon you in the name of Mylitta.' (The Assyrians call Aphrodite Mylitta.) The greatness of the coin may be what it may, for it is not lawful to reject it, since this money, once it is thrown, becomes sacred. The woman must follow the first man who throws the money into her lap and may reject none. Once she has lain with him, she has fulfilled her ob-

nature is said to have been observed in some parts of the Island of Cyprus.*

The infidelity of a married woman is naturally viewed in a different light, and, upon account of the inconveniencies with which it is attended, is often regarded as an offence that deserves to be severely punished. To introduce a spurious offspring into the family; to form a connexion with a stranger, by which the wife is diverted from her proper employments and duties, and by which she may be influenced to embezzle the goods committed to her charge; these are circumstances, that, even in a rude period, are apt to awaken the jealousy of the husband, and to excite his indignation and resentment. There are nations, however, who have disregarded even these considerations, and who have looked upon the strict preservation of conjugal fidelity as a matter of no consequence.

Among the ancient Massagetae, it was usual for persons who resided in the same part of the country to possess their wives in common.† The same custom is said, by Diodorus Siculus, to have taken place among the ancient Troglodites, and the Icthyophagi, inhabiting the coast of the Red Sea.‡

Caesar observes that, in Britain, ten or a dozen persons, chiefly near relations, were accustomed to maintain a community of wives; but that the off-<25>spring of such promiscuous intercourse was reputed to belong to that man who had been first connected with the mother.

Some authors, from a laudable desire of vindicating our forefathers, have called this fact in question, and have been willing to believe, that, in this particular, Caesar was imposed upon by the simple accommodation of those persons who lodged in the same cottage. But it is difficult to conceive that the judicious and well informed conqueror of Gaul, who had been long acquainted with the manners of rude people, and was of a disposition to look upon this as a matter of curiosity, would have made so slight an

---

ligation to the goddess and gets gone to her home. From that time forth you cannot give her any sum large enough to get her. Those women who have attained to great beauty and height depart quickly enough, but those who are ugly abide there a great while, being unable to fulfil the law. Some, indeed, stay there as much as three or four years." David Grene, trans.]]

  * Herodot. lib. 1. [[Ibid.]]
  † Herodot. Ibid. [[I.216.]]
  ‡ Diod. Sicul. hist. lib. 1. [[Actually III.32.]]

inquiry, or satisfied himself with so superficial an examination, as might expose him to such a gross deception.*

The custom of lending a wife to a friend, that he might have children by her, appears to have been universal among the ancient Greeks and Romans, and even when these nations had become wealthy and civilized, was openly countenanced by persons of the highest rank and character. It is said to have been recommended, in a particular manner, to the Spartans, by the celebrated institutions of Lycurgus.† <26>

---

* "Uxores habent deni duodenique inter se communes, et maxime fratres cum fratribus, parentesque cum liberis: sed si qui sunt ex his nati, eorum habentur liberi, quo primum virgo quaeque deducta est." [["Groups of ten or twelve men have wives together in common, and particularly brothers along with brothers, and fathers with sons; but the children born of the unions are reckoned to belong to the particular house to which the maiden was first conducted." Edwards, trans.]] Caesar de bell. Gall. lib. 5. §. 14.

† Plutarch. in vita Lycurg. [[XV [13].]]

> Interea, Phoebo gelidas pellente tenebras,
> Pulsatae sonuere fores: quas sancta relicto
> Hortensi moerens irrumpit Marcia busto;
> Quondam virgo toris melioris juncta mariti;
> Mox ubi connubii pretium, mercesque soluta est,
> Tertia jam soboles, alios fecunda penates
> Impletura datur, geminas, et sanguine matris
> Permixtura domos. Sed postquam condidit urna
> Supremos cineres, miserando concita vultu,
> Effusas laniata comas, contusaque pectus
> Verberibus crebris, cineresque ingesta sepulchri,
> Non aliter placitura viro, sic moesta profatur:
> Dum sanguis inerat, dum vis materna, peregi
> Jussa, Cato, et geminos excepi foeta maritos.
> Visceribus lassis partuque exhausta, revertor
> Jam nulli tradenda viro. Da foedera prisci
> Inlibata tori:———
>   Hae flexere virum voce, &c. Lucan. Pharsal. lib. 2.
> [[Now 'gan the sun to lift his dawning light
> Before him fled the colder shades of night,
> When lo, the sounding doors are heard to turn—
> Chaste Marcia comes from dead Hortensius' urn
> Once to a better husband's happier bed
> With bridal rites a virgin was she led.
> When every debt of love and duty paid,
> And thrice a parent by Lucina made,

In the country of Kamtschatka, there are several tribes of savages, who esteem it an ordinary mark of politeness, when they entertain a friend, to offer him the enjoyment of their wife or their daughter; and whosoever refuses a civility of this kind, to his guest, is supposed to have intended an affront; and his behaviour is resented accordingly. In Louisiana, upon the coast of Guinea, in several parts of the East Indies, in Pegu, Siam, Cochinchina, and Cambodia, the inhabitants are, in like manner, accustomed, for a small present, to make an offer of their women to all strangers who have occasion to visit the country.* <27>

Among all men who have made any considerable advances towards refinement, sentiments of modesty are connected with the intercourse of the sexes. These sentiments are derived from the very different manner in which individuals are affected, when under the immediate influence of desire, and upon other occasions. After the violence of passion has subsided, and when the mind returns to its usual state of tranquillity, its former emotions appear, in some measure, extravagant, and disproportioned to the object which excited them. But if, with all our partiality, the recollection of our

---

The teeming matron, at her lord's command,
To glad Hortensius gave her plighted hand,
With a fair stock his barren house to grace,
And mingle by the mother's side the race.
At length this husband in his ashes laid,
And every rite of due religion paid,
Forth from his monument the mournful dame,
With beaten breasts and locks dishevelled, came;
Then with a pale, dejected, rueful look,
Thus pleasing, to her former lord she spoke:
"While nature yet with vigour fed my veins,
And made me equal to a mother's pains,
To thee obedient, I thy house forsook,
And to my arms another husband took;
My powers at length with genial labours worn,
Weary to thee and wasted I return.
At length a barren wedlock let me prove—
. . . She said. The hero's manly heart was moved.
     Lucan, *Civil War,* trans. Nicholas Rowe, II.326–42]]
  * [[Krasheninnikov,]] History of Kamtschatka. [[p. 224.]]—Dampier's travels. [[William Dampier, *Voyage around the World,* chap. XIV, p. 395.]]

own appetites, in the case here alluded to, be seldom agreeable even to our-selves, we have good reason to conclude that an open display of them will be extremely offensive to others. Those who are not actuated by the same desires must behold our enjoyment with disgust: those who are, must look upon it with jealousy and rivalship. It is to be expected, therefore, that, according as men become sensible of this, they will endeavour to remove such disagreeable appearances. They will be disposed to throw a veil over those pleasures, and to cover from the public eye those thoughts and in-clinations, which, they know by experience, would expose them to con-tempt and aversion. The dictates of nature, in this respect, are inculcated by the force of education; our own feelings are continually gathering strength by a comparison with those of the people around us; and we blush at every deviation from that conceal-< 28 >ment and reserve which we have been taught to maintain, and which long practice has rendered habitual. Certain rules of decency and decorum with relation to dress, the modes of expression, and general deportment, are thus introduced; and as these con-tribute, in a high degree, to improve and embellish the commerce of society, they are regarded as peculiarly indispensible to that sex, in which, for ob-vious reasons, the greatest delicacy and propriety is required.

But mere savages are little acquainted with such refinements. Their sit-uation and manner of life prevent them, either from considering the in-tercourse of the sexes as an object of importance, or from attending to those circumstances which might suggest the propriety of concealing it. Con-scious of nothing blameable in that instinct which nature has bestowed upon them, they are not ashamed of its ordinary gratifications; and they effect no disguise, as to this particular, either in their words or in their actions.

From the account given by Herodotus of the Massagetae, it appears that those barbarians were strangers to reserve or modesty in the commerce of the sexes.* The same circumstance is mentioned by Caesar, in describing the ancient Germans; a people who had made some improvements < 29 >

* Της γαρ επιθυμῆσει γυναικός Μασσαγέτης ανηρ, τον Φαρετρεωνα απικρεμασας προς της ἁμαξας, μίσγεται αδεως. Herodot. B. I. [["When a man of the Massagetae desires a woman, he hangs his quiver on the front of her wagon and lies with her, fear-lessly." I.216. David Grene, trans.]]

in their manner of life.* The form of courtship among the Hottentots, by which the lover is permitted to overcome the reluctance of his mistress, may be considered as a plain indication of similar manners, and exhibits a striking picture of primitive rudeness and simplicity.†

When Mr. Banks was in the island of Otaheite, in 1769, he received a visit from some ladies, who made him a present of cloth, attended with very uncommon ceremonies, of which the following account is published by Dr. Hawkesworth. "There were nine pieces; and having laid three pieces one upon another, the foremost of the women, who seemed to be the principal, and who was called Oorattooa, stepped upon them, and taking up her garments all round her to the waist, turned about, and with great composure and deliberation, and with an air of perfect innocence and simplicity, three times: when this was done, she dropped the veil, and stepping off the cloth, three more pieces were laid on, and she repeated the ceremony: then stepping off as before, the last three were laid on, and the ceremony was repeated in the same manner the third time."‡ <30>

Though the inhabitants of that country are, almost without labour, supplied with great plenty of food, and may therefore be supposed more addicted to pleasure than is usual among savages in a colder climate, yet they appear to have no such differences of wealth as might restrain the free in-

---

* Cujus rei nulla est occultatio; quod et promiscue in fluminibus perluuntur, et pellibus, aut parvis renonum tegumentis utuntur, magna corporis parte nuda. Caes. de bell. Gall. lib. 6. [["And there is no secrecy in the matter, for both sexes bathe in the river and wear skins or small cloaks of reindeer hide, leaving great part of the body bare." Edwards, trans., VI.21.]]

† [[Peter Kolb]] Kolben. present state of Cape of Good Hope, ch. 13.

‡ [[Hawkesworth, ed.,]] Voyages for making discoveries in the Southern Hemisphere, vol. 2. chap. 12.

In the same publication, an account of a still more remarkable exhibition, made in that Island, is given as follows: "A young man, near six feet high, performed the rites of Venus with a little girl about eleven or twelve years of age, before several of our people, and a great number of the natives, without the least sense of its being indecent or improper, but, as appeared, in perfect conformity to the custom of the place. Among the spectators were several women of superior rank, particularly Oberea, who may properly be said to have assisted at the ceremony; for they gave instructions to the girl how to perform her part, which, young as she was, she did not seem to stand in need of." Ibid.

dulgence of their appetites, and by that means produce a degree of refinement in their passions.

Upon the discovery of the new world by Columbus, the natives appeared to have no idea of clothing as a matter of decency; for, though the men made use of a garment, the women, it is said had not the least covering.* The nakedness, however, of these Indians, when authorised by custom, had probably no more tendency to promote debauchery than similar circumstances can be supposed to have upon inferior animals. Rude nations are usually <31> distinguished by greater freedom and plainness of behaviour, according as they are farther removed from luxury and intemperance.

In the Odyssey, when Telemachus arrives at Pylos, he is stripped naked, bathed, and annointed by the king's daughter.

> While these officious tend the rites divine,
> The last fair branch of the Nestorian line,
> Sweet Polycaste, took the pleasing toil
> To bathe the prince, and pour the fragrant oil.
> O'er his fair limbs a flowery vest he threw,
> And issued, like a god, to mortal view.†

A remarkable instance of this plainness and simplicity occurs in the behaviour of Ruth to Boaz her kinsman.

"And when Boaz had eaten and drunk, and his heart was merry, he went to lie down at the end of the heap of corn: and she came softly, and uncovered his feet and laid her down.

"And it came to pass at midnight, that the man was afraid, and turned himself: and behold a woman lay at his feet.

"And he said, Who art thou? And she answered, I am Ruth, thine handmaid: spread therefore thy skirt over thine handmaid, for thou art a near kinsman."‡ <32>

The influence of such manners must be extremely unfavourable to the

---

* Columbus's voyages. Herrera says, that both men and women were perfectly naked. [[Herrera y Tordesillas, *The General History of . . . America,* I:48; *A Curious Collection,* 13.]]

† Pope's translation of the Odyssey, b. 4. l. 58.

‡ Ruth, chap. iii. ver. 7, 8, 9.

rank and dignity of the women; who are deprived of that consideration and respect which, in a polished nation, they are accustomed to derive from the passion between the sexes. It is, at the same time, impossible, in a rude age, that they should procure esteem by such talents as they are capable of acquiring, or by their usefulness in such employments as they have any occasion to exercise.

Among those who are almost continually employed in war, or in hunting, and who, by their manner of life, are exposed to numberless hardships and dangers, activity, strength, courage, and military skill, are the chief accomplishments that are held in high estimation. These accomplishments, which in all ages excite a degree of admiration, are, in a barbarous country, the principal sources of rank and dignity; as they are most immediately useful to the people in procuring food, and in providing for their personal safety, the two great objects which they have constantly in view.[1] When the members of a rude tribe return from an expedition, every man is respected in proportion to the actions which he has performed; and that person is distinguished at the feast who has been so fortunate as to signalize himself in the field. The various incidents of the battle, or of the chase, occupy their thoughts, and become an interesting subject of conversation. Those who are old take <33> pleasure in relating the deeds of former times, by which their own reputation has been established, and in communicating to the young those observations which they have treasured up, or those rules of conduct which appear most worthy of attention. The son, when he goes out to battle, is armed with the sword of his fathers, and, when he calls to mind the renown which they have acquired, is excited to a noble emulation of their achievements.

The inferiority of the women, in this respect, may be easily imagined. From their situation, indeed, they naturally acquire a degree of firmness and intrepidity which appears surprising to persons only acquainted with the manners of polished nations. It is usual for them to accompany the

---

1. "It is indeed observable, that, among all uncultivated nations, who have not as yet had full experience of the advantages attending beneficence, justice, and the social virtues, courage is the predominant excellence; what is most celebrated by poets, recommended by parents and instructors, and admired by the public in general" (Hume, *Enquiry Concerning the Principles of Morals*, VII:255).

men in their expeditions either for hunting or for war; and it sometimes happens that individuals are excited, by the general spirit of the times, to engage in battle, so as even to gain a reputation by their exploits. But whatever may have happened in some extraordinary cases, we may venture to conclude, that the female character is by no means suited to martial employments; and that, in barbarous, as well as in refined periods, the women are, for the most part, incapable of rivaling the other sex in point of strength and courage. Their attention, therefore, is generally limited to an humbler province. It falls upon them to manage all the inferior concerns of the household, and to perform such domestic offices as the particular circumstances of the people <34> have introduced: offices which, however useful, yet requiring little dexterity or skill, and being attended with no exertion of splendid talents, are naturally regarded as mean and servile, and unworthy to engage the attention of persons who command respect by their military accomplishments.

From these observations we may form an idea of the state and condition of the women in the ages most remote from improvement. Having little attention paid them, either upon account of those pleasures to which they are subservient, or of those occupations which they are qualified to exercise, they are degraded below the other sex, and reduced under that authority which the strong acquire over the weak: an authority, which, in early periods, is subject to no limitation from the government, and is therefore exerted with a degree of harshness and severity suited to the dispositions of the people.

We accordingly find that, in those periods, the women of a family are usually treated as the servants or slaves of the men.* Nothing can exceed the dependence and subjection in which they are kept, or the toil and drudgery which they are obliged to undergo. They are forced to labour without intermission in digging roots, in drawing water, in carrying wood, in milking the cattle, in dressing the victuals, in rearing the children, and <35> in those other kinds of work which their situation has taught them

---

* Ἐν δὲ τοῖς βαρβάροις τὸ θῆλυ καὶ δουλον τὴν αὐτὴν ἐχεὶ τάξιν. Aristot. Polit. lib. I. cap. 2. [["Yet among barbarians the female and the slave have the same rank" (Aristotle, *Politics,* Rackham, trans., I.1 [1252b1]).]]

to perform. The husband, when he is not engaged in some warlike exercise, indulges himself in idleness, and devolves upon his wife the whole burden of his domestic affairs. He disdains to assist her in these employments: she sleeps in a different bed, and is seldom permitted to have any conversation or correspondence with him.*

Among the negroes upon the slave-coast, the wife is never allowed to appear before the husband, or to receive any thing from his hands, without putting herself into a kneeling posture.†

In the empire of Congo, and in the greater part of those nations which inhabit the southern coast of Africa, the women of a family are seldom allowed to eat with the men. The husband sits alone at table, and the wife commonly stands at his back, to guard him from the flies, to serve him with his victuals, or to furnish him with his pipe and his tobacco. After he has finished his meal, she is allowed to eat what remains; but without sitting down, which it seems would be inconsistent with the inferiority and submission that is thought suitable to her sex.‡ <36> When a Hottentot and his wife have come into the service of a European, and are entertained in the same house, the master is under the necessity of allotting to each of them a distinct portion of victuals; which, out of regard to the general usage of their country, they always devour at a distance from one another.§

In the account lately given by Commodore Byron of the Indians of South America, we are told, that "the men exercise a most despotic authority over their wives, whom they consider in the same view they do any other part of their property; and dispose of them accordingly: even their common treatment of them is cruel; for though the toil and hazard of procuring food lies entirely upon the women, yet they are not suffered to touch any part of it till the husband is satisfied; and then he assigns them

---

* See Kolben's voyage to the Cape of Good Hope. [[XIV.3, 161.]]—Histoire generale des voyages, tom. 5. liv. 14. chap. 3 §. 4. Ibid. tom. 3. liv. 7. chap. 13. §. 1. Ibid. tom. 4. liv. 10. ch. 4.—Sale's voyage to North America. [[Robert Cavelier, sieur de la Salle (1643–87).]]

† Hist. gener. des voy. tom. 4. liv. 10. ch. 3.

‡ Histoire generale des voyages, tom. 4. liv. 13. ch. 3. §. 2. Ibid. tom. 3. liv. 7. chap. 13. §. 1.

§ Kolben's voyage to the Cape of Good Hope, chap. 15. §. 6.

their portion, which is generally very scanty, and such as he has not a stomach for himself." The same author informs us, that he observed a like arbitrary behaviour in many other nations of savages with whom he has since become acquainted.*

From the servile condition of the women in barbarous countries, they are rendered in a great measure incapable of property, and are supposed <37> to have no share in the estate of that particular family to which they belong. Whatever has been acquired by their labour is under the sole administration and disposal of those male relations and friends, by whom they are protected, and from whom they receive a precarious subsistence. Upon the death of a proprietor, his estate is continued in the possession of his sons, or transmitted to his other male relations; and his daughters are so far from being entitled to a share of the succession, that they are even considered as a part of the inheritance, which the heir has the power of managing at pleasure.

At the Cape of Good Hope, in the kingdom of Benin, and in general upon the whole southern and western coast of Africa, no female is ever admitted to the succession of any estate, either real or personal.†

The same custom is said to be observed among the Tartars; and there is some reason to believe that it has been anciently established among all the inhabitants of Chaldea and Arabia.‡

From the famous decision of this point related by Moses, it appears that, in his time, the succession of females had been without a precedent; and, <38> by his appointment, they were only permitted to inherit upon a failure of males of the same degree.

"Then came the daughters of Zelophehad—and they stood before Moses, and before Eleazar the priest, and before the princes, and all the congregation, by the door of the tabernacle of the congregation, saying,

"'Our father died in the wilderness, and he was not in the company of

---

* Byron's Narrative [[143]].

† See Kolben's voyage. [[XIII.7, pp. 156–57.]]—Modern Universal History, vol. 16. [[p. 374.]] Ibid. vol. 17.—Hist. gen. des voy. tom. 3. 4.

‡ Histoire generale des voyages, tom. 9. liv. 4. chap. 2. §. 6. page 318.—Vide Perizon de leg. Vocon. [[Jacobus Perizonius, "Dissertation II. De Lege Voconia Feminarumque apud Veteres Hereditatibus," p. 133 in *Ant. Fil. Dissertationes Septem.*]]

them that gathered themselves together against the Lord in the company of Korah; but died in his own sin, and had no sons.

" 'Why should the name of our father be done away from among his family, because he hath no son? Give unto us therefore a possession among the brethren of our father.'

"And Moses brought their cause before the Lord.

"And the Lord spake unto Moses, saying,

" 'The daughters of Zelophehad speak right; thou shalt surely give them a possession of an inheritance among their father's brethren, and thou shalt cause the inheritance of their father to pass unto them.

" 'And thou shalt speak unto the children of Israel, saying, If a man die, and have no son, then ye shall cause his inheritance to pass unto his daughter.' "* <39>

In all those German nations which over-ran and subdued the different provinces of the Roman empire, the same notions were entertained concerning the inferiority of the woman; and the same rules of succession were naturally introduced. It is probable that, according to the original customs which prevailed in all these nations, daughters, and all other female relations, were entirely excluded from the right of inheritance; but that afterwards, when the increase of opulence and luxury had raised them to higher consideration, they were admitted to succeed after the males of the same degree.†

In a country where the women are universally regarded as the slaves of the other sex, it is natural to expect that they should be bought and sold, like any other species of property. To marry a wife must there be the same thing as to purchase a female servant, who is to be intrusted, under the husband's direction, with a great part of the domestic economy.

Thus, in all savage nations, whether in Asia, Africa, or America, the wife is commonly bought by the husband from the father, or those other relations who have an authority over her; and the conclusion of a bargain of this nature, together with the payment of the price, has therefore become

---

* Numbers, chap. xxvii. ver. 1, 2, 3, 4, 5, 6, 7, 8.
† Tacit. de mor. German [[20.3]].

the most usual form or solemnity in the celebration of their marriages.*
<40>

This appears to be the real foundation of what is related by historians; that in some parts of the world it is usual for the husband to give a dowery to the wife or her relations, instead of the wife bringing along with her a dowery to the husband.

"Dotem non uxor marito, sed uxori maritus offert," is the expression used by Tacitus in speaking of this practice among the ancient German nations.†

When Shechem wanted to marry the daughter of Jacob—"He said unto her father, and unto her brethren, Let me find grace in your eyes, and what ye shall say unto me I will give.

"Ask me never so much dowery and gift, And I will give according as ye shall say unto me: but give me the damsel to wife."‡

When David married the daughter of king <41> Saul, he was obliged to pay a dowery of a very singular nature.§

This ancient custom, that the husband should buy his wife from her relations, remains at present among the Chinese; who, notwithstanding their opulence, and their improvement in arts, are still so wonderfully tenacious of the usages introduced in a barbarous period.‖

Sir Thomas Smith takes notice, that, according to the old law of En-

---

* This practice obtains in the kingdom of Pegu. See Modern Universal Hist. vol. 7 [[pp. 52–53]].—In Siberia. See professor Gmelin's travels into Siberia, vol. 1. p. 29.—Among the Tartars. Dr. Cooke's travels through the Russian empire, &c. vol. 2. chap. 21. Hist. gen. des voy. tom. 9.—Among the negroes on the coast of Guinea. Ibid. tom. 4.—Among the Arabs. See D'Arvieux travels. [[d'Arvieux, *The Travels of the Chevalier d'Arvieux*, 230.]]

"Illud etiam praesenti lege placuit contineri, ut si mulier maritum habens sine filiis hac luce transierit, maritus defunctae *uxoris pretium,* quod pro illa datum fuerit, non requirat." Leges Burgundior. tit. 14. l. 3. [["De Succesionibus et sanctimonialibus," in *Monumentae Germaniae Historica: Leges,* ed. G. H. Pertz (Hanover, 1863), III.539. The Lex Burgundionum was the legal code of the Kingdom of Burgundy promulgated by Gundobad in the early sixth century.]]

† Tacit. de mor. German. [[18.2: "The wife does not bring a dowry to the husband, but the husband offers a dowry to the wife."]]

‡ Genesis, chap. xxiv. ver. 11, 12.

§ 1 Samuel, chap. xviii. ver. 25.

‖ See P. Le Compte's Memoirs of China [[p. 267]].

gland, "the woman, at the church-door, was given of her father, or some
other man of the next of her kin, into the hands of the husband; and he laid
down *gold* and *silver* for her upon the book, *as though he did buy her.*"* In
the early history of France we meet with a similar practice; of which there
are traces remaining in the present marriage ceremony of that country.†

Upon the same principle, the husband is generally understood to have
the power of selling his wife, or of putting her away at pleasure.‡ <42>

It may however be remarked, that this is a privilege, which, from the
manners of a rude people, he seldom has reason to exercise. The wife, who
is the mother of his children, is generally the most proper person to be
employed in the office of rearing and maintaining them. As she advances
in years, she is likely to advance in prudence and discretion; a circumstance
of too much importance to be counterbalanced by any considerations relating to the appetite between the sexes. Nothing but some extraordinary
crime that she has committed, will move the husband to put away so useful
a servant, with whom he has long been acquainted, and whose labour, attention, and fidelity, are commonly of more value than all the money she
will bring in a market. Divorces are therefore rarely to be met with in the
history of early nations.

But though the wife is not apt to incur the settled displeasure of her
husband, which might lead him to banish her from the family, she may
often experience the sudden and fatal effects of his anger and resentment.
When unlimited power is committed to the hands of a savage, it cannot

---

* The Common-wealth of England, b. 3. chap. 8. [[Sir Thomas Smith (1513–77),
classicist, Regius Professor of Law at Cambridge, secretary of state under Queen Elizabeth. *De Republica Anglorum* (1583) was the most important Tudor account of the English Constitution and was used extensively by Millar in volume II of the *Historical
View.*]]

† "Le futur epoux devoit offrir une somme aux parens de la fille." M. L'Abbe Velly
Hist. de France, tom. 1. 8vo, p. 268. [["The future groom had to give a sum of money
to the parents of the girl."]]

‡ This is the case in the kingdom of Congo. Modern Univer. Hist. [[XVI:406.]]—
Upon the slave coast. Hist. gen. des voy. Among the Samoiedes, Le Brun. Observ. on
Russia [[Le Brun is included in Weber, *The Present State of Russia,* II:382.]]—The Os-
tiacks. Present state of Russia. pub. 1722 [[II:72]].—At Bantam—and in the island of
Banda. Recueil des voyages qui ont servi a l'etablissement de la comp. des Indes Orient.
dans les Païs Bas, 8vo, tom. 2. p. 41. p. 216.

fail, upon many occasions, to be grossly abused. He looks upon her in the same light with his other <43> domestic servants, and expects from her the same implicit obedience to his will. The least opposition kindles his resentment; and, from the natural ferocity of his temper, he is frequently excited to behave with a degree of brutality which, in some cases, may prove the unhappy occasion of her death.

Among the ancient inhabitants of Gaul, the husband exercised the power of life and death over his wives, and treated them with all the severity of an absolute and tyrannical master. In that country, whenever a person of distinction was thought to have died a violent death, his wives lay under the same suspicion of guilt with his other domestic servants; and in order to discover who had committed the crime, they were all subjected to the torture.*

But of all the different branches of power with which in a rude age the husband is usually invested, we meet with the fullest and most complete illustration in the ancient law of the Romans. By that law, a wife was originally considered as, in every respect, the slave of her husband.† She <44> might be sold by him, or she might be put to death by an arbitrary exertion of his authority. From the ceremonies which were used in the more solemn and regular celebration of marriage, it seems probable that, in early times, the wife was purchased with a real price from her relations.‡ She was held

* "Viri in uxores, sicuti in liberos, vitae necisque habent potestatem; et quum paterfamilias illustriore loco natus decessit, ejus propinqui conveniunt, et de morte, si res in suspicionem venit, de uxoribus in servilem modum quaestionem habent." Caes. de bell. Gall. lib. 6. §. 18. [[Actually VI.19: "Men have the power of life and death over their wives, as over their children; and when the father of a house, who is of distinguished birth, has died, his relatives assemble, they make inquisition of his wives as they would of slaves." Edwards, trans.]]

† She was said "conveniri in manum mariti," [["to come into the power of her husband"; cf. table VI, fragment 4]] and was precisely in the same condition with a "filia-familias." [[A daughter under the power of the father.]]

‡ The ceremonies of "coemptio." [[The ceremony of *coemptio*—a kind of Roman marriage in which the husband gained a sort of property ownership (*manus*) of the wife and from which the wife needed to be emancipated in order to change this status—was a simulated purchase. *Coemptio* was distinguished from two other kinds of marriage in which a woman was transferred from the *manus* of her father to her husband: *confarreatio,* which involved an elaborate ceremony but no bridal purchase, and *usus,* which could be invoked after a year of cohabitation.]]

incapable of having any estate of her own, and whatever she possessed at the time of her marriage, became the absolute property of her husband.*

It will be thought, perhaps, a mortifying picture that is here presented to us, when we contemplate the barbarous treatment of the female sex in early times, and the rude state of those passions which may be considered as the origin of society. But this rudeness and barbarism, so universally discovered in the early inhabitants of the world, is not unsuitable to the mean condition in which they are placed, and to the numberless hardships and difficulties which they are obliged to encounter. When men are in danger of perishing for hunger; when they are exerting their utmost efforts to procure the bare necessaries of life; when they are unable to shelter themselves from beasts of prey, or from enemies of their own kind, no less ferocious; their constitution would surely be ill adapt-<45>ed to their circumstances, were they endowed with a refined taste of pleasure, and capable of feeling the delicate distresses and enjoyments of love, accompanied with all those elegant sentiments, which, in a civilized and enlightened age, are naturally derived from that passion. Dispositions of this nature would be altogether misplaced in the breast of a savage: They would even be exceedingly hurtful, by turning his attention from real wants, to the pursuit of imaginary, and what, in his situation, must be accounted fantastical gratifications. Neither will it escape observation, that this refinement would be totally inconsistent with the other parts of his character. Nations who have so little regard to property as to live in the continual exercise of theft and rapine; who are so destitute of humanity, as, in cold blood, to put their captives to death with the most excruciating tortures; who have the shocking barbarity to feed upon their fellow-creatures, a practice rarely to be found among the fiercest and most rapacious of the brute animals; such nations, it is evident, would entirely depart from their ordinary habits and principles of action, were they to display much tenderness or benevolence, in consequence of that blind appetite which unites the sexes. It ought, at the same time to be remembered, that, how poor and wretched soever the aspect of human nature in this early state, it contains the seeds of improvement, <46> which, by long care and culture, are capable of being brought

---

* Vide Heinec. antiq. Roman. [[I.x.6.]]

to maturity; so that the lower its primitive condition, it requires the greater exertions of labour and activity, and calls for a more extensive operation of those wonderful powers and faculties, which, in a gradual progression from such rude beginnings, have led to the noblest discoveries in art or science, and to the most exalted refinement of taste and manners. <47>

SECTION II

The influence acquired by the mother of a family,
before marriage is completely established.

Such are the natural effects of poverty and barbarism, with respect to the passions of sex, and with respect to the rank in society which the women are permitted to enjoy. There is one circumstance, however, in the manners of a rude age, that merits particular attention; as it appears, in some countries, to have produced a remarkable exception to the foregoing observations.

Although marriage, for the reasons formerly mentioned, is undoubtedly a very early institution, yet some little time and experience are necessary before it can be fully established in a barbarous community; and we read of several nations, among whom it is either unknown, or takes place in a very imperfect and limited manner.

To a people who are little acquainted with that institution it will appear, that children have much more connexion with their mother than with their father. If a woman has no notion of attachment or fidelity to any particular person, if notwithstanding her occasional intercourse with different individuals she continues to live by herself, or with her own relations, the child which she has borne, and <48> which she maintains under her own inspection, must be regarded as a member of her own family; and the father, who lives at a distance, can have no opportunity of establishing an authority over it. We may in general conclude, that the same ideas which obtain in a polished nation, with regard to bastards, will, in those primitive times, be extended to all, or the greater part of the children produced in the country.

Thus, among the Lycians, children were accustomed to take their names from their mother, and not from their father; so that if any person was desired to give an account of the family to which he belonged, he was naturally led to recount his maternal genealogy in the female line. The same custom took place among the ancient inhabitants of Attica; as it does at present among several tribes of the natives of North America, and of the Indians upon the coast of Malabar.* <49>

In this situation, the mother of a numerous family, who lives at a distance from her other relations, will often be raised to a degree of rank and dignity to which, from her sex, she would not otherwise be entitled. Her children being, in their early years, maintained and protected by her care and tenderness, and having been accustomed to submit to her authority, will be apt, even after they are grown up, and have arrived at their full strength and vigour, to behave to her with some degree of reverence and filial affection.

---

* Herodot. hist. lib. 1.—See Goguet's Origin of Laws, &c. vol. 2. book. 1.—Charlevoix Journal historique d'un voyage de l'Amer. [[Letter XVIII (III:268).]] [[Bossu,]] nouveaux voyage aux Indes Orientales, tom. 2 p. 20. [[The actual title is *Nouveaux voyages aux Indes Occidentales.*]]—Mod. Univ. Hist. vol. 6. [["Account of the Inhabitants of the Coast of Malabar"]] p. 561.

Vestiges of the same practice are also to be found in the writings of the Roman Lawyers. "Qui ex duobus igitur campanis parentibus natus est, campanus est. Sed si ex patre compano, matre puteolana, aeque municeps campanus est: nisi forte privilegio aliquo materna origo censeatur: tunc enim maternae originis erit municeps. Utputa illiensibus concessum est, *ut qui matre iliense est, sit eorum municeps.* Etiam Delphis hoc idem tributum et conservatum est. Celsus etiam refert, Ponticis ex beneficio Pompeii magni competere, *ut qui Pontica matre natus esset, Ponticus esset:* quod beneficium ad vulgo quaesitos solos pertinere quidam putant: quorum sententiam Celsus non probat: neque enim debuisse caveri ut vulgo quaesitus matris conditionem sequeretur: quam enim aliam originem hic habet? sed ad eos qui ex diversarum civitatum parentibus orirentur," l. 1. §. 2. Dig. ad Municipal. [["Anyone who is born from two parents who are Campani is a Campanus. But if he is born from a father who is a Campanus and a mother who is a Puteolana, he is still a *municeps* Campanus, unless it happens that by some special dispensation the place of origin of the mother is taken into account; for then he will be a *municeps* [citizen] of the place of origin of the mother. Thus, for instance, it has been granted to the Iliensis that anyone who is born from a mother who is an Iliensis is one of their *municeps.* This dispensation has been granted to Delphi and also still exists there. Celsus also reports that the people of Pontus, by a grant of Pompeius Magnus, can regard anyone who is born from a mother from Pontus as being from Pontus. Some people hold that this grant only relates to children born out of wedlock; Celsus, however, does not agree with this view. For it would have been necessary to observe that a child born out of wedlock should have the status of the mother; for what other provenance can such a person have? But the grant relates to those who are born from parents of different communities" (*The Digest of Justinian,* L.1.2).]] See also l. 51. l. 61. [[These two references seem to be mistaken.]] Cod. Theod. de decurion. [[*Codex Theodosianus* V.2.2.]]

Although they have no admiration of her military talents, they may respect her upon account of her experience and wisdom; and although they should not themselves be always very scrupulous in paying her an implicit obedience, they will probably be disposed to espouse her quarrel, or to support her interest against every other person.

We are informed, indeed, that when a young Hottentot is of age to be received into the society of *men,* it is usual for him to beat and abuse his <50> mother, by way of triumph at being freed from her tuition. Such behaviour may happen in a rude country, where, after marriage is established, the superior strength of the husband has raised him to the head of his family, and where his authority has of course annihilated that of the wife, or at least greatly reduced her consideration and importance. But in a country where children have no acquaintance with their father, and are not indebted to him for subsistence and protection, they can hardly fail, during a considerable part of their life, to regard their mother as the principal person in the family.

This is in all probability the source of that influence which appears to have been possessed by the women in several rude and barbarous parts of the world.

In the island of Formosa, it is said, that in forming that slight and transient union between the sexes, to which our travellers, in conformity to the customs of Europe, have given the name of marriage, the husband quits his own family, and passes into that of his wife, where he continues to reside as long as his connection with her remains.* The same custom is said to be established among the people called Moxos, in Peru.† <51>

In the Ladrone islands the wife is absolute mistress of the house, and the husband is not at liberty to dispose of any thing without her permission. She chastises him, or puts him away, at pleasure; and whenever a separation happens, she not only retains all her moveables, but also her children, who consider the next husband she takes as their father.‡

---

* Du Halde, vol. 1. p. 179. [[*The General History of China.*]]

† See the extract of a Spanish relation, printed by order of the Bishop of the city Della Paz, published in the Travels of the Jesuits, by Mr. Lockman, vol. 2. p. 446.

‡ Father Gobien's history of the Ladrone or Marian islands. [[II:59–61.]]—See Callender's coll. vol. 3. p. 51, 52.

The North American tribes are accustomed to admit their women into their public councils, and even to allow them the privilege of being first called to give their opinion upon every subject of deliberation. Females, indeed, are held incapable of enjoying the office of chief, but through them the succession to that dignity is continued; and therefore, upon the death of a chief, he is succeeded, not by his own son, but by that of his sister; and in default of the sister's son, by his nearest relation in the female line. When his whole family happens to be extinct, the right of naming a successor is claimed by the noblest matron of the village.

It is observed, however, by an author, who has given us the fullest account of all these particulars, that the women of North America do not arrive at this influence and dignity till after a certain age, and after their children are in a condition to procure <52> them respect; that before this period they are commonly treated as the slaves of the men; and that there is no country in the world where the female sex is in general more neglected and despised.*

Among the ancient inhabitants of Attica, the women had, in like manner, a share in public deliberations. This custom continued till the reign of Cecrops, when a revolution was produced, of which the following fabulous relation has been given by historians. It is said that, after the building of Athens, Minerva and Neptune became competitors for the honour of giving a name to the city, and that Cecrops called a public assembly of the men and women in order to determine the difference. The women were interested upon the part of Minerva; the men upon that of Neptune; and the former carried the point by the majority of one vote. Soon after, there happened an inundation of the sea, which occasioned much damage, and greatly terrified the inhabitants, who believed that this calamity proceeded from the vengeance of Neptune for the affront he had suffered. To appease him, they resolved to punish the female sex, by whom the offence was committed, and determined that no woman should for the future be admitted into the public assemblies, nor any child be allowed to bear the name of its mother.† <53>

---

* Charlevoix, journal historique de l'Amer. let. 19.
† See Goguet's origin of laws, &c. vol. 2. book 1.

It may explain this piece of ancient mythology to observe, that in the reign of Cecrops marriage was first established among the Athenians. In consequence of this establishment the children were no longer accustomed to bear the name of their mother, but that of their father, who, from his superior strength and military talents, became the head and governor of the family; and as the influence of the women was thereby greatly diminished, it was to be expected that they should, in a little time, be entirely excluded from those great assemblies which deliberated upon public affairs.

Among the ancient Britons we find, in like manner, that the women were accustomed to vote in the public assemblies. The rude and imperfect institution of marriage, and the community of wives, that anciently took place in Britain, must have prevented the children from acquiring any considerable connexion with their father, and have disposed them to follow the condition of their mother, as well as to support her interest and dignity.

When a woman, by being at the head of a large family, is thus advanced to influence and authority, and becomes a sort of female chief, she naturally maintains a number of servants, and endeavours to live with suitable splendour and magnificence. In proportion to her affluence, she has the greater temptation to indulge her sensual appetites; and, in a period when the sexes are but little accustomed to controul or disguise their inclinations, she <54> may, in some cases, be led into a correspondence with different male retainers, who happen to reside in her family, and over whom she exercises an authority resembling that of a master.

The above remark may account for what is related by historians; that, in some provinces of the ancient Median empire, it was customary for women to entertain a number of husbands, as in others, it was usual for men to entertain a number of wives or concubines.* The dominion of the ancient Medes comprehended many extensive territories; in some of which, the inhabitants were extremely barbarous; in others, no less opulent and luxurious.

This unusual kind of polygamy, if I may be allowed to use that expres-

---

* Strabo, lib. ii. [[*Geography*, XI.13.12.]]

sion, is established at present upon the coast of Malabar,* as well as in some cantons of the Iroquois in North America;† and though there is no practice more inconsistent with the views and manners of a civilized nation, it has in all probability been adopted by many individuals, in every country where the inhabitants were unacquainted with the regular institution of marriage.‡ <55>

It is highly probable, that the celebrated traditions of the *Amazons,* inhabiting the most barbarous regions of Scythia, and the relations of a similar people in some parts of America, have arisen from the state of manners now under consideration. Though these accounts are evidently mixed with fable, and appear to contain much exaggeration, we can hardly suppose that they would have been propagated by so many authors, and have created such universal attention, had they been entirely destitute of real foundation.§ In a country where marriage is unknown, females are commonly exalted to be the heads of families, or chiefs, and thus acquire an authority, which, notwithstanding their inferiority in strength, may extend to the direction of war, as well as of other transactions. So extraordinary a spectacle as that of a military <56> enterprise conducted by women, and where the men acted in a subordinate capacity, must have filled the enemy with wonder and astonishment, and might easily give rise to those fictions of a *female*

---

* Modern Universal History, vol. 16. [[It is in fact VI:561.]]—Capt. Hamilton says, that upon the coast of Malabar a woman is not allowed to have more than twelve husbands.

† Charlevoix, journal hist. [[Letter XIX.]]

‡ Father Tachard, superior of the French Missionary Jesuits in the East Indies, gives the following account of the inhabitants in the neighbourhood of Calicut. "In this country," says he, called Malleami, "there are *castes,* as in the rest of India. Most of them observe the same customs; and, in particular, they all entertain a like contempt for the religion and manners of the Europeans. But a circumstance, that perhaps is not found elsewhere, and which I myself could scarce believe, is, that among these barbarians, and *especially the noble castes,* a woman is allowed, by the laws, to have several husbands. Some of these have had ten husbands together, all whom they look upon as so many slaves that their charms have subjected." [[*Travels of the Jesuits.*]] Lettres edifiantes et curieuses, translated by Mr. Lockman, vol. 1. p. 168.

§ Vide Petit. dissert. de Amazon. [[Petit, *De Amazonibus dissertatio, passim.*]]

republic, and of other circumstances equally marvellous, which we meet
with in ancient writers.

> Ducit Amazonidum lunatis agmina peltis
> Penthesilea furens, mediisque in millibus ardet,
> Aurea subnectens exsertae cingula mammae,
> Bellatrix, audetque viris concurrere virgo.[2] <57>

---

2. Virgil *Aeneid* II.490–93.

> Penthisilea in her fury leads,
> The ranks of crescent-shielded Amazons.
> She flashes through her thousands; underneath
> Her naked breast, a golden girdle; soldier,
> Virgin and queen, daring to war with men.
>   (Mandelbaum, trans.)

SECTION III

The refinement of the passions of Sex, in the Pastoral Ages.

When we examine the circumstances which occasion the depression of the women, and the low estimation in which they are held, in a simple and barbarous age, we may easily imagine in what manner their condition is varied and improved in the subsequent periods of society. Their condition is naturally improved by every circumstance which tends to create more attention to the pleasures of sex, and to increase the value of those occupations that are suited to the female character; by the cultivation of the arts of life; by the advancement of opulence; and by the gradual refinement of taste and manners. From a view of the progress of society, in these respects, we may, in a great measure, account for the diversity that occurs among different nations, in relation to the rank of the sexes, their dispositions and sentiments towards each other, and the regulations which they have established in the several branches of their domestic economy.

The invention of taming and pasturing cattle, which may be regarded as the first remarkable improvement in the savage life, is productive of <58> very important alterations in the state and manners of a people.

A shepherd is more regularly supplied with food, and is commonly subjected to fewer hardships and calamities than those who live by hunting and fishing. In proportion to the size of his family, the number of his flocks may in some measure be increased; while the labour which is requisite for their management can never be very oppressive. Being thus provided with necessaries, he is led to the pursuit of those objects which may render his situation more easy and comfortable; and among these the enjoyments derived from the intercourse of the sexes claim a principal share, and become an object of attention.

The leisure, tranquillity, and retirement of a pastoral life, seem calculated, in a peculiar manner, to favour the indulgence of those indolent gratifications. From higher notions of refinement a nicer distinction is made
with regard to the objects of desire; and the mere animal pleasure is more
frequently accompanied with a correspondence of inclination and sentiment. As this must occasion a great diversity in the taste of individuals, it
proves, on many occasions, an obstruction to their happiness, and prevents
the lover from meeting with a proper return to his passion. But the delays
and the uneasiness to which he is thereby subjected, far from repressing the
ardour of his wishes, serve only to increase it; and, amid the idleness and
<59> freedom from other cares which his situation affords, he is often
wholly occupied by the same tender ideas, which are apt to inflame his
imagination, and to become the principal subject of such artless expressive
songs as he is capable of composing for his ordinary pastime and amusement.

In consequence of these improvements the virtue of chastity begins to
be recognized; for when love becomes a passion, instead of being a mere
sensual appetite, it is natural to think that those affections which are not
dissipated by variety of enjoyment, will be the purest and the strongest.

The acquisition of property among shepherds has also a considerable
effect upon the commerce of the sexes.

Those who have no other fund for their subsistence but the natural fruits
of the earth, or the game which the country affords, are acquainted with
no other distinctions in the rank of individuals, but such as arise from their
personal accomplishments; distinctions which are never continued for any
length of time in the same family, and which therefore can never be productive of any lasting influence and authority. But the invention of taming
and pasturing cattle gives rise to a more remarkable and permanent distinction of ranks. Some persons, by being more industrious or more fortunate than others, are led in a short time to acquire more numerous herds
and flocks, and are thereby enabled to live in greater affluence, to maintain
a <60> number of servants and retainers, and to increase, in proportion,
their power and dignity. As the superior fortune which is thus acquired by
a single person is apt to remain with his posterity, it creates a train of de-
pendance in those who have been connected with the possessor; and the

influence which it occasions is gradually augmented, and transmitted from one generation to another.

The degree of wealth acquired by single families of shepherds is greater than may at first be imagined. In the eastern parts of Tartary, where the inhabitants are chiefly maintained upon the flesh of rein-deer, many of the rich possess ten or twenty thousand of those animals; and one of the chiefs of that country, according to an account lately published, was proprietor of no less than an hundred thousand.

The introduction of wealth, and the distinction of ranks with which it is attended, must interrupt the communication of the sexes, and, in many cases, render it difficult for them to gratify their wishes. As particular persons become opulent, they are led to entertain suitable notions of their own dignity; and, while they aim at superior elegance and refinement in their pleasures, they disdain to contract an alliance with their own dependents, or with people of inferior condition. If great families, upon an equal footing, happen to reside in the same neighbourhood, they are frequently engaged in mutual depredations, and are <61> obliged to have a watchful eye upon the conduct of each other, in order to defend their persons and their property. The animosities and quarrels which arise from their ambition or desire of plunder, and which are fomented by reciprocal injuries, dispose them, in all cases, to behave to one another with distance and reserve, and sometimes prove an insuperable bar to their correspondence.

Among persons living upon such terms, the passions of sex cannot be gratified with the same facility as among hunters and fishers. The forms of behaviour, naturally introduced among individuals jealous of each other, have a tendency to check all familiarity between them, and to render their approaches towards an intimacy proportionably slow and gradual. The rivalship subsisting between different families, and the mutual prejudices which they have long indulged, must often induce them to oppose the union of their respective relations: And thus the inclinations of individuals having in vain been smothered by opposition, will break forth with greater vigour, and rise at length to a higher pitch, in proportion to the difficulties which they have surmounted.

Upon the eastern coast of Tartary, it is said that such tribes as are accustomed to the pasturing of cattle discover some sort of jealousy with regard to the chastity of their women; a circumstance regarded as of no importance by those inhabitants of <62> the same country who procure their subsistence merely by fishing.*

From what is related of the patriarch Jacob, it would seem that those families or tribes of shepherds which were anciently scattered over the country of Arabia, had attained some degree of improvement in their manners.

"And Jacob loved Rachel; and said, I will serve thee seven years for Rachel thy younger daughter.

"And Laban said, It is better that I give her to thee than that I should give her to another man: abide with me.

"And Jacob served seven years for Rachel: and they seemed unto him but a few days, for the love he had to her."†

In the compositions of Ossian, which describe the manners of a people acquainted with pasturage, there is often a degree of tenderness and delicacy of sentiment which can hardly be equalled in the most refined productions of a civilized age. Some allowance no doubt must be made for the heightening of a poet possessed of uncommon genius and sensibility; but, at the same time, it is probable, that the real history of his countrymen was the groundwork of those events which he has related, <63> and of those tragical effects which he frequently ascribes to the passion between the sexes.‡

---

* History of Kamtschatka [[215, 223]].

† Genesis, chap. xxix. ver. 18, 19, 20.

‡ [[James Macpherson, "The Battle of Lora, a Poem," in *The Poems of Ossian and Related Works,* ed. Howard Gaskill (Edinburgh: Edinburgh University Press, 1996), 122–23. James Macpherson (1736–96) was a poet of Highland origins who wrote a series of poems, putatively sung by a bard named Ossian and putatively belonging to a larger epic, that drew on Gaelic sources but were mainly the product of Macpherson's own imagination. The poems, combining Gaelic imagery and a long list of Gaelic names with a *faux* Homeric style, presented many of the leading lights of the Scottish Enlightenment—John Home, Hugh Blair, Lord Kames, and others—with the primitive, natural rough-hewn genius they had hoped for. Hume dissented from acclaiming the poem, but Millar clearly viewed it as genuine.]] As this poet was chiefly employed in describing grand and sublime objects, he has seldom had occasion to introduce any images taken from the pastoral life. From the following passages, however, there can be no doubt that, in his time, the people in the West-Highlands of Scotland, as well as upon the neighbouring coast of Ireland, were acquainted with pasturage. "The deer

"Lorma sat in Aldo's hall, at the light of a flaming oak: the night came, but he did not return, and the soul of Lorma is sad.—What detains thee, Hunter of Cona? for thou didst promise to return.—Has the deer been distant far, and do the dark winds sigh round thee on the <64> heath? I am in the land of strangers, where is my friend, but Aldo? Come from thy echoing hills, O my best beloved!

"Her eyes are turned towards the gate, and she listens to the rustling blast. She thinks it is Aldo's tread, and joy rises in her face:—but sorrow returns again, like a thin cloud on the moon.—And thou wilt not return, my love? Let me behold the face of the hill. The moon is in the east. Calm and bright is the breast of the lake! When shall I behold his dogs returning from the chace? When shall I hear his voice loud and distant on the wind? Come from thy echoing hills, Hunter of Woody Cona!

"His thin ghost appeared on a rock, like the watery beam of the moon, when it rushes from between two clouds, and the midnight shower is on the field.—She followed the empty form over the heath, for she knew that her hero fell.—I heard her approaching cries on the wind, like the mournful voice of the breeze, when it sighs on the grass of the cave.

"She came, she found her hero: her voice was heard no more: silent she rolled her sad eyes; she was pale as a watery cloud, that rises from the lake to the beam of the moon.

"Few were her days on Cona: she sunk into the tomb: Fingal commanded his bards, and they sung over the death of Lorma. The daughters

---

descend from the hill. No hunter at a distance is seen. No whistling *cow-herd* is nigh." Carric-thura.

"Let Cuchullin," said Cairbar, "divide the *herd* on the hill. His breast is the seat of justice. Depart, thou light of beauty. I went and *divided the herd.* One bull of snow remained. I gave that bull to Cairbar. The wrath of Deugala rose." Fingal, B. II. [[Ibid., 69.]]

I am informed that, in the Erse language, the word used to denote a man who has nothing, signifies properly one who has no *head of cattle;* which affords a presumption that, in the countries where this language was spoken, pasturage was nearly coeval with property. It is, at the same time, difficult to imagine, that people should possess the art of managing a chariot drawn by horses, without having previously learnt something of the management of herds and flocks: Not to mention, that, in those parts of Britain which were known to the Romans, the pasturing of cattle was understood for ages before the time when Ossian is supposed to have lived.

<65> of Morven mourned her for one day in the year, when the dark winds of autumn returned."*

In the agreeable pictures of the *golden age,* handed down from remote antiquity, we may discover the opinion that was generally entertained of the situation and manners of shepherds. Hence that particular species of poetry, which is now appropriated by fashion, to describe the pleasures of rural retirement, accompanied with innocence and simplicity, and with the indulgence of all the tender passions. There is good reason to believe, that these representations of the pastoral life were not inconsistent with the real condition of shepherds, and that the poets, who were the first historians, have only embellished the traditions of early times. In Arcadia, in Sicily, and in some parts of Italy, where the climate was favourable to the rearing of cattle, or where the inhabitants were but little exposed to the depredations of their neighbours, it is probable that the refinement natural to the pastoral state was carried to a great height. This refinement was the more likely to become the subject of exaggeration and poetical embellishment; as, from a view of the progressive improvements in society, it was contrasted, on the one hand, with the barbarous manners of mere savages; and, on the other, with the opposite style of behaviour in polished nations, who, being con-<66>stantly engaged in the pursuit of gain, and immersed in the cares of business, have contracted habits of industry, avarice, and selfishness.

> Nondum caesa suis, peregrinum ut viseret orbem,
> Montibus, in liquidas pinus descenderat undas:
> Nullaque mortales, praeter sua littora norant.
> Nondum praecipites cingebant oppida fossae:
> Non tuba directi, non aeris cornua flexi,
> Non galeae, non ensis erant. Sine militis usu
> Mollia securae peragebant otia gentes:
> Ipsa quoque immunis, rastroque intacta, nec ullis
> Saucia vomeribus, per se dabat omnia tellus;
> Contentique cibis, nullo cogente, creatis,
> Arbuteos foetus, montanaque fraga legebant;

* The battle of Lora. [[Ibid., 123.]]

Cornaque, et in duris haerentia mora rubetis;
Et quae deciderant patula Jovis arbore glandes;
Ver erat eternum, placidique tepentibus auris
Mulcebant Zephyri, natos sine semine flores.[3] <67>

3. Ovid *Metamorphoses* I.94–108.

In those times,
Upon its native mountain heights stood unfilled;
no wood had yet been hauled
Down to the limpid waves, that it might sail
To foreign countries; and the only coasts
That mortals knew in that age were their own.
The towns were not yet girded by steep moats;
There were no curving horns of brass, and no
Brass trumpets—straight, unbent; there were no swords,
No helmets. No one needed warriors;
The nations lived at peace, in tranquil ease.
Earth of itself—and uncompelled—untouched
By hoes, not torn by ploughshares, offered all
That one might need: men did not have to seek:
They simply gathered mountain strawberries
And the arbutus' fruit and cornel cherries;
And thick upon prickly stems, blackberries;
And acorns fallen from Jove's sacred tree.
There spring was never-ending. The soft breeze
Of tender zephyrs wafted and caressed
The flowers that sprang unplanted, without seed.
                              (Mandelbaum, trans.)

SECTION IV

The consequences of the introduction of Agriculture,
with respect to the intercourse of the Sexes.

The passions which relate to the commerce of the sexes may be still raised
to a greater height, when men are acquainted with the cultivation of the
ground, and have made some progress in the different branches of husbandry.

The improvement of agriculture, which in most parts of the world has
been posterior to the art of taming and rearing cattle, is productive of very
important alterations in the state of society; more especially with respect
to the subject of our present inquiry. Although this employment requires
greater industry and labour than is necessary among men who have only
the care of herds and flocks; yet, by producing plenty of vegetable as well
as of animal food, it multiplies the comforts and conveniencies of life, and
therefore excites in mankind a stronger desire of obtaining those pleasures
to which they are prompted by their natural appetites. It also obliges men
to fix their residence in the neighbourhood of that spot where their labour
is chiefly to be employed, and thereby gives rise to property in land, the
most valuable and permanent species of wealth; by the unequal distribution
of <68> which a greater disproportion is made in the fortune and rank of
individuals, and the causes of their dissension and jealousy are, of course,
extended.

In the heroic times of Greece, we may, in some measure, discern the
effect of these circumstances upon the character and manners of the people.

The inhabitants of that country were then divided into clans or tribes,
who, having for the most part begun the practice of agriculture, had quitted
the wandering life of shepherds, and established a number of separate independent villages. As those little societies maintained a constant rivalship

with each other, and were frequently engaged in actual hostilities, they were
far from being in circumstances to encourage a familiar correspondence;
and when in particular cases a formal visit had produced an interview between them, it was often attended with such consequences as might be
expected from the restraints to which they were usually subjected. A man
of wealth and distinction, having conceived a violent passion for the wife
or the daughter of a neighbouring prince, was disposed to encounter every
danger in order to gratify his desires; and, after seducing the lady, or carrying
her away by force, he was generally involved in a war with her relations,
and with such as chose to assist them in vindicating the honour of their
family. Disorders of this kind were for a considerable time the source of
the chief animosities among the different states of Greece, as well as between them and <69> the inhabitants of Asia Minor; and the rape of Io,
of Europa, of Medea, and of Helen, are mentioned as the ground of successive quarrels, which in the end were productive of the most distinguished
military enterprise that is recorded in the history of those periods.

But notwithstanding these events, from which it appears that the passions of sex had often a considerable influence upon the conduct of the
people, there is no reason to imagine that the Greeks, in those times, had
entirely shaken off their ancient barbarous manners, or in their ideas with
respect to the women, had attained any high degree of delicacy.

In the Iliad, the wife of Menelaus is considered as of little more value
than the treasure which had been stolen along with her. The restitution
of the lady and of that treasure is always mentioned in the same breath,
and seems to be regarded as a full reparation of the injury which Menelaus
had sustained: and though it was known that Helen had made a voluntary elopement with Paris, yet her husband neither discovers any resentment upon that account, nor seems unwilling to receive her again into
favour.*

Even the wife of Ulysses, whose virtue in refusing the suitors is highly
celebrated in the Odyssey, is supposed to derive her principal merit from
<70> preserving to her husband's family the dowery which she had brought

* Iliad, book 3. l. 100. 127. 355.

along with her, and which, it seems, upon her second marriage, must have been restored to her father Icarius.*

And though Telemachus is always represented as a pious and dutiful son, we find him reproving his mother in a manner which shews he had no very high notion of her dignity, or of the respect which belonged to her sex.

> Your widowed hours, apart, with female toil,
> And various labours of the loom, beguile;
> There rule, from palace cares remote and free;
> That care to man belongs, and most to me.†

Penelope, so far from being offended at this language, appears to consider it as a mark of uncommon prudence and judgment in so young a person.

> Mature beyond his years, the queen admires
> His sage reply, and with her train retires.

In all parts of the world, where the advancement of agriculture has introduced the appropriation of landed estates, it will be found that the manners of the inhabitants are such, as indicate considerable improvements in the commerce of the sexes. <71>

But the acquisition of property in land, the jealousy arising from the distinction of ranks, and the animosities which are apt to be produced by the neighbourhood of great independent families, appear to have been attended with the most remarkable consequences in those barbarous nations, who, about the fifth century, invaded the Roman empire, and afterwards settled in the different provinces which they had conquered.

As those nations were small, and as they acquired an extensive territory, the different tribes or families of which they were composed spread themselves over the country, and were permitted to occupy very large estates. Particular chieftains or heads of families became great and powerful in proportion to their wealth, which enabled them to support a numerous train

---

* How to Icarius, in the bridal hour,
  Shall I, by waste undone, refund the dower!
                    Pope's Odyss. book 2. *l.* 153

† Pope's Odyssey, book 1. l. 453.

of retainers and followers. A great number of these were united under a sovereign; for the different parts of a Roman province, having a dependence upon one another, fell naturally into the hands of the same military leader, and were erected into one kingdom. But, in a rude age, unaccustomed to subordination, the monarch could have little authority over such wide dominions. The opulent proprietors of land, disdaining submission to regular government, lived in the constant exercise of predatory incursions upon their neighbours; and every separate family, being in a great measure left without protection from the public, was under the necessity of provid-<72>ing for its own defence. The disorders arising from private wars between different families of the same kingdom, were not effectually repressed for many centuries; during which time the same causes continued to operate in forming the character and manners of the people, and gave rise to a set of customs and institutions of which we have no example in any other age or country.

The high notions of military honour, and the romantic love and gallantry, by which the modern nations of Europe have been so much distinguished, were equally derived from those particular circumstances.

As war was the principal employment of those nations, so it was carried on in a manner somewhat peculiar to themselves. Their military enterprises were less frequently undertaken against a foreign enemy than against the inhabitants of a neighbouring district; and on these latter occasions, the chief warriors of either party, were, from the smallness of their numbers, known to each other, and distinguished by the respective degrees of strength or valour which they possessed. The members of different families, who had long been at variance, were therefore animated with a strong personal animosity; and as, in the time of an engagement, they were disposed to single out one another, a battle was frequently nothing more than a number of separate duels between combatants inspired with mutual jealousy, and contending for <73> superiority in military prowess. As the individuals of different parties were inflamed by opposition, those of the same party, conscious of acting under the particular observation of all their companions, were excited to vie with each other in the performance of such exploits as might procure admiration and applause. In this situation they not only contracted habits which rendered them cool and intrepid in danger, but at the same time acquired a remarkable generosity of sentiment in the exercise of their mutual hostilities. Persons, who aspired to superior rank and influence, fought merely to obtain a reputation in arms, and affected to look upon every other consideration as mean and ignoble. Having this object in view, they thought it disgraceful to assault an enemy when unprepared for his defence, or without putting him upon his guard by a previous challenge; and they disdained to practise unfair means in order to gain a victory, or to use it with insolence and barbarity. These notions of honour were productive of certain rules and maxims, by which the gentry were directed in their whole manner of fighting, and from which they never deviated without bringing an indelible stain upon their character.

The ideas of personal dignity, which were thus raised to so high a pitch among neighbouring families, were incompatible with any regular distribution of justice. Men of wealth and distinction were unwilling to apply to a magistrate in order <74> to procure redress for the injuries or affronts which they sustained; because this would have amounted to a confession that they were unable to assert their character and rank, by taking vengeance upon the offender. If a law-suit had arisen in matters of property, it commonly happened in the progress of the dispute, that one of the parties gave such offence to the other, as occasioned their deciding the difference by the sword. The judge, who found himself incapable of preventing this determination, endeavoured to render it less hurtful to society, by discouraging the friends of either party from interfering in the quarrel. With this view, he assumed the privilege of regulating the forms, and even became a spectator of the combat; which in that age, no less prone to superstition than intoxicated with the love of military glory, was considered as an immediate appeal to the judgment of heaven. These judicial combats, though they did not introduce the custom of duelling, had certainly a tendency to render it more universal, and to settle a variety of observances with which it came to be attended.

The diversions of a people have always a relation to their general character and manners. It was therefore to be expected that such warlike nations would be extremely addicted to martial exercises, and that the members of different tribes or families, when not engaged in actual hostilities, would be accustomed to challenge one another to <75> a trial of their strength, activity, or military skill. Hence the origin of jousts and tournaments; those images of war, which were frequently exhibited by men of rank, and which tended still farther to improve those nice punctilios of behaviour that were commonly practised by the military people in every serious contest.

From this prevailing spirit of the times, the art of war became the study of every one who was desirous of maintaining the character of a gentleman. The youth were early initiated in the profession of arms, and served a sort of apprenticeship under persons of distinguished eminence. The young squire became in reality the servant of that leader to whom he had attached himself, and whose virtues were set before him as a model for imitation. He was taught to perform with ease and dexterity those exercises which were either ornamental or useful; and, at the same time, he endeavoured to acquire those talents and accomplishments which were thought suitable to his profession. He was taught to look upon it as his duty to check the insolent, to restrain the oppressor, to protect the weak and defenceless; to behave with frankness and humanity even to an enemy, with modesty and politeness to all. According to the proficiency which he had made, he was honoured with new titles and marks of distinction, till at length he arrived at the dignity of knighthood; a dignity which even the greatest <76> potentates were ambitious of acquiring, as it was supposed to ascertain the most complete military education, and the attainment of such qualifications as were then universally admired and respected.

The same ambition, in persons of an exalted military rank, which gave rise to the institution of chivalry, was afterwards productive of the different *orders of knighthood,* by which, from a variety of similar establishments in the several kingdoms of Europe, a subdivision was made in the degrees of honour conferred upon individuals.

The situation of mankind in those periods had also a manifest tendency to heighten and improve the passion between the sexes. It was not to be expected that those opulent chiefs, who maintained a constant opposition to each other, would allow any sort of familiarity to take place between the members of their respective families. Retired in their own castles, and surrounded with their numerous vassals, they looked upon their neighbours either as inferior to them in rank, or as enemies. They behaved to each other with that ceremonious civility which the laws of chivalry required; but, at the same time, with that reserve and caution which a regard to their own safety made it necessary for them to observe. The young knight, as he marched to the tournament, saw at a distance the daughter of the chieftain by whom the show was exhibited; and it was even with difficulty that <77> he could obtain access to her, in order to declare the sentiments with which she had inspired him. He was entertained by her relations with that cold respect which demonstrated that their dignity was alarmed by his aspiring to contract an alliance with them. The lady herself was taught to assume the pride of her family, and to think that no person was worthy of her affection who did not possess an exalted rank and character. To have given way to a sudden inclination would have disgraced her for ever in the opinion of all her kindred; and it was only by a long course of attention, and of the most respectful service, that the lover could hope for any favour from his mistress.*

The barbarous state of the country at that time, and the injuries to which the inhabitants, especially those of the weaker sex, were frequently exposed, gave ample scope for the display of military talents; and the knight, who had nothing to do at home, was encouraged to wander from place to place, and from one court to another, in quest of adventures; in which he endeavoured to ad-<78>vance his reputation in arms, and to recommend himself to the fair of whom he was enamoured, by fighting with every person who was so inconsiderate as to dispute her unrivalled beauty, virtue, or personal accomplishments. Thus, while his thoughts were constantly fixed upon the same object, and while his imagination, inflamed by absence and repeated disappointments, was employed in heightening all those charms by which his desires were continually excited, his passion was at length wrought up to the highest pitch, and uniting with the love of fame,

---

* Among the Franks, so early as the compilation of the Salique law, it appears that a high degree of reserve was practised between the sexes. M. L'Abbé Velly quotes, from that ancient code, the following article, *"Celui qui aura serré la main d'une femme libre, sera condamné à une amende de quinze sous d'or."* [[*"He who has shaken the hand of a free woman, shall pay a fine of fifteen golden sous."*]] And he adds, "On conviendra que si notre siecle est plus poli que celui de nos anciens legislateurs, il n'est du moins ni fi respectueux, ni sì reservè." [["One will agree that while our century is more polite than that of our ancient legislators, it is neither as respectful, nor as reserved."]] Histoire de France, tom. I. p. 134.

became the ruling principle, which gave a particular turn and direction to all his sentiments and opinions.

As there were many persons in the same situation, they were naturally inspired with similar sentiments. Rivals to one another in military glory, they were often competitors, as it is expressed by Milton, "to win her grace whom all commend";[4] and the same emulation which disposed them to aim at pre-eminence in the one respect, excited them with no less eagerness to dispute the preference in the other. Their dispositions and manner of thinking became fashionable, and were gradually diffused by the force of education and example. To be in love was looked upon as one of the necessary qualifications of a knight; and he was no less ambitious of showing his constancy and fidelity to his mistress, than of displaying his military virtues. He assumed the title of her slave, or servant. By <79> this he distinguished himself in every combat; and his success was supposed to redound to her honour, no less than to his own. If she had bestowed upon him a present to be worn in the field of battle in token of her regard, it was considered as a pledge of victory, and as laying upon him the strongest obligation to render himself worthy of the favour.

The sincere and faithful passion, which commonly occupied the heart of every warrior, and which he professed upon all occasions, was naturally productive of the utmost purity of manners, and of great respect and veneration for the female sex. The delicacy of sentiment which prevailed, had a tendency to divert the attention from sensual pleasure, and created a general abhorrence of debauchery. Persons who felt a strong propensity to magnify and exalt the object of their own wishes, were easily led to make allowance for the same disposition in their neighbours; and such individuals as made a point of defending the reputation and dignity of that particular lady to whom they were devoted, became extremely cautious, lest by any insinuation or impropriety of behaviour, they should hurt the character of another, and be exposed to the just resentment of those by whom she was protected. A woman who deviated so far from the established maxims of the age as to violate the laws of chastity, was indeed deserted by every body,

4. Milton, "L'Allegro," p. 124.

and < 80 > was universally contemned and insulted.* But those who adhered to the strict rules of virtue, and maintained an unblemished reputation, were treated like beings of a superior order. The love of God and of the ladies was one of the first lessons inculcated upon every young person who was initiated into the military profession. He was instructed with care in all those forms of behaviour which, according to the received notions of gallantry and politeness, were settled with the most frivolous exactness. He was frequently put under the tuition of some matron of rank and distinction, who in this particular directed his education, and to whom he was under a necessity of revealing all his sentiments, thoughts, and actions. An oath was imposed upon him, by which he became bound to vindicate the honour of the ladies, as well as to de-<81>fend them from every species of injustice; and the uncourteous knight who behaved to them with rudeness, or who ventured to injure and insult them, became the object of general indignation and vengeance, and was treated as the common enemy of all those who were actuated by the true and genuine principles of chivalry.†

The sentiments of military honour, and the love and gallantry so universally diffused among those nations, which were displayed in all the amusements and diversions of the people, had necessarily a remarkable influence upon the genius and taste of their literary compositions. Men were pleased with a recital of what they admired in real life; and the first poetical

---

* M. de la Curne de Sainte Palaye has collected some extraordinary instances of that zeal with which those who enjoyed the honour of knighthood endeavoured to expose any lady who had lost her reputation—"Et vous diray encore plus," says an old author, "comme j'ay ouy racompter à plusieurs Chevaliers qui virent celluy Messire Geoffroy, qui disoit que quant il chevauchoit par les champs, et il veoit le chasteau ou manoir de quelque Dame, il demandoit tousjours à qui il estoit; et quant on lui disoit, *il est a celle,* se la Dame estoit *blasmee de son honneur,* il se fust plustost detournè d'une demie lieue qu'il ne fust venu jusques devant la porte; et là prenoit ung petit de croye qu'il portoit, et notoit cette porte, et y faisoit ung signet, et l'en venoit." [["And you will say too, as I heard from many knights who saw Sir Geoffroy, that when he went riding in the fields, and saw the castle or manor of a Lady, he always asked who it belonged to; and when he was told that it belonged to a Lady who had been 'blamed in her honor,' he would rather ride a half [*lieue*] further than pass in front of her door; he would also take out a piece of chalk and mark the door, before leaving" (I:124–25 [note 43]).]]

    † Memoires sur l'ancienne chevalrie, par M. de la Curne de Ste. Palaye. [[I:118 (note 40).]]

historians endeavoured to embellish those events which had struck their imagination, and appeared the most worthy of being preserved.

Such was the employment of the bards,* who about the eleventh century are said, along with their minstrels,† to have attended the festivals and entertainments of princes, and to have sung, with the accompaniment of musical instruments, a variety of small poetical pieces of their own composition, describing the heroic sentiments, as well as the love and gallantry of the times.‡ <82>

They were succeeded by the writers of romance, who related a longer and more connected series of adventures, in which were exhibited the most extravagant instances of valour and generosity, of patience and fortitude, of respect to the ladies, of disinterested love, and inviolable fidelity; subjects the most capable of warming the imagination, and of producing the most sublime and refined descriptions; but which were often disgraced by the unskilfulness of the author, and by that excessive propensity to exaggeration, and turn for the marvellous, which prevailed in those ages of darkness and superstition. These performances, however, with all their faults, may be regarded as striking monuments of the Gothic taste and genius, to which there is nothing similar in the writings of antiquity, and at the same time as useful records, that contain some of the outlines of the history, together with a faithful picture of the manners and customs of those remarkable periods.

This observation is in some measure applicable to the Epic poetry which followed, and which, with little more correctness, but with the graces of versification, described the same heroic and tender sentiments, though tinctured by the peculiar genius and character of different writers.

The romance of Charlemain and his twelve peers, ascribed to archbishop Turpin, a cotemporary of that monarch, but which is supposed to be a work of the eleventh century,[5] furnished mate-<83>rials for the *Morgante,* the

---

* *Trouverres* ou *Troubadours.*
† *Chanterres* et *Iongleoürs.* [[Singers and Jugglers.]]
‡ Histoire du theatre François, par. M. de Fontenelle. [[*Oeuvres,* III:2–3.]]
5. *La Chanson de Roland.*

Orlando Innamorato, and the *Orlando Furioso.*[6] The last of these poems, which entirely eclipsed the reputation of the two former, whatever may be its merit to an Italian, in easiness and harmony of expression, is a bundle of incoherent adventures, discovering neither unity of design, nor any selection of such objects as are fitted to excite admiration. The *Gierusalemme Liberata,* to the system of enchantment, and the romantic exploits which modern times had introduced, has united the regularity of the ancient Greek and Roman poets; and though the author's talents for the pathetic seem inferior to his powers of description, the whole structure of his admirable poem is sufficient to show the advantages, in point of sublimity, derived from the manners and institutions of chivalry.[7] The fabulous legends of Prince Arthur, and his knights of the round table, suggested the ground-work of Spenser's *Fairy Queen;*[8] but the writer, instead of improving upon the Gothic model, has thought proper to cover it with a veil of allegory; which is too dark to have much beauty of its own; and which, notwithstanding the strength of imagery frequently displayed, destroys the appearance of reality, necessary, in works of imagination, to interest the affections.

When the improvement of public shows had given rise to dramatic performances, the same sort of manners was adopted in those entertainments; <84> and the first tragedies, unless when founded upon religious subjects, represented love as the grand spring and mover of every action, the source of all those hopes and fears with which the principal persons were successively agitated, and of that distress and misery in which they were finally involved. This is the more remarkable, because, from the rigid morals of that age, women were not permitted to act in those representations; and therefore the parts allotted to them, which were performed by men, were usually so conducted by the poet as to bear a very small proportion to the rest of the piece.

6. Luigi Pulci's *Morgante* (1480), Matteo Maria Boiardo's *Orlando Innamorato* (1483), and Ludovico Ariosto's continuation of Boiardo's poem, *Orlando Furioso,* were three of the greatest comic works of the Italian Renaissance.

7. Torquato Tasso's epic poem, published in 1581, describing the First Crusade.

8. Millar had a further reference to Edmund Spenser's poem (1590) in the earlier edition of the *Ranks.*

The first deviation from this general taste of composition in works of entertainment may be discovered in Italy, where the revival of letters was early attended with some relaxation of the Gothic institutions and manners.

The advancement of the Italian states in commerce and manufactures so early as the thirteenth century, had produced a degree of opulence and luxury, and was followed, soon after, by the cultivation of the fine arts, and the improvement of taste and science. The principal towns of Italy came thus to be filled with tradesmen and merchants, whose unwarlike dispositions, conformable to their manner of life, were readily communicated to those who had intercourse with them. To this we may add the influence of the clergy, who resorted in great numbers to Rome, as the fountain of ecclesiastical pre-<85>ferment, and who, embracing different views and principles from those of the military profession, were enabled to propagate their opinions and sentiments among the greater part of the inhabitants.

The decay of the military spirit among the Italians was manifest from their disuse of duelling, the most refined method of executing private revenge, and from their substituting, in place of it, the more artful but cowardly practice of poisoning. Their taste of writing was in like manner varied according to this alteration of their circumstances; and people began to relish those ludicrous descripions of low life and of licentious manners which we meet with in the tales of Boccace, and many other writers, entirely repugnant to the gravity and decorum of former times, and which appear to have taken their origin from the monks, in consequence of such dispositions and habits as their constrained and unnatural situation had a tendency to produce. This kind of composition, however, appears to have been the peculiar growth of Italy; and those authors who attempted to introduce it into other countries, as was done by Chaucer in England, are only servile imitators, or rather mere translators of the Italians.

In the other countries of Europe, the manners introduced by chivalry were more firmly rooted, and acquiring stability from custom, may still be observed to have a good deal of influence upon the taste and sentiments even of the present age. <86> When a change of circumstances, more than the inimitable ridicule of Cervantes, had contributed to explode the ancient romances, they were succeeded by those serious novels which, in France and England, are still the favourite entertainment, and which represent, in a more moderate degree, the sentiments of military honour, as well as the love and gallantry which prevailed in the writings of a former period. The fashion of those times has also remained with us in our theatrical compositions; and scarce any author, till very lately, seems to have thought that a tragedy without a love-plot could be attended with success.

The great respect and veneration for the ladies, which prevailed in a former period, has still a considerable influence upon our behaviour towards them, and has occasioned their being treated with a degree of politeness, delicacy, and attention, that was unknown to the Greeks and Romans, and perhaps to all the nations of antiquity. This has given an air of refinement to the intercourse of the sexes, which contributes to heighten the elegant pleasures of society, and may therefore be considered as a valuable improvement, arising from the extravagance of Gothic institutions and manners. <87>

Changes in the condition of women, arising from the
improvement of useful Arts and Manufactures.

One of the most remarkable differences between man and other animals consists in that wonderful capacity for the improvement of his faculties with which he is endowed. Never satisfied with any particular attainment, he is continually impelled by his desires from the pursuit of one object to that of another; and his activity is called forth in the prosecution of the several arts which render his situation more easy and agreeable. This progress however is slow and gradual; at the same time that, from the uniformity of the human constitution, it is accompanied with similar appearances in different parts of the world. When agriculture has created abundance of provisions, people extend their views to other circumstances of smaller importance. They endeavour to be clothed and lodged, as well as maintained, in a more comfortable manner; and they engage in such occupations as are calculated for these useful purposes. By the application of their labour to a variety of objects, commodities of different kinds are produced. These are exchanged for one another, according to the demand of different individuals; and thus <88> manufactures, together with commerce, are at length introduced into a country.

These improvements are the source of very important changes in the state of society, and particularly in relation to the women. The advancement of a people in manufactures and commerce has a natural tendency to remove those circumstances which prevented the free intercourse of the sexes, and contributed to heighten and inflame their passions. From the cultivation of the arts of peace, the different members of society are more and more united, and have occasion to enter into a greater variety of transactions for their mutual benefit. As they become more civilized, they per-

ceive the advantages of establishing a regular government; and different
tribes who lived in a state of independence, are restrained from injuring
one another, and reduced under subjection to the laws. Their former animosities, the cause of so much disturbance, are no longer cherished by fresh
provocation, and at length are buried in oblivion. Being no longer withheld
by mutual fear and jealousy, they are led by degrees to contract an acquaintance, and to carry on a more intimate correspondence. The men and
women of different families are permitted to converse with more ease and
freedom, and meet with less opposition to the indulgence of their inclinations.

But while the fair sex become less frequently the objects of those romantic and extravagant pas-<89>sions, which in some measure arise from
the disorders of society, they are more universally regarded upon account
of their useful or agreeable talents.

When men begin to disuse their ancient barbarous practices, when their
attention is not wholly engrossed by the pursuit of military reputation,
when they have made some progress in arts, and have attained to a proportional degree of refinement, they are necessarily led to set a value upon
those female accomplishments and virtues which have so much influence
upon every species of improvement, and which contribute in so many different ways to multiply the comforts of life. In this situation, the women
become, neither the slaves, nor the idols of the other sex, but the friends
and companions. The wife obtains that rank and station which appears
most agreeable to reason, being suited to her character and talents. Loaded
by nature with the first and most immediate concern in rearing and maintaining the children, she is endowed with such dispositions as fit her for
the discharge of this important duty, and is at the same time particularly
qualified for all such employments as require skill and dexterity more than
strength, which are so necessary in the interior management of the family.
Possessed of peculiar delicacy, and sensibility, whether derived from original constitution, or from her way of life, she is capable of securing the
esteem and <90> affection of her husband, by dividing his cares, by sharing
his joys, and by soothing his misfortunes.

The regard, which is thus shown to the useful talents and accomplishments of the women, cannot fail to operate in directing their education,

and in forming their manners. They learn to suit their behaviour to the circumstances in which they are placed, and to that particular standard of propriety and excellence which is set before them. Being respected upon account of their diligence and proficiency in the various branches of domestic economy, they naturally endeavour to improve and extend those valuable qualifications. They are taught to apply with assiduity to those occupations which fall under their province, and to look upon idleness as the greatest blemish in the female character. They are instructed betimes in whatever will qualify them for the duties of their station, and is thought conducive to the ornament of private life. Engaged in these solid pursuits, they are less apt to be distinguished by such brilliant accomplishments as make a figure in the circle of gaiety and amusement. Accustomed to live in retirement, and to keep company with their nearest relations and friends, they are inspired with all that modesty and diffidence which is natural to persons unacquainted with promiscuous conversation; and their affections are neither dissipated by pleasure, nor corrupted by the vicious customs of the world. As their attention is principally bestowed upon the <91> members of their own family, they are led, in a particular manner, to improve those feelings of the heart which are excited by these tender connections, and they are trained up in the practice of all the domestic virtues.

The celebrated character, drawn by Solomon, of the virtuous woman, is highly expressive of those ideas and sentiments, which are commonly entertained by a people advancing in commerce and in the arts of life.

"She seeketh wool and flax, and worketh willingly with her hands.

"She is like the merchant ships, she bringeth her food from afar.

"She riseth also while it is yet night, and giveth meat to her household, and a portion to her maidens.

"She considereth a field and buyeth it: with the fruit of her hands she planteth a vineyard.

"She perceiveth that her merchandise is good: her candle goeth not out by night.

"She layeth her hands to the spindle, and her hands hold the distaff.

"She stretcheth out her hand to the poor; yea, she reacheth forth her hands to the needy.

"She is not afraid of the snow for her household: for all her household are clothed with scarlet.

"She maketh herself coverings of tapestry, her clothing is silk and purple. <92>

"Her husband is known in the gates, when he sitteth among the elders of the land.

"She maketh fine linen, and selleth it, and delivereth girdles unto the merchant.

"Strength and honour are her clothing, and she shall rejoice in time to come.

"She openeth her mouth with wisdom, and in her tongue is the law of kindness.

"She looketh well to the ways of her household, and eateth not the bread of idleness."*

In many of the Greek states, during their most flourishing periods, it appears that the women were viewed nearly in the same light, and that their education was chiefly calculated to improve their industry and talents, so as to render them useful members of society. Their attention seems to have been engrossed by the care of their own families, and by those smaller branches of manufacture which they were qualified to exercise. They were usually lodged in a remote apartment of the house, and were seldom visited by any person except their near relations. Their modesty and reserve, and their notions of a behaviour suited to the female character, were such as might be expected from their retired manner of life. They never appeared abroad without being covered with a veil, and were not allowed to be present at any public entertainment.† "As for you, women," <93> says Pericles, in one of the orations in Thucydides, "it ought to be the constant aim of your sex to avoid being talked of by the public; and it is your highest commendation that you should never be the objects either of applause or censure."‡

Lysias, in one of his orations, has introduced a widow, the mother of

* Proverbs, chap. xxxi. ver. 13, &c.
† Cornel. Nep. pref. [[*De Viris Illustribus* 6–8.]]—Cicero in Verrem. [[The most likely passage is III.xxxiii–xxxxv.]]
‡ Thucydides, lib. 2. [[II.xlv [2].]]

several children, who considers her appearing in public as one of the most desperate measures to which she could be driven by her misfortunes. She prays and entreats her son-in-law to call together her relations and friends, that she might inform them of her situation. "I have," says she, "never before been accustomed to speak in the presence of men; but I am compelled by my sufferings to complain of the injuries I have met with."*

In another oration, composed by the same author, a citizen, accused of murdering his wife's gallant, gives the following simple narrative of his domestic economy.

"When I first entered into the married state, Athenians! I endeavoured to observe a medium between the harsh severity of some husbands, and the easy fondness of others. My wife, though treated with kindness, was watched with attention. As a husband, I rendered her situation agreeable; but as a woman, she was left <94> neither the entire mistress of my fortune, nor of her own actions. When she became a mother, this new endearment softened and overcame the prudent caution of my former conduct, and engaged me to repose in her an unlimited confidence. During a short time, Athenians! I had no occasion to repent of this alteration: she proved a most excellent wife; and, highly circumspect in her private behaviour, she managed my affairs with the utmost diligence and frugality. But since the death of my mother, she has been the cause of all my calamities. *Then she first got abroad to attend the funeral,* and being observed by Eratosthenes, was soon after seduced by him. This he effected by means of our female slave, whom he watched going to market, and whom, by fair promises and flattery, he drew over to his designs.

"It is necessary you should be informed, Athenians! that my house consists of two floors; the floor above is laid out in a similar manner to that below; *this lodges the men, that above is destined for the women.* Upon the birth of our son, my wife suckled him herself; and to relieve her from the fatigue of going below stairs as often as it was necessary to bathe him, I yielded up the ground floor to the women, and kept above stairs myself. She still continued, however, to sleep with me during the night; and when

* Lys. Orat. cont. Diagit. [["On an Indictment against Diogeiton," in Gillies, *The Orations of Lysias,* 456.]]

the child was peevish, and fell a-cry-<95>ing, she frequently went below stairs, and offered it the breast. This practice was long continued without any suspicion on my part, who, simple man that I was! regarded my spouse as a prodigy of virtue."*

Solon is said to have made regulations for preventing the women from violating those decorums which were esteemed essential to their character. He appointed that no matron should go from home with more than three garments, nor a larger quantity of provisions than could be purchased for an obolus. He also provided, that when any matron went abroad, she should always have an attendant, and a lighted torch carried before her.†

At Athens, a man was not permitted to approach the apartment of his step-mother, or her children, though living in the same house; which is given, by Mr. Hume, as the reason why, by the Athenian laws, one might marry his half-sister by the father; for as these relations had no more intercourse than the men and women of different families, there was no greater danger of any criminal correspondence between them.[9]

It is probable, that the recluse situation of the Grecian women, which was adapted to the circumstances of the people upon their first advancement in arts, was afterwards maintained from an inviol-<96>able respect to their ancient institutions. The democratical form of government, which came to be established in most parts of Greece, had, at the same time, a tendency to occupy the people in the management of public affairs, and to engage them in those pursuits of ambition, from which the women were naturally excluded. It must however be admitted that, while such a state of manners might be conducive to the more solid enjoyments of life, it undoubtedly prevented the two sexes from improving the arts of conversation, and from giving a polish to the expression of their thoughts and sentiments. Hence it is, that the Greeks, notwithstanding their learning and good sense, were remarkably deficient in delicacy and politeness, and were so little judges of propriety in wit and humour, as to relish the low ribaldry of an Aristophanes, at a period when they were entertained with the sublime el-

---

* See the oration of Lysias, in defence of Euphiletus, translated by Dr. Gillies [[420]].
† See Potter's Greek antiquities [[I:171]].
9. Hume, *Enquiry Concerning the Principles of Morals,* IV:208.

oquence of a Demosthenes, and with the pathetic compositions of a Euripides and a Sophocles.

The military character in ancient Greece, considered with respect to politeness, and compared with the same character in modern times, seems to afford a good illustration of what has been observed. Soldiers, as they are men of the world, have usually such manners as are formed by company and conversation. But in ancient Greece they were no less remarkable for rusticity and ill-manners, than in the modern nations of Europe they <97> are distinguished by politeness and good-breeding; for Menander, the comic poet, says, that he can hardly conceive such a character as that of a polite soldier to be formed even by the power of the Deity.*

When the Romans, towards the middle of the Commonwealth, had become in some degree civilized, it is probable that the condition of their women was nearly the same with that of the Greeks in the period above mentioned. But it appears that, at Rome, the circumstances of the people underwent very rapid changes in this particular. By the conquest of many opulent nations, great wealth was suddenly imported into the capital of the empire; which corrupted the ancient manners of the inhabitants, and produced a great revolution in their taste and sentiments.

In the modern nations of Europe, we may also observe, that the introduction of arts, and of regular government, had an immediate influence upon the relative condition and behaviour of the sexes. When the disorders incident to the Gothic system had subsided, the women began to be valued upon account of their useful talents and accomplishments; and their consideration and rank, making allowance for some remains of that romantic spirit which had prevailed in a former period, came to be chiefly determined by the importance of those departments <98> which they occupied, in carrying on the business and maintaining the intercourse of society. The manners introduced by such views of the female character are still in some measure preserved, in those European countries which have been least affected by the late rapid advances of luxury and refinement. <99>

---

* Menander apud Stobaeum. [[Millar appears to have taken this reference wholesale from Hume, "Of National Characters," *Essays*, 99, n. 2. (I.xxi).]]

*The effects of great opulence, and the culture of the
elegant arts, upon the relative condition of the sexes.*

The progressive improvements of a country are still attended with farther
variations in the sentiments and manners of the inhabitants.

The first attention of a people is directed to the acquisition of the mere
necessaries of life, and to the exercise of those occupations which are most
immediately requisite for subsistence. According as they are successful in
these pursuits, they feel a gradual increase of their wants, and are excited
with fresh vigour and activity to search for the means of supplying them.
The advancement of the more useful arts is followed by the cultivation of
those which are subservient to pleasure and entertainment. Mankind, in
proportion to the progress they have made in multiplying the conveniencies
of their situation, become more refined in their taste, and luxurious in their
manner of living. Exempted from labour, and placed in great affluence,
they endeavour to improve their enjoyments, and become addicted to all
those amusements and diversions which give an exercise to their minds,
and relieve them from languor and weariness, the <100> effects of idleness
and dissipation. In such a state, the pleasures which nature has grafted upon
the love between the sexes, become the source of an elegant correspondence, and are likely to have a general influence upon the commerce of
society. Women of condition come to be more universally admired and
courted upon account of the agreeable qualities which they possess, and
upon account of the amusement which their conversation affords. They
are encouraged to quit that retirement which was formerly esteemed so
suitable to their character, to enlarge the sphere of their acquaintance, and
to appear in mixed company, and in public meetings of pleasure. They lay
aside the spindle and the distaff, and engage in other employments more

agreeable to the fashion. As they are introduced more into public life, they are led to cultivate those talents which are adapted to the intercourse of the world, and to distinguish themselves by polite accomplishments that tend to heighten their personal attractions, and to excite those peculiar senti-ments and passions of which they are the natural objects.

These improvements, in the state and accomplishments of the women, might be illustrated from a view of the manners in the different nations of Europe. They have been carried to the greatest height in France, and in some parts of Italy, where the fine arts have received the highest cultivation, and where a taste for refined and elegant amusement has been generally diffused. The same im-<101>provements have made their way into En-gland and Germany; though the attention of the people to the more nec-essary and useful arts, and their slow advancement in those which are sub-servient to entertainment, has, in these countries, prevented the intercourse of the sexes from being equally extended. Even in Spain, where, from the defects of administration, or from whatever causes, the arts have for a long time been almost entirely neglected, the same effects of refinement are at length beginning to appear, by the admission of the women to that freedom which they have in the other countries of Europe.

Thus we may observe, that in refined and polished nations there is the same free communication between the sexes as in the ages of rudeness and barbarism. In the latter, women enjoy the most unbounded liberty, because it is thought of no consequence what use they shall make of it. In the for-mer, they are entitled to the same freedom, upon account of those agreeable qualities which they possess, and the rank and dignity which they hold as members of society.

It should seem, however, that there are certain limits beyond which it is impossible to push the real improvements arising from wealth and opu-lence. In a simple age, the free intercourse of the sexes is attended with no bad consequences; but in opulent and luxurious nations, it gives rise to licentious and dissolute manners, inconsistent <102> with good order, and with the general interest of society. The love of pleasure, when carried to excess, is apt to weaken and destroy those passions which it endeavours to gratify, and to pervert those appetites which nature has bestowed upon mankind for the most beneficial purposes. The natural tendency, therefore, of great luxury and dissipation is to diminish the rank and dignity of the women, by preventing all refinement in their connection with the other sex, and rendering them only subservient to the purposes of animal enjoyment.

> Prima peregrinos obscena pecunia mores
> Intulit; et turpi fregerunt secula luxû
> Divitiae molles. Quid enim Venus ebria curat?[10]

The voluptuousness of the Eastern nations, arising from a degree of advancement in the arts, joined, perhaps, to the effect of their climate, and the facility with which they are able to procure subsistence, has introduced the practice of polygamy; by which the women are reduced into a state of slavery and confinement, and a great proportion of the inhabitants are employed in such offices as render them incapable of contributing, either to the population, or to the useful improvements of the country.* <103>

The excessive opulence of Rome, about the end of the Commonwealth, and after the establishment of the despotism, gave rise to a degree of debauchery of which we have no example in any other European nation. This did not introduce polygamy, which was repugnant to the regular and well-established police of a former period; though Julius Caesar is said to have prepared a law by which the *emperour* should be allowed to have as many wives as he thought fit.† But the luxury of the people, being restrained in this way, came to be the more indulged in every other; and the common

---

* What is here said with respect to polygamy is only applicable to that institution as it takes place among opulent and luxurious nations; for in barbarous countries, where it is introduced in a great measure from motives of conveniency, and where it is accompanied with little or no jealousy, it cannot have the same consequences.

† "Helvius Cinna Trib, pleb. plerisque confessus est, habuisse scriptam paratamque legem, quam Caesar ferre jussisset, cum ipse abesset, uti uxores liberorum quaerendorum causa, quas et quot vellet, ducere liceret." Suetonius in Julio, c. 52. [["Helvius Cinna, tribune of the plebeians, had confessed to many that he had written and prepared a law for approval, that Caesar had ordered him to present, while he himself was absent, allowing Caesar to marry whomever he might like, and how many wives he might like, in order to produce legal heirs" (*De Vita Caesarum* LII [3]).]]

10. Juvenal *Satire* VI.298–300. ("Filthy money imported obscene foreign morals. Effeminate wealth has shattered our age with venal luxury. When Venus is drunk she's ready for anything.")

prostitution of the women was carried to a height that must have been extremely unfavourable to the multiplication of the species; while the liberty of divorce was so much extended and abused, that, among persons of condition, marriage became a very slight and transient connection.* <104>

The frequency of divorce, among the Romans, was attended with bad consequences, which were felt in every part of their domestic economy. As the husband and wife had a separation constantly in view, they could repose little confidence in each other, but were continually occupied by separate considerations of interest. In such a situation, they were not likely to form a strong attachment, or to bestow much attention to the joint concerns of their family. So far otherwise, the practice of <105> stealing from each other, in expectation of a divorce, became so general that it was not branded with the name of theft, but, like other fashionable vices, received a softening appellation.†

The bad agreement between married persons, together with the com-

---

* By the Roman law, about this period, divorces were granted upon any pretence whatever, and might be procured at the desire of either party. At the same time, the manners, which produced this law, disposed the people very frequently to lay hold of the privilege which it gave them; in so much that we read of few Romans of rank who had not been once divorced, if not oftener. To mention only persons of the gravest and most respectable character: M. Brutus repudiated his wife Claudia, though there was no stain upon her reputation. Cicero put away his wife Terentia, after she had lived with him thirty years, and also his second wife Publilia, whom he had married in his old age. His daughter Tullia was repudiated by Dolabella. Terentia, after she was divorced from Cicero, is said to have had three successive husbands, the first of whom was Cicero's enemy, Sallust the historian. It was formerly mentioned that M. Cato, after his wife Marcia had brought him three children, gave her away to his friend Hortensius. Many of those trifling causes which gave rise to divorce are taken notice of by Valerius Maximus. Seneca declares that some women of illustrious rank were accustomed to reckon their years, not by the number of consuls, but of husbands [De beneficiis [[III.16]].] As a further proof of the profligacy of that age, it is observed that men were sometimes induced to marry from the prospect merely of enriching themselves by the forfeiture of the wife's dower, when she committed adultery. Valer. Max. lib. 6. c. 3.

† The action for the recovery of such stolen goods was not called *conditio furtiva* [[an action against a thief or the heirs of a thief for the recovery of property, whether they still possessed it or not (*Institutes* IV.1.19)]], but *actio rerum amotarum* [[actions for property unlawfully removed, specifically when the wife removed property in expectation of a divorce and after the divorce the husband wished to recover the property granted him (*Digest* XXV:2); the "softening" Millar describes is from theft (*furtiva*) to removal (*amotarum*)]].

mon infidelity of the wife, had a natural tendency to alienate the affections of a father from his children, and led him, in many cases, not only to neglect their education, but even to deprive them of their paternal inheritance. This appears to have been one great cause of that propensity, discovered by the people, to convey their estates by *will;* which, from the many statutes that were made, and the equitable decisions of judges that were given, in order to rectify the abuse, has rendered that branch of the Roman law, relating to testaments, more extensive and complicated than any other. The frequency of such deeds, to the prejudice of the heirs at law, created swarms of those legacy-hunters,* whose trade, as we learn from Horace, afforded the most infallible means of growing rich; and the same circumstance gave also great encouragement to the forgery or falsification of *wills,* a species of fraud which is much taken notice of by the writers of those times, <106> and which has been improperly regarded as one of the general effects of opulence and luxury.†

In those voluptuous ages of Rome, it should seem that the inhabitants were too much dissipated by pleasure to feel any violent passion for an individual, and the correspondence of the sexes was too undistinguishing to be attended with much delicacy of sentiment. It may accordingly be remarked, that the writers of the Augustan age, who have afforded so many

---

* *Heredipetae.*
† ————Tu protenus, unde
    Divitias aerisque ruam, dic augur, acervos.
    Dixi equidem, et dico. Captes astutus ubique
    Testamenta senum; neu, si vafer unus et alter
    Insidiatorem praeroso fugerit hamo,
    Aut spem deponas, aut artem illusus omittas.

[["Tell me, augur, tell me pronto, how I can scrape together a heap of riches and money. I've said it before and I'll say it again. Angle about, cunningly, for the wills of old men. If one or another sly lurker escapes by nibbling the bait off the hook, don't lose hope, or stop purveying this art" (*Satires* II.5, 21–26).]] [See the whole of the 5th Satire, B. 2. of Horace.]

The Volpone, of Johnson, is entirely founded upon this part of ancient manners; but the ridicule of that performance is in a great measure lost, as the original from which it is drawn, and of which it is a faithful copy, has no place in any modern country. [[In Ben Jonson's (1572–1637) *Volpone* (1606), the protagonist convinces his acquisitive neighbors that he is dying so that they will bring him gifts in hope of getting into his will. It is unclear why Millar thinks this is no longer a comprehensible plot device!]]

models of composition in other branches, have left no work of imagination, describing the manners of their own countrymen, in which love is supposed to be productive of any tragical, or very serious effects. Neither that part of the Eneid which relates to the death of Dido, nor the love-epistles of Ovid, both of which are founded upon events in a remote age, and in distant countries, can properly be considered as exceptions to what is here alleged. It also merits <107> attention, that when the Roman poets have occasion to represent their own sentiments in this particular, the subject of their description, not to mention more irregular appetites, is either the love of a concubine, or an intrigue with a married woman. This is not less apparent from the grave and tender Elegies of Tibullus and Propertius, than from the gay and more licentious writings of Horace, of Ovid, and of Catullus. The style of those compositions, and the manners from which it was derived, while they degraded the women of virtue, contributed, no doubt, to exalt the character of a kept-mistress. The different situation of modern nations, in this respect, is perhaps the reason why they have no term corresponding to that of *amica* in Latin.

The acquisition of great wealth, and the improvement of the elegant arts, together with the free intercourse of the sexes, have, in some of the modern European nations, had similar consequences to what they produced in ancient Rome, by introducing a strong disposition to pleasure. This is most especially remarkable in France and Italy, the countries in which opulence was first acquired, and in which the improvements of society are supposed to have made the greatest advances. But in these countries, the authority obtained by the clergy after the establishment of the Christian religion, and the notions which they endeavoured to inculcate with regard to abstinence from every sensual gratification, have concurred with the influ-<108>ence of the former usage and laws, not only to exclude polygamy, but in a great measure to prevent the dissolution of marriage by voluntary divorce. Many disorders, therefore, which were felt in the luxurious ages of Rome, have thus been avoided; and in modern Europe, the chief effect of debauchery, beside the encouragement given to common prostitution, has been to turn the attention, from the pursuits of business or ambition, to the amusements of gallantry; or rather to convert these last into a serious occupation.

It is not intended, however, in this discourse, to consider those variations, in the state of women, which arise from the civil or religious government of a people, or from such other causes as are peculiar to the inhabitants of different countries. The revolutions that I have mentioned, in
the condition and manners of the sexes, are chiefly derived from the progress of mankind in the common arts of life, and therefore make a part in
the general history of society. <109>

Of the Jurisdiction and Authority of a Father over His Children

SECTION I

The power of a father in early ages.

The jurisdiction and authority which, in early times, a father exercised over his children, was of the same nature with that of a husband over his wife. Before the institution of regular government, the strong are permitted to oppress the weak; and in a rude nation, every one is apt to abuse that power which he happens to possess.

After marriage is completely established in a community, the husband, as has been formerly observed, becomes the head of his family, and assumes the direction and government of all its members. It is to be expected, indeed, that in the exercise of this authority, he should have an inclination to promote the welfare and prosperity of his children. The helpless and miserable state in which they are produced, can hardly fail to excite his pity, and to solicit, in a peculiar manner, the protection of that person from whom they have derived their existence. Being thereby induced to undertake the burden of rearing and maintain-<110>ing them, he is more warmly engaged in their behalf in proportion to the efforts which he has made for their benefit, and his affection for them is increased by every new mark of his kindness. While they grow up under his culture and tuition, and begin to lisp the endearing names of a parent, he has the satisfaction of observing their progress towards maturity, and of discovering the seeds of those dispositions and talents, from the future display of which he draws the most flattering expectations. By retaining them afterwards in his family, which is the foundation of a constant intercourse, by procuring their assistance in the labour to which he is subjected, by connecting them with all his plans and views of interest, his attachment is usually continued and strengthened from the same habits and principles which, in other cases, give rise to friendship or acquaintance. As these sentiments are felt in common by the father and mother, it is natural to suppose that their affection for each other will be, in some measure, reflected upon their offspring, and will become an additional motive of attention to the objects of their united care and tenderness.

Such is, probably, the origin of that parental fondness, which has been found so extensive and universal that it is commonly regarded as the effect of an immediate propensity. But how strongly soever a father may be disposed to promote the happiness of his children, this disposition, in the breast <III> of a savage, is often counteracted by a regard to his own preservation, and smothered by the misery with which he is loaded. In many cases he is forced to abandon them entirely, and suffer them to perish by hunger, or be devoured by wild beasts. From his necessitous circumstances, he is sometimes laid under the temptation of selling his children for slaves. Even those whom the father finds it not convenient to support, are subjected to a variety of hardships from the natural ferocity of his temper; and if on some occasions they are treated with the utmost indulgence, they are, on others, no less exposed to the sudden and dreadful effects of his anger. As the resentment of a savage is easily kindled, and raised to an excessive pitch; as he behaves like a sovereign in his own family, where he has never been accustomed to bear opposition or controul, we need not wonder that, when provoked by unusual disrespect or contradiction, he should be roused and hurried on to commit the most barbarous of all actions, the murder of his own child.

The children in their early years, are under the necessity of submitting to the severe and arbitrary will of their father. From their inferiority in strength, they are in no condition to dispute his commands; and being incapable of maintaining themselves, they depend entirely upon him for subsistence. To him they must apply for assistance, whenever they are exposed to danger, or <112> threatened with injustice; and looking upon him as the source of all their enjoyments, they have every motive to court his favour and to avoid his displeasure.

The respect and reverence which is paid to the father, upon account of his wisdom and experience, is another circumstance that contributes to support his power and authority.

Among savages, who are strangers to the art of writing, and who have scarcely any method of recording facts, the experience and observation of each individual are almost the only means of procuring knowledge; and the only persons who can attain a superior degree of wisdom and sagacity are those who have lived to a considerable age.

It also merits attention that, in rude and ignorant nations, the least superiority in knowledge and wisdom is the source of great honour and distinction. The man who understands any operation of nature, unknown to the vulgar, is beheld with superstitious awe and veneration. As they cannot penetrate into the ways by which he has procured his information, they are disposed to magnify his extraordinary endowments; and they feel an unbounded admiration of that skill and learning which they are unable to comprehend. They suppose that nothing is beyond the compass of his abilities, and apply to him for counsel and direction in every new and difficult emergency. They are apt to imagine that he holds commerce <113> with invisible beings, and to believe that he is capable of seeing into futurity, as well as of altering the course of human events by the wonderful power of his art. Thus, in the dark ages, a slight acquaintance with the heavenly bodies gave rise to the absurd pretensions of judicial astrology; and a little knowledge of chemistry, or medicine, was supposed to reveal the invaluable secret of rendering ourselves immortal.

As in all barbarous countries old men are distinguished by their great experience and wisdom, they are upon this account universally respected, and commonly attain superior influence and authority.

Among the Greeks, at the siege of Troy, the man who had lived three ages was treated with uncommon deference, and was their principal adviser and director in all important deliberations.

"Dost thou not see, O Gaul," says Morni, in one of the poems of Ossian, "how the steps of my age are honoured? Morni moves forth, and the young meet him with reverence, and turn their eyes, with silent joy, on his course."*

The Jewish lawgiver, whose system of laws was in many respects accommodated to the circumstances of an early people, has thought proper to enforce the respect due to old age, by making it the subject of a particular precept. "See that <114> thou rise up before the hoary head, and honour the face of the old man."†

"I am young," says the son of Barachel, "and ye are very old, wherefore I was afraid, and durst not show you mine opinion. I said days should speak, and multitude of years teach wisdom."‡

When any of the Tartar nations have occasion to elect a khan or leader, they regard experience and wisdom more than any other circumstance; and for that reason they commonly prefer the oldest person of the royal family.§ It is the same circumstance that, in the infancy of government, has given rise to a senate or council of the elders, which is commonly invested with the chief direction and management of all public affairs.||

So inseparably connected are age and authority in early periods, that in the language of rude nations the same word which signifies an old man is generally employed to denote a ruler or magistrate.¶

Among the Chinese, who, from their little intercourse with strangers, are remarkably attached to their ancient usages, the art of writing, notwith-<115>standing their improvement in manufactures, is still beyond the reach of the vulgar. This people have accordingly preserved that high admiration of the advantages arising from long experience and observation, which we commonly met with in times of ignorance and simplicity. Among them,

---

* Lathmon. [[*Poems of Ossian,* 177.]]

† Leviticus, chap. xix. ve. 32.

‡ Job, chap. xxxii.

§ Histoire generale des voyages. [[*Histoire Generale des Voyages* volume XIX contains Gmelin's *Travels,* but I have been unable to find the passage in question.]]

|| This was the case among the Jews.—Among the North Americans, see Charlevoix [[*Histoire et description générale,* letter XVII]].—Among the ancient Romans the elders formed the senate, and were called *Patres.*

¶ In the language of the Arabs, see D'Arvieux trav. Arab. [[*The Chevalier d'Arvieux's Travels,* 99.]] This also is the case in the German and most of the modern languages of Europe.

neither birth, nor riches, nor honours, nor dignities, can make a man forget that reverence which is due to grey hairs; and the sovereign himself never fails to respect old age, even in persons of the lowest condition.

The difference in this particular, between the manners of a rude and polished nation may be illustrated from the following anecdote concerning two Grecian states, which, in point of what is commonly called refinement, were remarkably distinguished from each other.

"It happened, at Athens, during a public representation of some play, exhibited in honour of the commonwealth, that an old gentleman came too late for a place suitable to his age and quality. Many of the young gentlemen, who observed the difficulty and confusion he was in, made signs to him that they would accommodate him, if he came where they sat. The good man bustled through the crowd accordingly; but when he came to the seats to which he was invited, the jest was to sit close, and, as he stood out of countenance, expose him to the whole audience. The frolic went round all the <116> Athenian benches. But on those occasions there were also particular places assigned for foreigners: when the good man skulked towards the boxes appointed for the Lacedemonians, that honest people, more virtuous than polite, rose up all to a man, and with the greatest respect received him among them. The Athenians, being suddenly touched with a sense of the Spartan virtue and their own degeneracy, gave a thunder of applause; and the old man cried out, The Athenians understand what is good, but the Lacedemonians practise it."*

We may easily imagine that this admiration and reverence, which is excited by wisdom and knowledge, must in a particular manner affect the conduct of children with respect to their father. The experience of the father must always appear greatly superior to that of his children, and becomes the more remarkable, according as he advances in years, and decays in bodily strength. He is placed in a situation where that experience is constantly displayed to them, and where, being exerted for their preservation

---

* Notwithstanding that old men are commonly so much respected among savages, they are sometimes put to death when so far advanced in years as to have lost the use of their faculties. This shows, that the estimation in which they are held does not proceed from a principle of humanity, but from a regard to the useful knowledge they are supposed to possess. [[The anecdote is from Cicero *De Senectute* 18.]]

and welfare, it is regarded in the most <117> favourable light. From him they learn those contrivances which they make use of in procuring their food, and the various stratagems which they put in practice against their enemies. By him they are instructed in the different branches of their domestic economy, and are directed what measures to pursue in all those difficulties and distresses in which they may be involved. They hear with wonder the exploits he has performed, the precautions he has taken to avoid the evils with which he was surrounded, or the address and dexterity he has employed to extricate himself from those misfortunes which had befallen him; and, from his observation of the past, they treasure up lessons of prudence, by which they may regulate their future behaviour. If ever they depart from his counsel, and follow their own headstrong inclination, they are commonly taught by the event to repent of their folly and rashness, and are struck with new admiration of his uncommon penetration and foresight. They regard him in the light of a superior being, and imagine that the gifts of fortune are at his disposal. They dread his curse, as the cause of every misfortune; and they esteem his blessing of more value than the richest inheritance.

When Phenix, in the Iliad, bewails his misfortune in having no children, he imputes it to the curse of his father, which he had incurred in his youth. <118>

> My sire with curses loads my hated head,
> And cries, ye furies! barren be his bed!
> Infernal Jove, the vengeful Fiends below,
> And ruthless Proserpine confirmed his vow.*

"And Esau said unto his father, Hast thou but one blessing, my father? Bless me, even me also, O my Father! And Esau lift up his voice and wept."†

To these observations it may be added, that the authority of the father is confirmed and rendered more universal, by the force and influence of custom.

We naturally retain, after we are old, those habits of respect and sub-

---

* Pope's translation of the Iliad, book 9. l. 582.
† Genesis, chap. xxvii. ver. 38.

mission which we received in our youth; and we find it difficult to put ourselves upon a level with those persons whom we have long regarded as greatly our superiors. The slave, who has been bred up in a low situation, does not immediately, upon obtaining his freedom, lay aside those sentiments which he has been accustomed to feel. He retains for some time the idea of his former dependence, and, notwithstanding the change of his circumstances, is disposed to continue that respect and reverence which he owed to his master. We find that the legislature, in some countries, has even regarded and enforced these natural sentiments. By the Roman law a freed man was, through the whole <119> of his life, obliged to pay to his patron certain attendance on public occasions, and to show him particular marks of honour and distinction.* If ever he failed in the observance of these duties, he was thought unworthy of his liberty, and was again reduced to be the slave of that person to whom he had behaved in so unbecoming a manner.†

A son who, in a barbarous age, has been accustomed from his infancy to serve and to obey his father, is in the same manner disposed for the future to continue that service and obedience. Even after he is grown up, and has arrived at his full strength of body, and maturity of judgment, he retains the early impressions of his youth, and remains in a great measure under the yoke of that authority to which he has hitherto submitted. He shrinks at the angry countenance of his father, and trembles at the power of that arm whose severe discipline he has so often experienced, and of whose valour and dexterity he has so often been a witness. He thinks it the highest presumption to dispute the wisdom and propriety of those commands to which he has always listened, as to an oracle, and which he has been taught to regard as the infallible rule of his conduct. He is <120> naturally led to acquiesce in that jurisdiction which he has seen exerted on so many different occasions, and which he finds to be uniformly acknowledged by all the members of the family. In proportion to the rigour with which he is treated,

---

* Operae officiales. [[This is the technical term in Roman law for the relation Millar describes in the body of the text.]]

† Vide Heineccii antiq. Rom. lib. 1. Tit. 6. §. 9. Dig. Tit. de oper. libert. [[*Digest* XXXVIII.1 "De operas libertorum."]] Inst. §. 1. de cap. deminut. l. un. [[I.xvii. De capitis minutione.]] Cod. de ingrat. liber. [[*Codex* VIII.49 "De Ingratis Liberis."]]

his temper will be more thoroughly subdued, and his habits of implicit submission and obedience will be the stronger. He looks upon his father as invested by Heaven with an unlimited power and authority over all his children, and imagines that, whatever hardships they may suffer, their rebellion against him, or resistance to his will, would be the same species of impiety, as to call in question the authority of the Deity, and arraign the severe dispensations with which, in the government of the world, he is sometimes pleased to visit his creatures.

From these dispositions, which commonly prevail among the members of his family, the father can have no difficulty to enforce his orders, wherever compulsion may be necessary. In order to correct the depravity, or to conquer the rebellious disposition of any single child, he can make use of that influence which he possesses over the rest, who will regard the disobedience of their brother with horror and detestation, and be ready to contribute their assistance in punishing his transgression.

In the history of early nations, we meet with a great variety of facts, to illustrate the nature and <121> extent of that jurisdiction and authority which originally belonged to the father, as the head and governor of his family.

We are informed by Caesar, that among the Gauls the father had the power of life and death over his children;* and there is reason to believe, that, in the ancient German nations, his jurisdiction was no less extensive.†

By the early laws and customs of Arabia, every head of a family seems, in like manner, to have enjoyed an absolute power over his descendants. When the sons of Jacob proposed to carry their brother Benjamin along with them into Egypt, and their father discovered an unwillingness to part with him, "Reuben spake unto his father, saying, Slay my two sons, if I bring him not to thee: deliver him into my hand, and I will bring him to thee again."‡ Moses appears to have intended that the father should not, in ordinary cases, be at liberty to take away the life of his children in private; as may be concluded from this particular institution, that a stubborn and

* Caesar de bel. Gall. lib. 6.
† See Heineccius elem. jur. German. [[*Elementa Iuris Germanici, Tum Veteris, Tum Hodierni* (Naples, 1770), I.VI § CXXXV.]]
‡ Genesis, chap. xlii. ver. 37.

rebellious son should be stoned to death before the elders of the city.* It was further enacted by this legislator, that a man might sell his daughter for a slave or concubine to those of his own nation, though he was not permitted to dispose of her to a stranger. <122>

"If a man sell his daughter to be a maid-servant, she shall not go out as the men-servants do.

"If she please not her master, who hath betrothed her to himself, then shall he let her be redeemed: to sell her to a strange nation he shall have no power, seeing he hath dealt deceitfully with her."†

In the empire of Russia, the paternal jurisdiction was formerly understood to be altogether supreme and unlimited.‡ Peter the Great appears to have been so little aware that the customs of his own country might differ from those of other nations, that in his public declaration to his clergy, and to the states civil and military, relative to the trial of his son, he appeals to all the world, and affirms, that, according to all laws human and divine, and, above all, according to those of Russia, a father, even among private persons, has a full and absolute right to judge his children, without appeal, and without taking the advice of any person.§

Among the Tartars, nothing can exceed the respect and reverence which the children usually pay to their father. They look upon him as the sovereign lord and master of his family, and consider it as their duty to serve him upon all occasions. In those parts of Tartary which have any inter-<123>course with the great nations of Asia, it is also common for the father to sell his children of both sexes; and from thence the women and eunuchs, in the harams and seraglios, belonging to men of wealth and distinction in those countries, are said to be frequently procured.‖

Upon the coast of Africa, the power of the father is carried to the most

---

* Deuteronomy, chap. xxi. ver. 18.

† Exodus, chap. xxi. ver. 7.

‡ Sigon. de antiq. jur. civ. Roman. lib. 1. cap. 10. [[Carlo Sigonio, *De Antiquo Iure Civium Romanorum Libri Duo.*]]

§ See [[Friedrich Christian Weber]] Present State of Russia, published 1722 [[201, 221]].

‖ Histoire generale des voyages [[vol. IX]].—Chardin. tom. 1. [[Jean Chardin, *Journal du Voyage du chevalier Chardin* (no passage corresponds exactly).]]

excessive pitch, and exercised with the utmost severity. It is too well known to be denied, that, in order to supply the European market, he often disposes of his own children for slaves; and that the chief part of a man's wealth is supposed to consist in the number of his descendants. Upon the slave-coast, the children are accustomed to throw themselves upon their knees, as often as they come into the presence of their father.*

The following account, given by Commodore Byron, may serve, in some measure, to show the spirit with which the savages of South America are apt to govern the members of their family.

"Here," says he, "I must relate a little anecdote of our Christian Cacique. He and his wife had gone off, at some distance from the shore, in their canoe, when she dived for sea-eggs; but not meeting with great success, they returned a good deal out of humour. A little boy of theirs, <124> about three years old, whom they appeared to be doatingly fond of, watching for his father and mother's return, ran into the surf to meet them: the father handed a basket of sea-eggs to the child, which being too heavy for him to carry, he let it fall; upon which the father jumped out of the canoe, and catching the boy up in his arms, dashed him with the utmost violence against the stones. The poor little creature lay motionless and bleeding, and in that condition was taken up by the mother, but died soon after. She appeared inconsolable for some time; but the brute his father shewed little concern about it."†

The exposition of infants, so common in a great part of the nations of antiquity, is a proof that the different heads of families were under no restraint or controul in the management of their domestic concerns. This barbarous practice was probably introduced in those rude ages when the father was often incapable of maintaining his children, and from the influence of old usage, was permitted to remain in later times, when the plea of necessity could no longer be urged in its vindication. How shocking soever it may appear to us, the custom of exposing infant-children was universal among the ancient inhabitants of Greece, and was never abolished

---

* Histoire generale des voyages, tom. 4. liv. 10. chap. 3.
† Narrative of the honourable John Byron [[148–49]].

even by such of the Greek states as were <125> most distinguished for their learning and politeness.*

According to the laws and customs of the Romans, the father had anciently an unlimited power of putting his children to death, and of selling them for slaves. While they remained in his family, they were incapable of having any estate of their own, and whatever they acquired, either by their own industry, or by the donations of others, became immediately the property of their father. Though with respect to every other person they were regarded as free, yet with respect to their father they were considered as in a state of absolute slavery and subjection; and they could neither marry, nor enter into any other contract, without his approbation and consent.†

In one respect, the power of a father over his sons appears, in ancient Rome, to have extended even farther than that of a master over his slaves. <126> If upon any occasion a son had been sold by his father, and had afterwards obtained his freedom from the purchaser, he did not thereby become independent, but was again reduced under the paternal dominion. The same consequence followed, if he had been sold and manumitted a second time; and it was only after a third purchase, that the power of his father was altogether dissolved, and that he was permitted to enjoy any real and permanent advantage from the bounty of his master.

---

* Aelian mentions the Thebans alone as having made a law forbidding the exposition of infants under a capital punishment, and ordaining, that if the parents were indigent, their children, upon application to the magistrate, should be maintained and brought up as slaves. Aelian var. hist. lib. 2. cap. 7. [[Aelian *Varia Historia.* See also Smith, *Theory of Moral Sentiments,* V.2.15.]]

† Dion. Halicar. lib. 11. l. 11. Dig. de lib et postum. § 3. [[*Digest* XXVIII.2 "De liberis et postumis heredibus instituendis vel exheredandis."]] Inst. per quas person. cuiq. adquir. l. ult. [[*Institutes* II.9 "Per quas personas nobis adquiritur."]] Cod. de impub. et al. subst. l. 4. [[*Codex* "De impuberum et de aliis sustitutionibus."]] Dig. de judic. § 6. [[*Digest* VI.26 "De iudiciis: ubi quisque agere vel conveneri debeat."]] Inst. de inut. stip. [[*Institutes* III.19 "De inutilibus stipulationibus."]]

Upon the same principle a father might claim his son from any person, by the ordinary action upon property, lib. 1. § 2. Dig. de rei vind. [[*Digest* VI.1 "De rei vindicatione."]] If a son had been stolen from his father, the "actio furti" was given against the thief, l. 38. Dig. de furt. [[*Digest* 47.2 "De furtis."]] When children were sold by their father, the form of conveyance was the same which was used in the transference of that valuable property which was called "res mancipi," Cai Inst. l. 6. 3. [[Gaius's *Commentary* I.18–19 on *Institutes* I.6 "Qui quibus et causis manumittere non possunt."]]

This peculiarity is said to have been derived from a statute of Romulus, adopted into the laws of the twelve tables, and affords a sufficient proof that the Romans had anciently no idea of a child living in the family, without being considered as the slave of his father.*

In those early ages, when this practice was first introduced, the Roman state was composed of a few clans, or families of barbarians, the members of which had usually a strong attachment to one another, and were at variance with most of their <127> neighbours. When a son therefore had been banished from his family by the avarice of his father, we may suppose that, as soon as he was at liberty, he would not think of remaining in a foreign tribe, or of submitting to the hardships of procuring his food in a state of solitude, but that he would rather choose to return to his own kindred, and again submit to that jurisdiction, which was more useful from the protection it afforded, than painful from the service and obedience which it required.

It is probable, however, that if in this manner a child had been frequently separated from the company of his relations, he would at length grow weary of returning to a society in which he was the object of so little affection, and in which he was treated with so much contempt. How long he would be disposed to maintain his former connexions, and how often he would be willing to restore that property which his father had abandoned, seems, from the nature of the thing, impossible to ascertain. But whatever might be the conduct of the son, it seems to have been intended by the statute of Romulus, that, after a third sale, the property of the father should be finally extinguished, and that he should never afterwards recover a power which he had exercised with such immoderate severity. <128>

---

* This statute, which was afterwards transferred into the twelve tables, is thus handed down to us. "Endo liberis justis jus vitae, necis, venumdandique potestas ei esto. Si pater filium ter venumduit, filius a patre liber esto." Ulp. frag. 10. 1. [["Concerning the right of life or death and the power of selling, belonging to just free men. If the father sells the son three times, the son is free from the father." This is from the fourth of the twelve tables, the oldest extant written Roman Law, which is preserved only in fragments. The writings of Ulpian (d. 228), one of the most important Roman jurists and legal editors, make up a large portion of the *Digest*.]]

SECTION II

The influence of the improvement of arts
upon the jurisdiction of the father.

Such was the power, in early times, possessed by the head of a family. But the gradual advancement of a people in civilized manners, and their subjection to regular government, have a natural tendency to limit and restrain this primitive jurisdiction. When different families are united in a larger society, the several members of which have an intimate correspondence with each other, it may be expected that the exercise of domestic authority will begin to excite the attention of the public. The near relations of a family, who have a concern for the welfare of the children, and who have an opportunity of observing the manner in which they are treated, will naturally interpose by their good offices, and endeavour to screen them from injustice and oppression. The abuses which, on some occasions, are known and represented with all their aggravating circumstances, will excite indignation and resentment, and will at length give rise to such regulations as are necessary for preventing the like disorders for the future.

Those improvements in the state of society, which are the common effects of opulence and refinement, <129> will at the same time dispose the father to use his power with greater moderation. By living in affluence and security, he is more at leisure to exert the social affections, and to cultivate those arts which tend to soften and humanize the temper. Being often engaged in the business and conversation of the world, and finding, in many cases, the necessity of conforming to the humours of those with whom he converses, he becomes less impatient of contradiction, and less apt to give way to the irregular sallies of passion. His parental affection, though not perhaps more violent, becomes at least more steady and uniform; and while it prompts him to undergo the labour that may be requisite in providing

169

for his family, it is not incompatible with that discretion which leads him to bear with the frowardness, the folly, and imprudence of his children, and in his behaviour towards them, to avoid equally the excess of severity and of indulgence.

On the other hand, the progress of arts and manufactures will contribute to undermine and weaken his power, and even to raise the members of his family to a state of freedom and independence.

In those rude and simple periods when men are chiefly employed in hunting and fishing, in pasturing cattle, or in cultivating the ground, the children are commonly brought up in the house of their father; and continuing in his family as long as he <130> lives, they have no occasion to acquire any separate property, but depend entirely for subsistence upon that hereditary estate, of which he is the sole disposer and manager. Their situation, however, in this, as well as in many other respects, is greatly altered by the introduction of commerce and manufactures. In a commercial country, a great part of the inhabitants are employed in such a manner as tends to disperse the members of a family, and often requires that they should live at a distance from one another.

The children, at an early period of life, are obliged to leave their home, in order to be instructed in those trades and professions by which it is proposed they should earn a livelihood, and afterwards to settle in those parts of the country which they find convenient for prosecuting their several employments. By this alteration of circumstances, they are emancipated from their father's authority. They are put in a condition to procure a maintainance without having recourse to his bounty, and by their own labour and industry are frequently possessed of opulent fortunes. As they live in separate families of their own, of which they have the entire direction, and are placed at such a distance from their father, that he has no longer an opportunity of observing and controuling their behaviour, it is natural to suppose that their former habits will be gradually laid aside and forgotten. <131>

When we examine the laws and customs of polished nations, they appear to coincide with the foregoing remarks, and leave no room to doubt that, in most countries, the paternal jurisdiction has been reduced within narrower bounds, in proportion to the ordinary improvements of society.

The Romans, who for several centuries were constantly employed in war, and for that reason gave little attention to the arts of peace, discovered more attachment to their barbarous usages than perhaps any other nation that arose to wealth and splendour; and their ancient practice, with respect to the power of the father, was therefore permitted to remain in the most flourishing periods of their government. The alterations in this particular, which were at length found expedient, having, for the most part, occurred in times of light and knowledge, are recorded with some degree of accuracy, and, as they mark the progress of a great people in an important branch of policy, may deserve to be particularly considered.

We know nothing with certainty concerning the attempts which, in a very remote period, are supposed to have been made for restraining the exposition of infants. By a law of Romulus, parents are said to have been obliged to maintain their male children, and the eldest female, unless where a child was, by two of the neighbours called for the purpose, declared to be a monster. A regulation of the same nature is mentioned among the laws of <132> the twelve tables; but there is ground to believe that little regard was paid to it; and even under the emperors, the exposing of new-born children, of either sex, appears to have been exceedingly common.*

The first effectual regulations in favour of children were those which bestowed upon them a privilege of acquiring property independent of their father. During the free government of Rome, as war was the chief employment in which a Roman citizen thought proper to engage, and by which he had any opportunity of gaining a fortune, it appeared highly reasonable, that when he hazarded his person in the service of his country, he should be allowed to reap the fruit of his labour, and be entitled to the full enjoyment of whatever he had acquired. With this view, it was enacted by Julius and by Augustus Caesar, that whatever was gained by a son, in the

---

* See the treatise of Noodt, entitled Julius Paulus.—And that of Binckershook de jure occidendi liberos. [[In 1719 Cornelius van Bijnkershoek wrote *Opusculum de Jure Occidendi Liberos* against Gerard de Noodt's *Julius Paulus* concerning the power of the father to expose infants in ancient Rome and Greece. The natural lawyer De Noodt had argued that positive laws had their value insofar as they responded to and expressed the natural law. Bijnkershoek felt that de Noodt had undermined the authority of the *Corpus Juris* by stressing the legality of the obviously immoral practice of exposure.]]

military profession, should be considered as his own estate, and that he should be at liberty to dispose of it at pleasure.*

Some time after, when the practice of the law had also become a lucrative profession, it was further established, that whatever a son acquired in the exercise of this employment, should in like manner become his own property, and should in no respect belong to the father.† <133>

In a later age, when no employment was considered as too mean for the subjects of the Roman empire, the son became proprietor of what he could procure by the practice of the mechanical arts, and of whatever he obtained by donations, or by succession to his mother or maternal relations; though the *usufruct*[1] of those acquisitions was, in ordinary cases, bestowed upon the father.‡

It is uncertain at what time the Romans first began to limit the father in the power of selling his children for slaves. It appears, that before the reign of the emperor Dioclesian this privilege was entirely abolished, except in a singular case, in which it remained to the latest periods of the empire. To remove the temptation of abandoning new-born children, a permission was given to sell them, but with provision that they might, at any time after, be redeemed from the purchaser, by restoring the price which he had paid.§

Exclusive of infants, the power over the life of children was first sub-

---

* It was called "peculium castrense." [[A *peculium* was essentially an allowance given a slave or son under parental power by the head of the household. The *peculium castrense,* or "military peculium," was, unlike an ordinary *peculium,* within the power of the son, as was the *peculium quasi castrense.* Cf. *Digest* XV and XLIX.17.]]

† Peculium quasi castrense. [[See previous note.]]

‡ The subject so acquired was called *peculium adventitium.* Constantine made the first regulations concerning it, which were extended by his successors, especially by the emperor Justinian. Vid. Tit. Cod. de bon. matern. [[*Codex* VI.60 "De bonis maternis et materni generis."]]—Tit. de bon. quae lib. [[*Codex* VI.61 "De bonis quae liberis in potestate patris."]]

§ L. 1. C. de pat. qui fil. distrax. l. 2. eod. [[*Codex* IV.43 "De patribus qui filios distraxerunt." The chronology of the abolishment of the right of the father to sell his children as slaves is interesting insofar as it downplays the role of Christianity and shows the limiting of paternal power to have come about through a gradual process stretching from Hadrian (117–38) at the height of the pagan empire to the first Christian emperor Constantine (280–337).]]

1. "Usufruct" is the right to use without impairing the substance, in this case the right of the father to use what the son has acquired (*Digest* VII.1).

jected to any limitation in the reign of Trajan, and of Hadrian his successor, who interposed, in some particular cases, to punish the wanton exercise of paternal authority. In the <134> time of the emperor Severus, the father was not allowed to put his children to death in private, but when they committed a crime of an atrocious nature, was directed to accuse them before a magistrate, to whom he was empowered, in that case, to prescribe the particular punishment which he chose to have inflicted. At length this part of his jurisdiction was finally abolished by the emperor Constantine, who ordained, that if a father took away the life of his child, he should be deemed guilty of parricide.*

These were the principal steps by which the Romans endeavoured to correct this remarkable part of their ancient law. It was natural to begin with the reformation of those particulars in which the greatest abuses were committed, and thence to proceed to others, which, however absurd in appearance, were less severely felt, and less productive of disorder and oppression. It seldom happened that a father, though permitted by law, was so hardened to the feelings of humanity and natural affection, as to be capable of embruing his hands in the blood of a child whom he had brought up in his family; and accordingly no more than three or four instances of that nature are mentioned in the whole Roman history.[2] He might oftener be tempted to neglect his children immediately after their birth, or be reconciled to the measure of reaping a certain <135> profit at the expence of their freedom. But the part of his prerogative which he would probably exert in the most arbitrary manner, was that which related to the maintenance of his family, and the management of that property which had been procured by their industry and labour. Thus we find that, beside the early and ineffectual attempts to prevent the neglect of infants, the interpositions of the Roman legislature were directed first to secure the

---

* L. 3. C. ne patr. potest. l. un. [[*Codex* VIII.46 "De patria potestate."]] C. de his qui parent. [[*Codex* IX.17 "De his qui parentes vel liberos occiderunt."]]

2. The case that Millar's readers would have in mind would be Brutus's killing of his sons for attempting to overthrow the republic and restore the Tarquin tyranny (cf. Livy *Ab Urbe Condita* [*History of Rome*] II.5).

property, afterwards the liberty, and last of all the life and personal safety of the children.*

Upon comparing the manners of different countries, with regard to the subject of our present inquiry, it will be found that wherever polygamy is established, the authority enjoyed by the head of every family is usually carried to a greater height, and is more apt to remain in its full force, notwithstanding the improvements which, in other respects, the people may have attained. By the institution of polygamy, the children belonging to a person of opulent fortune, are commonly rendered so numerous as greatly to diminish the influence of paternal affection: not to mention that the confinement of his wives, and the jealousy, hatred, and dissension, which prevail among them, are productive of such intrigues to supplant or destroy one another, and to promote the interest of their respective children, that the husband, in order to repress these dis-<136>orders, finds it necessary to preserve a strict discipline in his family, and to hold all its members in extreme subjection. This will suggest a reason for what is observed by Aristotle, that among the Persians, in his time, the power of a father over his children was no less absolute as that of a master over his slaves.†

In the empire of China, the same circumstance, together with that aversion which the people discover to every sort of innovation, has also enabled the father to maintain a great part of his original jurisdiction.‡ The father is said to have there the privilege of selling his children whenever he thinks proper; but if he intends to put them to death, it is necessary that he should bring them before a magistrate, and publicly accuse them. At the same time, whatever be the crime of which they are accused, they are held to be guilty, without any other proof but the bare assertion of the father.§

The custom of exposing infants was not restrained in China till very lately. Father Noel, in a relation presented to the general of the Jesuits, in 1703, takes notice, that at Pekin a number of children were usually dropt

---

* Vid. l. ult. Cod. de. pat. Potest.

† Aristot. Ethic. lib. 6. cap. 10.

‡ Though in China a man is not allowed to have more wives than one, yet he may have any number of concubines; which, in the point under consideration, must have nearly the same effect. Le Compte's memoirs of China. [[Le Comte, *Memoirs,* 302.]]

§ Ibid.

or exposed every morning <137> in the streets. "As Pekin is excessively populous," continues that pious and Catholic father, "and those who have more children than they can maintain do not scruple to drop them in places of public resort, where they either die miserably, or are devoured by beasts; one of our first cares is to send, every morning, catechists into the different parts of that great city, in order to baptize such of those children as are not dead. About twenty or thirty thousand children are exposed yearly, and of these our catechists baptize about three thousand; and had we twenty or thirty catechists, few of the children in question would die unbaptized."*

In those European nations which have made the greatest improvements in commerce and manufactures, great liberty is usually enjoyed by the members of every family; and the children are no farther subjected to the father than seems necessary for their own advantage. When they come to be of age, they have the full enjoyment and disposal of any separate property which they happen to acquire; and even during their father's life, they are in some cases entitled to a fixed provision out of the family estate.

It can hardly be doubted that these regulations, <138> which tend to moderate the excessive and arbitrary power assumed by the head of a family, are supported by every consideration of justice and utility. The opinion of Sir Robert Filmer, who founds the doctrine of passive obedience to a monarch, upon the unlimited submission which children owe to their father, seems, at this day, unworthy of the serious refutation which it has met with, and could only have gained reputation when men were just beginning to reflect upon the first principles of government.[3] To say that a king ought to enjoy absolute power because a father has enjoyed it, is to defend one system of oppression by the example of another.

The interest of those who are governed is the chief circumstance which ought to regulate the powers committed to a father, as well as those committed to a civil magistrate; and whenever the prerogative of either is further

---

* Travels of the Jesuits, compiled from their letters, translated by Lockman, vol. I. p. 448.

3. Cf. Robert Filmer, *Patriarcha* (1588–1653), *passim* (published posthumously in 1680). The best known responses to Filmer were James Tyrell's *Patriarcha Non Monarcha* (1680), Algernon Sidney's *Discourse Concerning Government* (1698), and John Locke's *First Treatise on Government* (1689).

extended than is requisite for this great end, it immediately degenerates into usurpation, and is to be regarded as a violation of the natural rights of mankind.

The tendency, however, of a commercial age is rather towards the opposite extreme, and may occasion some apprehension that the members of a family will be raised to greater independence than is consistent with good order, and with a proper domestic subordination. As, in every country, the laws enforced by the magistrate are in a great <139> measure confined to the rules of justice, it is evident that further precautions are necessary to guard the morals of the inhabitants, and that, for this purpose, the authority of parents ought to be such as may enable them to direct the education of their children, to restrain the irregularities of youth, and to instil those principles which will render them useful members of society. <140>

The Authority of a Chief over the Members of a Tribe or Village

SECTION I

The origin of a Chief, and the degrees of influence which he is enabled to acquire.

Having considered the primitive state of a family during the life of the father, we may now examine the changes which happen in their situation, upon the death of this original governor, and the different species of authority to which they are then commonly subjected.

When the members of a family become too numerous to be all maintained and lodged in the same house, some of them are under the necessity of leaving it, and providing themselves with a new habitation. The sons, having arrived at the age of manhood, and being disposed to marry, are led by degrees to have a separate residence, where they may live in a more comfortable manner. They build their huts very near one to another, and each of them forms a distinct family; of which he assumes the direction, and which he endeavours to supply with the means of subsistence. Thus the original society is gradually enlarged into a village <141> or tribe; and according as it is placed in circumstances which favour population, and render its condition prosperous and flourishing, it becomes proportionably extensive, and is subdivided into a greater multiplicity of branches.

From the situation of this early community, it is natural to suppose that an uncommon degree of attachment will subsist between all the different persons of which it is composed. As the ordinary life of a savage renders him hardy and robust, so he is a stranger to all those considerations of utility, by which, in a polished nation, men are commonly induced to restrain their appetites, and to abstain from violating the possessions of each other. Different clans or tribes of barbarians are therefore disposed to rob and plunder one another, as often as they have an opportunity of doing it with success; and the reciprocal inroads and hostilities in which they are engaged become the source of continual animosities and quarrels, which are prosecuted with a degree of fury and rancour suited to the temper and disposition of the people. Thus the members of every single clan are frequently at variance with all their neighbours around them. This makes it necessary that they should be constantly upon their guard, in order to repel the numerous attacks to which they are exposed, and to avoid that barbarous treatment, which they have reason to expect, were they ever to fall under the power of their enemies. As they are divided from <142> the rest of the world, so they are linked together by a sense of their common danger, and by a regard to their common interest. They are united in all their pastimes and amusements, as well as in their serious occupations; and when they go out upon a military enterprise, they are no less prompted to show their friendship for one another, than to gratify their common passions of enmity and resentment. As they have been brought up together from their infancy, and have little intercourse with those of a different community, their affections are raised to a greater height, in proportion to the narrowness of that circle to which they are confined. As the uniformity of their life supplies them with few occurrences, and as they have no opportunity of acquiring any great variety of knowledge, their thoughts are the more fixed upon those particular objects which have once excited their attention; they retain more steadily whatever impressions they have received, and become the more devoted to those entertainments and practices with which they have been acquainted.

Hence it is, that a savage is never without difficulty prevailed upon to abandon his family and friends, and to relinquish the sight of those objects to which he has been long familiar. To be banished from them is accounted the greatest of all misfortunes. His cottage, his fields, the faces and conversation of his kindred and companions, recur incessantly to his memory,

and prevent him from <143> relishing any situation where these are wanting. He clings to those well-known objects, and dwells upon all those favourite enjoyments which he has lost. The poorer the country in which he
has lived, the more wretched the manner of life to which he has been accustomed, the loss of it appears to him the more insupportable. That very
poverty and wretchedness, which contracted the sphere of his amusements,
is the chief circumstance that confirms his attachment to those few gratifications which it afforded, and renders him the more a slave to those particular habits which he has acquired. Not all the allurements of European
luxury could bribe a Hottentot to resign that coarse manner of life which
was become habitual to him; and we may remark, that the "maladie du
pays," which has been supposed peculiar to the inhabitants of Switzerland,
is more or less felt by the inhabitants of all countries, according as they
approach nearer to the ages of rudeness and simplicity.* <144>

Those tribes that inhabit the more uncultivated parts of the earth being
almost continually at war with their neighbours, and finding it necessary
to be always in a posture of defence, have constant occasion for a leader to
conduct them in their various military enterprises.

---

* Mr. Kolben relates, that one of the Dutch governors at the Cape of Good Hope
brought up an Hottentot according to the fashions and customs of the Europeans, teaching him several languages, and instructing him fully in the principles of the Christian
religion, at the same time clothing him handsomely, and treating him in all respects as
a person for whom he had an high esteem, and whom he designed for some beneficial
and honourable employment. The governor afterwards sent him to Batavia, where he
was employed under the commissary for some time, till that gentleman died; and then
he returned to the Cape of Good Hope. But having paid a visit to the Hottentots of his
acquaintance, he threw off all his fine clothes, bundled them up, laid them at the governor's feet, and desired he might be allowed to renounce his Christianity, and to live
and die in the religion and customs of his ancestors; only requesting that he might be
permitted to keep the hanger and collar which he wore, in token of his regard to his
benefactor. While the governor was deliberating upon this, scarce believing the fellow
to be in earnest, the young Hottentot took the opportunity of running away, and never
afterwards came near the Cape, thinking himself happy that he had exchanged his European dress for a sheep-skin, and that he had abandoned the hopes of preferment for
the society of his relations and countrymen. [[Peter Kolben, *The Present State of the Cape
of Good-Hope*, VIII.7 (pp. 106–7).]]

The English East-India Company made the like experiment upon two young Hottentots, but with no better success.

Wherever a number of people meet together in order to execute any measures of common concern, it is convenient that some person should be appointed to direct their proceedings, and prevent them from running into confusion. It accordingly appears to be a regulation, uniformly adopted in all countries, that every public assembly should have a president, invested with a degree of authority suitable to the nature of the business committed to their care. But in no case is a regulation of this kind so necessary as in the conduct of a military <145> expedition. There is no situation in which a body of men are so apt to run into disorder, as in war; where it is impossible that they should co-operate, and preserve the least regularity, unless they are united under a single person, empowered to direct their movements, and to superintend and controul their several operations.

The members of a family having been usually conducted by the father in all their excursions of moment, are naturally disposed, even when their society becomes larger, to continue in that course of action to which they have been accustomed; and after they are deprived of this common parent, to fall under the guidance of some other person, who appears next to him in rank, and has obtained the second place in their esteem and confidence.

Superiority in strength, courage, and other personal accomplishments, is the first circumstance by which any single person is raised to be the leader of a tribe, and by which he is enabled to maintain his authority.

In that rude period, when men live by hunting and fishing, they have no opportunity of acquiring any considerable property; and there are no distinctions in the rank of individuals, but those which arise from their personal qualities, either of mind or body.

The strongest man in a village, the man who excels in running, in wrestling, or in handling those weapons which are made use of in war, is, in every <146> contest, possessed of an evident advantage which cannot fail to render him conspicuous, and to command respect and deference. In their games and exercises, being generally victorious, he gains an ascendency over his companions, which disposes them to yield him pre-eminence, and to rest fully satisfied of his superior abilities. When they go out to battle, he is placed at their head, and permitted to occupy that station where his behaviour is most likely to be distinguished and applauded. His exploits and feats of activity are regarded by his followers with pleasure and admiration;

and he becomes their boast and champion in every strife or competition with their neighbours. The more they have been accustomed to follow his banner, they contract a stronger attachment to his person, are more afraid of incurring his displeasure, and discover more readiness to execute those measures which he thinks proper to suggest. Instead of being mortified by his greatness, they imagine that it reflects honour upon the society to which he belongs, and are even disposed to magnify his prowess with that fond partiality which they entertain in favour of themselves.

In many savage tribes, the captain of an expedition is commonly chosen from the number of wounds he has received in battle. The Indians of Chili are said, in the choice of a leader, to regard only his superior strength, and to determine <147> this point according to the burden which he is able to carry.*

Montaigne gives an account of three West Indian savages, who came to Rouen when Charles IX. was there. "The king," says he, "discoursed a long time with them. They were shown our manner of living, our pomp, and the several beauties of that great city. Some time after, a gentleman asked what it was that struck them most among the various objects they had seen. They answered, three things. First, They thought it very strange that so many tall men, wearing beards, and standing round the king (these in all probability were his Swiss guards) should submit voluntarily to a child; and that they did not rather choose to be governed by one of themselves."† <148>

---

* "Lorsqu'ils se soulevérent, et qu'il fut question d'élire un capitaine entre eux, ils prirent une grosse poutre, le chargérent sur leur épaules tour a tour, et celui qui la soutint le plus long tems, eut le commandement sur eux. Il y en eut beaucoup qui la soutirent 4. 5. et 6. heures; mais enfin il y en eut un la soutint 24. heures; et celui-la fût reconnu pour chef." Voyage d'Olivier de Noort. Recueil de voy. qui ont. servi a l'etab. de la comp. dans les Indes Orient. des Pais Bas. [["Once they rose up, and needed to elect a captain amongst them, they took a heavy beam, each one bore it on their shoulders in turn, and he who held it the longest obtained the command of the others. Many could hold the beam for 4, 5 or 6 hours; but one held it for 24 hours, and he was recognized as chief" (*Voyage autour du monde*, 65).]]

† Montaigne's essays. p. 169. Paris, 1604, 8vo. [[The passage is from "On the Cannibals," in Michel de Montaigne, *The Complete Essays*, trans. M. A. Screech (London: Penguin, 1987), 240.]]

It has been remarked, that all animals which live in herds or flocks are apt to fall under the authority of a single leader of superior strength or courage. Of this a curious instance

But when a people have begun to make improvements in their manner of fighting, they are soon led to introduce a variety of stratagems, in order to deceive their enemy, and are often no less indebted to the art and address which they employ, than to the strength or courage which they have occasion to exert. Thus, military skill and conduct are raised to higher degrees of estimation; and the experience of a Nestor, or the cunning of a Ulysses, being found more useful than the brutal force of an Ajax, is frequently the source of greater influence and authority.

This, as has been formerly observed, is the foundation of that respect and reverence which <149> among early nations is commonly paid to old men. From this cause also it happens, that the leader of a barbarous tribe, is often a person somewhat advanced in years, who, retaining still his bodily strength, has had time to acquire experience in the art of war, and to obtain a distinguished reputation by his atchievements.

The effect of these circumstances, to raise and support the authority of a leader or chief, is sufficiently obvious, and is fully illustrated, not only from the uniform history of mankind in a barbarous state, but also from a variety of particulars which may be observed in the intercourse of polished society.

"And the people and princes of Gilead said one to another, What man is he that will begin to fight against the children of Ammon? He shall be head over all the inhabitants of Gilead.

---

is mentioned by the author of Commodore Anson's voyage. "The largest sea-lion," says he, "was the master of the flock; and, from the number of females he kept to himself, and his driving off the males, was stiled by the sea-men the bashaw. As they are of a very lethargic disposition, and are not easily awakened, it is observed, that each herd places some of their males at a distance in the manner of centinels, who always give the alarm whenever any attempt is made either to molest or approach them, by making a loud grunting noise like a hog, or snorting like a horse in full vigour. The males had often furious battles with each other, chiefly about the females; and the bashaw just mentioned, who was commonly surrounded by his females, to which no other male dared to approach, had acquired that distinguished pre-eminence by many bloody contests, as was evident from the numerous scars visible in all parts of his body." [[Anson, *A Voyage Around the World,* 174.]]

In a herd of deer, the authority of the master-buck, founded upon his superior strength, is not less conspicuous.

"Now Jephthah the Gileadite was a mighty man of valour, and he was the son of an harlot, and Gilead begat Jephthah.

"And Gilead's wife bare him sons; and his wife's sons grew up, and they thrust out Jephthah, and said unto him, Thou shalt not inherit in our father's house; for thou art the son of a strange woman.

"Then Jephthah fled from his brethren, and dwelt in the land of Tob; and there were gathered vain men to Jephthah, and went out with him. <150>

"And it came to pass, in process of time, that the children of Ammon made war against Israel.

"And it was so, that when the children of Ammon made war against Israel, the elders of Gilead went to fetch Jephthah out of the land of Tob.

"And they said unto Jephthah, Come, and be our captain, that we may fight with the children of Ammon.

"And Jephthah said unto the elders of Gilead, Did ye not hate me, and expel me out of my father's house? and why are ye come unto me now, when ye are in distress?

"And the elders of Gilead said unto Jephthah, Therefore we turn again to thee now, that thou mayest go with us, and fight against the children of Ammon, and be our head over all the inhabitants of Gilead.

"And Jephthah said unto the elders of Gilead, If ye bring me home again to fight against the children of Ammon, and the Lord deliver them before me, shall I be your head?

"And the elders of Gilead said unto Jephthah, The Lord be witness between us, if we do not so, according to thy words.

"Then Jephthah went with the elders of Gilead; and the people made him head and captain over them: and Jephthah uttered all his words before the Lord in Mizpeh."* <151>

When Saul was afterwards appointed king over the Jewish nation, we find that the prophet Samuel recommends him to the people, merely upon account of his superior stature, and the advantages of his person.

"And when he stood among the people, he was higher than any of the people from his shoulders and upward.

* Judges, chap. x. ver. 18; chap. xi. ver. 1. &c.

"And Samuel said to all the people, See ye him whom the Lord hath chosen, that there is none like him among all the people? And all the people shouted, and said, God save the king."*

In like manner, when the family of this prince was deprived of the crown, the minds of the people were prepared for that revolution by the opinion which they entertained of the superior valour and military accomplishments of his successor.

"And it came to pass, when David was returned from the slaughter of the Philistine, that the women came out of all the cities of Israel, singing and dancing, to meet king Saul, with tabrets, with joy, and with instruments of music.

"And the women answered one another as they played, and said, Saul hath slain his thousands, and David his ten thousands."†

After mankind have fallen upon the expedient of taming and pasturing cattle, in order to render <152> their situation more comfortable, there arises another source of influence and authority which was formerly unknown to them. In their herds and flocks they frequently enjoy considerable wealth, which is distributed in various proportions, according to the industry or good fortune of different individuals; and those who are poor become dependent upon the rich, who are capable of relieving their necessities, and affording them subsistence. As the pre-eminence and superior abilities of the chief are naturally exerted in the acquisition of that wealth which is then introduced, he becomes of course the richest man in the society; and his influence is rendered proportionably more extensive. According to the estate which he has accumulated, he is exalted to a higher rank, lives in greater magnificence, and keeps a more numerous train of servants and retainers, who, in return for that maintenance and protection which they receive from him, are accustomed in all cases to support his power and dignity.‡

The authority derived from wealth, is not only greater than that which

---

* 1 Samuel, chap. x. ver. 23, 24.

† 1 Samuel, chap. xviii. ver. 6, 7.

‡ The admiration and respect derived from the possession of superior fortune, is very fully and beautifully illustrated by the eloquent and ingenious author of the "Theory of Moral Sentiments." [[Smith, *Theory of Moral Sentiments,* I.iii.3.]]

arises from mere personal accomplishments, but also more stable and permanent. Extraordinary endowments, either of mind or body, can operate only during the life of the <153> possessor, and are seldom continued for any length of time in the same family. But a man usually transmits his fortune to his posterity, and along with it all the means of creating dependence which he enjoyed. Thus the son, who inherits the estate of his father, is enabled to maintain an equal rank, at the same time that he preserves all the influence acquired by the former proprietor, which is daily augmented by the power of habit, and becomes more considerable as it passes from one generation to another.

Hence that regard to genealogy and descent which we often meet with among those who have remained long in a pastoral state. From the simplicity of their manners, they are not apt to squander or alienate their possessions; and the representative of an ancient family is naturally disposed to be ostentatious of a circumstance which contributes so much to increase his power and authority. All the Tartars, of whatever country or religion, have an exact knowledge of the tribe from which they are descended, and are at great pains to ascertain the several branches into which it is divided."*

For the same reason the dignity of the chief, which in a former period was frequently elective, is, among shepherds, more commonly transmitted <154> from father to son by hereditary succession. As the chief possesses the largest estate, so he represents the most powerful family in the tribe; a family from which all the rest are vain of being descended, and the superiority of which they have been uniformly accustomed to acknowledge. He enjoys not only that rank and consequence which is derived from his own opulence, but seems entitled to the continuance of that respect and submission which has been paid to his ancestors; and it rarely happens that any other person, though of superior abilities, is capable of supplanting him, or of diverting the course of that influence which has flowed so long in the same channel.

The acquisition of wealth in herds and flocks, does not immediately give rise to the idea of property in land. The different families of a tribe are accustomed to feed their cattle promiscuously, and have no separate pos-

---

* Histoire generale des voyages, tom. 9. liv. 3. chap. 3. p. 33.

session or enjoyment of the ground employed for that purpose. Having exhausted one field of pasture, they proceed to another; and when at length they find it convenient to move their tents, and change the place of their residence, it is of no consequence who shall succeed them, and occupy the spot which they have relinquished.

"Is not the whole land before thee?" says Abraham to Lot his kinsman; "Separate thyself, I pray thee, from me: if thou wilt take the left hand, then I will go to the right; or if thou de-<155>part to the right hand, then I will go to the left."*

The wild Arabs, who inhabit a barren country, are accustomed to change their residence every fortnight, or at least every month.† The same wandering life is led by the Tartars; though, from the greater fertility of their soil, their migrations are perhaps less frequent.‡

If people in this situation, during their temporary abode in any one part of a country, should cultivate a piece of ground, this also, like that which is employed in pasture, will naturally be possessed in common. The management of it is regarded as an extraordinary and difficult work, in which it is necessary that they should unite and assist one another; and therefore, as each individual is entitled to the fruit of his own labour, the crop, which has been raised by the joint labour of all, is deemed the property of the whole society.§ <156>

Thus among the natives of the island of Borneo, it is customary, in time of harvest, that every family of a tribe should reap so much grain as is sufficient for their maintenance; and the remainder is laid up by the public, as a provision for any future demand.‖ Similar practices have probably taken place in most countries, when the inhabitants first applied themselves to

---

* Genesis, chap. xiii. ver 9.—We read, however, of Abraham's buying a field for the particular purpose of a burying place, and of his having weighed, as the price, four hundred shekels of silver, current money with the merchant.

† See D'Arvieux's travels [[182]].

‡ See Professor Gmelin's travels into Siberia [[chap. 15, I:303–4]].

§ That land is appropriated by tribes before it becomes the property of individuals, has been observed by Dr. Stuart, in his acute dissertation concerning the antiquity of the English constitution. [[Stuart, *Historical Dissertation,* 30–31.]]

‖ Modern universal history, vol. 9. [[“Conquests and Settlements of the Portuguese in the East Indies,” 333.]]

the cultivation of the earth. "The Suevi," according to Caesar, "are by far the greatest and most warlike of the German tribes. They are said to possess an hundred villages; from each of which a thousand armed men are annually led forth to war. The rest of the people remain at home; and cultivate the ground for both. These the following year take arms, and the former, in their turn, remain at home. Thus neither agriculture, nor the knowledge and practice of the military art is neglected. But they have no separate landed possessions belonging to individuals, and are not allowed to reside longer than a year in one place. They make little use of grain; but live chiefly upon milk and the flesh of their cattle, and are much addicted to hunting."*
<157>

But the settlement of a village in some particular place, with a view to the further improvement of agriculture, has a tendency to abolish this ancient community of goods, and to produce a separate appropriation of landed estates. When mankind have made some proficiency in the various branches of husbandry, they have no longer occasion to exercise them by the united deliberation and counsel of a whole society. They grow weary of those joint measures, by which they are subjected to continual disputes concerning the distribution and management of their common property, while every one is desirous of employing his labour for his own advantage, and of having a separate possession, which he may enjoy according to his own inclination. Thus, by a sort of tacit agreement, the different families of a village are led to cultivate different portions of land apart from one another, and thereby acquire a right to the respective produce arising from the labour that each of them has bestowed. In order to reap what they have sown, it is necessary that they should have the management of the subject upon which <158> it is produced; so that from having a right to the crop,

---

* Suevorum gens est longe maxima et bellicosissima Germanorum omnium. Ii centum pagos habere dicuntur: ex quibus quotannis singula millia armatorum, bellandi causa, suis ex finibus educunt. Reliqui domi manent: pro se atque illis colunt. Hi rursus invicem anno post in armis sunt: illi domi remanent. Sic neque agricultura, neque ratio, neque usus belli intermittitur. Sed privati et separati agri apud eos nihil est; neque longius anno remanere uno in loco, incolendi causa, licet: neque multum frumento, sed maximam partem lacte atque pecore vivunt, multumque sunt in venationibus. Caesar de bell. Gall. lib. 4. cap. 1.

they appear of course entitled to the exclusive possession of the ground itself. This possession, however, from the imperfect state of early cultivation, is at first continued only from the seed-time to the harvest; and during the rest of the year, the lands of a whole village are used in common for pasturing their cattle. Traces of this ancient community of pasture grounds, during the winter season, may still be discovered in several parts of Scotland. But after a person has long cultivated the same field, his possession becomes gradually more and more complete; it is continued during the whole year without interruption; and when by his industry and labour he has increased the value of the subject, he seems justly entitled, not only to the immediate crop that is raised, but to all the future advantages arising from the melioration of the soil.

The additional influence which the captain of a tribe or village is enabled to derive from this alteration of circumstances, may be easily imagined. As the land employed in tillage is at first possessed in common, the different branches of husbandry are at first carried on, and even the distribution of the produce is made, under the inspection of their leader, who claims the superintendence of all their public concerns.

Among the negroes upon the banks of the river Gambia, the seed-time is a period of much festivity. Those who belong to the same village unite in cul-<159>tivating the ground, and the chief appears at their head, armed as if he were going out to battle, and surrounded by a band of musicians, resembling the bards of the Celtic nations, who, by singing and playing upon musical instruments, endeavour to encourage the labourers. The chief frequently joins in the music; and the workmen accompany their labour with a variety of ridiculous gestures and grimace, according to the different tunes with which they are entertained.*

Upon the Gold Coast each individual must obtain the consent of the chief before he has liberty to cultivate so much ground as is necessary for his subsistence. At the same time when a person has been allowed to cultivate a particular spot, it should seem that he has the exclusive privilege of

* Histoire generale des voyages, tom. 3. liv. 7. chap. 13.

reaping the crop.* This may be considered as one step towards the appropriation of land.

When men are disposed to separate and divide their landed possessions, every family, according as it is numerous and powerful, will be in a condition to occupy and appropriate a suitable extent of territory. For this reason the chief, from his superior wealth in cattle, and the number of his domestics, as well as from his dignity and personal abilities, can hardly fail to acquire a much larger estate, than any other member of the community. His retainers must of consequence be increased in <160> proportion to the enlargement of his domain, and as these are either maintained in his family, or live upon his ground in the situation of tenants at will, they depend entirely upon him for subsistence. They become, therefore, necessarily subservient to his interest, and may at pleasure be obliged either to labour or to fight upon his account. The number of dependents whom he is thus capable of maintaining will be so much the greater, as, from the simplicity of his manners, he has no occasion to purchase many articles of luxury, and almost his whole fortune is consumed in supplying the bare necessaries of life.

The estate which is acquired by a chief, after the appropriation of land, is not only more extensive than what he formerly possessed in herds and flocks, but at the same time is less liable to be destroyed or impaired by accidents; so that the authority which is founded upon it becomes more permanent, and is apt to receive a continued accumulation of strength by remaining for ages in the same family. <161>

* Histoire generale des voyages, tom. 4. liv. 9. chap. 7. §. 5.

SECTION II

The powers with which the chief of a rude tribe
is commonly invested.

The powers which belong to this early magistrate, who is thus exalted to
the head of a rude society, are such as might be expected from the nature
of his office, and from the circumstances of the people over whom he is
placed.

He is at first the commander of their forces, and has merely the direction
of their measures during the time of an engagement. But having acted for
some time in this capacity, he finds encouragement to exert his authority
on other occasions, and is entrusted with various branches of public
administration.

From his peculiar situation, he is more immediately led to attend to the
defence of the society, to suggest such precautions as may be necessary for
that purpose, and to point out those enterprises which he thinks it would
be expedient for them to undertake. By degrees they are accustomed to
follow his opinion, in planning as well as in conducting their several expeditions. Warmly attached to his person, and zealous to promote his interest, they are disposed to accompany him for his own sake, and to espouse
his quarrel upon every <162> occasion. "The Germans," says Tacitus, "esteem it an inviolable duty to defend their chief, to maintain his dignity,
and to yield him the glory of all their exploits. The chiefs fight for victory:
the attendants only for the chief."* As the leader of a tribe affords protection
and security to all its members, so he expects that they should make a proper

* "Illum defendere, tueri, sua quoque fortia facta gloriae ejus assignare, praecipuum
sacramentum est. Principes pro victoria pugnant; comites pro principe." Tacit. de mor.
German. [[XIV.1.]]

return for these good offices by serving him in war. To refuse this service would not only expose them to his resentment, but be regarded as a mark of infidelity or cowardice that would disgrace them for ever in the opinion of all their kindred. When, on the other hand, they are willing to fulfil their duty, by appearing in the field as often as they are summoned, and by discharging with honour the trust that is reposed in them, they are admitted to be the friends and companions of the chief; they are entertained at his table, and partake in all his amusements; and after the improvement of agriculture has given rise to the appropriation of land, they obtain the possession of landed estates, proportioned to their merit, and suited to their rank and circumstances.

As the chief is, by his office, engaged in protecting and securing the members of his tribe from the hostile attacks of their neighbours, so he endea-<163>vours to prevent those disorders and quarrels which may sometimes arise among themselves, and which tend to weaken and disturb the society. When a dispute or controversy happens among those who belong to different families, he readily interposes by his good offices, in order to bring about a reconciliation between the parties; who at the same time, if they choose to avoid an open rupture, may probably be willing to terminate their difference by referring it to his judgment. To render his decisions effectual, he is, at first, under the necessity of employing persuasion and entreaty, and of calling to his assistance the several heads of families in the tribe. When his authority is better established, he ventures to execute his sentences by force; in which, from considerations of expediency, he is naturally supported by every impartial and unprejudiced member of the society. Having been accustomed to determine causes in consequence of a reference, and finding that persons, accused of injustice, are frequently averse to such determination, he is at length induced, when complaints are made, to summon parties before him, and to judge of their differences independent of their consent. Thus he acquires a regular jurisdiction both in civil and criminal cases; in the exercise of which particular officers of court are gradually set apart to enforce his commands: and when law-suits become numerous, a deputy-judge is appointed, from whom the people may expect more attention to <164> the dispatch of business than the chief is usually inclined to bestow.

Of this gradual progress in the judicial power of a magistrate, from the period when he is merely an arbiter, to that when he is enabled to execute his decrees, and to call parties before him, several vestiges are still to be found even in the laws of polished nations. Among the Romans, the civil judge had no power to determine a law suit, unless the parties had previously referred the cause to his decision, by a contract which was called *litis contestatio*.[1] In England, at this day, no criminal trial can proceed, until the culprit, by his *pleading,* has acknowledged the authority of the court. But while these practices were retained, from a superstitious regard to ancient usage, a ridiculous circuit was made, to avoid the inconveniencies of which they were manifestly productive. At Rome, the plaintiff, after having desired the defendant to come voluntarily into court, was, upon his refusal, permitted to drag him by the throat;* and by the English law, the defendant, who *stands mute,* is subjected to the *peine fort et dure,*[2] a species of torture intended to overcome the obstinacy of such as are accused of atrocious crimes.

According to the systems of religion which have prevailed in the unenlightened parts of the world, mankind have imagined that the Supreme Being is endowed with passions and sentiments resem-<165>bling their own, and that he views the extraordinary talents and abilities of their leader with such approbation and esteem as these qualities never fail to excite in themselves. The same person whom they look upon as the first of mortals, is naturally believed to be the peculiar favourite of Heaven, and is therefore regarded as the most capable to intercede in their behalf, to explain the will of the Deity, and to point out the most effectual means to avert his anger, or to procure his favour.

The admiration of a military leader in rude countries, has frequently proceeded so far as to produce a belief of his being sprung from a heavenly

---

* Obtorto collo. [[Literally, "with a twisted neck."]]

1. "Litis contestatio" was a sort of preliminary hearing with a judge in which the plaintiff and the defendant presented their assertions and the case was formulated between them, allowing the hearing to move forward toward a judgment. See Gaius *Institutionem iuris civilis Commentarii* III.180.

2. The defendant who refused to speak was put in a prone position and stones were piled on her/him until s/he testified, was crushed, or both.

original, and to render him the object of that adoration which is due to the Supreme Being.

In some of the American tribes, the chiefs carry the name of the sun, from whom they are supposed to be descended, and whom they are understood to represent upon earth.* The Yncas of Peru derived themselves, in like manner, from the sun. In the kingdom of Loango, the prince is worshipped as a god by his subjects. They give him the name or title usually bestowed upon the Deity; and they address him with the utmost solemnity for rain or fruitful seasons.† <166>

The superstition of the early Greeks, in this particular, is well known; which was carried to such a height, as enabled almost every family of distinction to count kindred with some one or other of the celestial deities. It is in conformity to this ancient mythology that Racine has put the following beautiful address into the mouth of Phedra.

> Noble et brillant auteur d'une triste famille,
> Toi, dont ma mére osoit se vanter d'être fille,
> Qui peut-être rougis du trouble où tu me vois,
> Soleil, je te viens voir pour la dernière fois![3]

The same principle has disposed men to deify those heroes who have rendered themselves illustrious by their public spirit, and their eminent abilities; to imagine that in another state of existence they retain their former patriotic sentiments, and being possessed of superior power, continue, with unremitting vigilance, to ward off the misfortunes, and to promote the happiness of their people.

When such are the prevailing dispositions of a people, the chief of a barbarous tribe is naturally raised to be their high priest; or if he does not

---

* This is particularly the case among the Hurons and Natchez. Journal historique d'une voyage de l'Amerique, par Charlevoix, let. 30. [[Bossu,]] Nouveaux voyage aux Indes orientales, tom. 1. p. 42.

† Modern Universal History, vol. 16. p. 300.

3. Noble and glorious progenitor of a sad line,
   You, whom my mother boasted to be your daughter,
   Who would likely blush to see me in this plight,
   Sun, I come to look on you for the last time!
            Racine, *Phédre*, 11.169–72.

himself exercise that office, he obtains at least the direction and superintendence of their religious concerns. For some time after the building of
Rome, the leader of each *curia,* or tribe, is said to have been their chief
ecclesiastical officer. A similar police in this respect appears to have been
<167> originally established in the cities of Greece, and has probably taken
place among the primitive inhabitants of most countries. It may easily be
conceived, that in ignorant nations, guided by omens and dreams, and subject to all the terrors of gross superstition, this branch of power, when added
to the conduct of war, and the distribution of justice, will be an engine of
great consequence to the magistrate, for carrying through his measures, and
for extending his authority.

As, in conducting the affairs of a community, in the management of
what relates to peace or war, and in the administration of justice, various
abuses are apt to be committed, and many more may still be apprehended,
the people are gradually led, by experience and observation, to introduce
particular statutes or laws, in order to correct or ascertain their practice for
the future. Even this legislative power, by which all the other branches of
government are controuled and directed, is naturally assumed by the chief,
after he has acquired considerable influence and authority. When the members of his tribe have become in a great measure dependent upon him with
regard to their property, they are in no condition to dispute his commands,
or to refuse obedience to those ordinances which he issues at pleasure, in
order to model or establish the constitution of the society.

From these observations, we may form an idea of that constitution of
government which is natu-<168>rally introduced among the members of
a rude tribe or village. Each of the different families of which it is composed
is under the jurisdiction of the father, and the whole community is subjected to a chief or leader, who enjoys a degree of influence and authority
according to the superior abilities with which he is endowed, or the wealth
which he has been enabled to acquire.

The rudest form of this government may be discovered among the Indians of America. As these people subsist, for the most part, by hunting or
fishing, they have no means of obtaining so much wealth as will raise any
one person greatly above his companions. They are divided into small independent villages, in each of which there is a chief, who is their principal

leader in war. He bears the name of that particular tribe over which he presides; and in their public meetings he is known by no other. His authority, though greater in some villages than in others, does not appear in any of them to be very considerable. If he is never disobeyed, it is because he knows how to set bounds to his commands. Every family has a right to name an assistant to the chief; and the several heads of families compose an assembly, or "council of the elders," which is accustomed to deliberate upon all matters of public importance.* <169>

* "L'autorité des chefs s'étend proprement sur ceux de leur tribu, qu'ils considerent comme leurs enfans."—"Leur pouvoir ne paroît avoir rein d'absolu, et il ne semble pas qu'ils ayent aucune voie de coaction pour se faire obeir en cas de résistance, on leur obéit cependant, et ils commandent avec autorité; leur commandement a force de prieres, et l'obeissance qu'on leur rend, paroît entierement libre."—"Bien que les chefs n'ayent aucune marque de destinction et de superiorité, qu'on ne puisse pas le distinguer de la foule par les honeurs qu'on devroit leur rendre, à l'exception de quelques cas particuliers, on ne laisse pas d'avoir pour eux un certain respect; mais, c'est surtout dans les affaires publiques que leur dignité se soûtient. Les conseils s'assemblent par leurs ordres; ils se tiennent dans leurs cabanes, à moins qu'il n'y ait une cabane publique, destinée uniquement pour les conseils, et qui est comme une maison de ville; les affaires se traitent en leur nom; ils président à toutes sortes d'assemblées; ils ont une part considerable dans les festins, et dans les distributions generales."—"De peur que le chefs n'usurpassent une autorité trop grande, et ne se rendissent trop absolus, on les a comme bridés, en leur donnant des adjoints, qui partagent avec eux la souveraineté de la terre, et se nomment *Agoianders* comme eux."—"Après les *Agoianders,* vient le *Sênat,* composé des vieillards, ou des anciens, nommés dans leur langue *Agokstenha:* le nombre des ces senateurs n'est point dèterminê: chacun a droit d'entrer au conseil pour y donner son suffrage." P. Lafitau moeurs de sauvages Ameriquains, 4to à Paris, 1724. tom. 1. p. 472–475. [["The authority of the chiefs extends to their tribe proper, whom they consider as their children";— "Their power does not appear to be absolute, and they do not seem to have any form of coercion at their disposal in case of resistance, yet they are obeyed, and they command with authority; their commands have the force of prayers, and the obedience they receive seems to be entirely free"—"Even though the chiefs have no marks of distinction or superiority, and one cannot distinguish them from others in a crowd by the honor due them, except in some particular cases, their people never cease to have a certain respect for them; but it is above all in public matters that their dignity is apparent. Councils are assembled by their orders; they are held in their cabins, unless there is a public cabin, intended solely for councils, and which is like a town hall; business is discussed in their name; they preside over all sorts of assemblies; they take considerable part in the feasts, and in the [general distributions.]"—"So as to prevent the chiefs from assuming too great an authority, of too absolute a kind, they have been partly thwarted by the attribution of adjuncts, who share with them the sovereignty over the earth, and are named *Agoian-*

Each individual is allowed, in ordinary cases, to "take up the hatchet," as it is called, or make war upon those who have offended him. Enterprises of moment, however, are seldom undertaken without the concurrence of the assembly. Each family has a jurisdiction over its own members. <170> But the members of different families are at liberty to settle their differences in what manner they please; and the chief, or council, interfere only as mediators, or as arbiters; unless upon the commission of those enormous and extraordinary crimes which excite the general indignation, and which, from a sudden impulse of resentment, are instantly punished with severity.*
<171>

---

ders like them"; "After the *Agoianders* comes the Senate, composed of the old ones or ancients, known in their tongue as *Agokstenha;* the number of these senators is not fixed; each one can sit in the council to give his suffrage."]]

* Ibid. tom. 2. p. 167.—"La décision des affaires criminelles apartient immédiatement à ceux de la cabane des coupables, par rapport aux coupables même, quand quelqu'un d'une cabane en a tué un autre de la même cabane: comme on suppose qu'ils ont droit de vie et de mort les uns sur les autres, le village semble ne prendre nul interêt au disordre qui est arrivé—L'affaire change bien de nature, si le meurtre a été commis à l'egard d'une personne d'une cabane differente, d'une autre tribu, d'une autre village et encore plus d'une nation étrangere; car alors cette mort funeste interesse tout le public; chacun prend fait et cause pour le défunt, et contribue en quelque chose pour refaire l'esprit (c'est leur expression) aux parens aigris par la perte qu'ils viennent de faire; tous s'interessent aussi pour sauver la vie au criminel, et pour mettre les parens de celui-ci à couvert de la vengeance des autres, qui ne manqueroit pas d'éclater tôt ou tard si on avoit manquè à faire la satisfaction prescrite, dans des cas semblables, par leurs loix, et par leurs usages."—"Il est des occasions où le crime est si noir, qu'on n'a pas tant d'egard pour garantir le meurtrier, et où le conseil, usant de son autorité suprême, prend soin d'en ordonner la punition."—Ibid. tom. 1. p. 486, 487, 490, 495. [["Decisions in criminal matters belong directly to those in the cabin of the guilty party, in relation to the guilty themselves, when someone in one cabin has killed another from the same cabin; as one assumes that they have the right of life and death over each other, the village does not seem to take much concern with such disorderly occurrences. The matter is quite different, however, if the murder victim was from a different cabin, tribe, village, or even more, from a foreign nation; then this untimely death is of concern to all; every one takes the side of the deceased party, and contributes something so as to 'remake the mind' (as they say) of the relatives who are embittered by their recent loss; all are also concerned with saving the life of the criminal, and protecting his relatives from the revenge of others, which would erupt without fail if satisfaction had not been given, according to their laws and customs." "There are cases when the crime is so heinous that less care is taken to

From the accounts which have been given of the wandering tribes of shepherds in different parts of the world, it would seem that their government is of the same nature, though the power of their leader is further advanced, according to the degrees of wealth which they enjoy. In proportion to the extent of his herds and flocks, the chief is exalted above all the other members of the tribe, and has more influence in directing their military operations, in establishing their forms of judicial procedure, and in regulating the several branches of their public administration. Thus the captain or leader of a tribe among the Hottentots, who have made but small progress in the pastoral life, and among the wild Arabs, who have seldom acquired considerable property, appears to have little more authority than among the savages of America.* The great riches, on the other hand, which <172> are frequently acquired by those numerous bands of shepherds inhabiting the vast country of Tartary, have rendered the influence of the chief proportionably extensive, and have bestowed upon him an almost unlimited power, which commonly remains in the same family, and is transmitted from father to son like a private inheritance.†

---

protect the murderer, and the council, by its supreme authority, is careful to order its punishment."]]

See also the view which is given of the state of government among the Americans, by P. Charlevoix Journal historique d'un voyage de l'Amerique, let. 13. 18.

* "The Arabian tribes, though they have been for many ages under the Turkish yoke, are rarely interrupted, either in what may concern the course of justice, or in the succession to those few offices and dignities that belong properly to themselves.—Every *Dou-war* (i.e. village or encampment) therefore may be looked upon as a little principality, over which it is usual for that particular family, which is of the greatest name, substance, and reputation, to preside. However, this honour does not always lineally descend from the father to son; but, as it was among their predecessors the Numidians, when the heir is too young, or subject to any infirmity, then they make choice of the uncle, or some other relation, who, for prudence and wisdom, is judged to be the fittest for that employ. Yet, notwithstanding the despotic power which is lodged in this person, all grievances and disputes are accommodated in as amicable a manner as possible, by calling to his assistance one person or two out of each tent; and as the offended is considered as a brother, the sentence is always given on the favourable side; and even in the most enormous crimes, rarely any other punishment is inflicted than banishment." Shaw's Travels, chap. 4. p. 310.

† See Kolben's History of the Cape of Good Hope.—[[VII.2, 85–86.]] Histoire general des voyages. [[The first edition of the *Ranks* lists 5, 6, 9 as the location.]]—Montesquieu, Esprit de Loix, liv. 18. chap. 19.

The ancient German nations, described by Caesar and Tacitus, may be ranked in a middle situation between these extremes; having probably had more wealth than the Hottentots, or most of the wild Arabs, and less than the greater part of the Tartars. While they remained in their own country, they were not altogether strangers to the cultivation of the ground; but they all led a wandering life, and seem to have had no idea of property in land; a sufficient proof that they drew their subsistence chiefly from their cattle, and regarded agriculture as only a secondary employment. Their <173> chiefs appear to have been either hereditary, or elected from those families who had been longest in the possession of opulent fortunes; but their military expeditions were frequently conducted by such inferior leaders, as happened to offer their service, and could persuade their companions to follow them. In time of peace, justice was administered by the respective chiefs, or leading men, of the different villages.* <174>

---

* "Reges ex nobilitate; duces ex virtute sumunt. Nec regibus infinita aut libera potestas; et duces exemplo potius quam imperio, si prompti, si conspicui: si ante aciem agant, admiratione praesunt." Tacitus de mor. German. §. 7. [["Kings they choose for their birth, generals for their valour. But the kings do not have unlimited power without restriction, while the generals lead more by example than command; if they are energetic and seen by all, if they are active in the front ranks, their men look up to them" (VII.1). Cited by Smith in the same context in *Lectures on Jurisprudence,* iv.14. The two passages from Tacitus which follow are discussed by Smith in iv.18, i.e., all within the same day's lecture.]] "De minoribus rebus principes consultant, de majoribus omnes. Ita tamen, ut ea quoque, quorum penes plebem arbitrium est, apud principes pertractentur.—Ut turbae placuit, considunt armati. Silentium per sacerdotes, quibus tum et coercendi jus est, imperatur. Mox rex vel principes prout aetas cuique, prout nobilitas, prout decus bellorum, prout facundia est, audiuntur, auctoritate suadendi magis quam jubendi potestate." Ibid. §. 11. [["The leading men take counsel over minor issues, the major ones involve them all; yet even those decisions that lie with the commons are considered in advance by the elite. Unless something unexpected suddenly occurs, they gather on set days.—At the command of the priest there is silence, since at this time too they have the right of enforcement. Then, according to his age, birth, military distinction, and eloquence, the king or leading man is given a hearing, more through his influence in persuasion than his power in command" (XI.1, 3).]] "Licet apud concilium accusare quoque, et discrimen capitis intendere. Distinctio poenarum ex delicto: proditores et transfugas arboribus suspendunt. Ignavos, et imbelles, et corpore infames, coeno ac palude, injecta insuper crate, mergunt.—Eliguntur in iisdem consiliis et principes, qui jura per pagos vicosque reddunt. Centeni singulis ex plebe comites, consilium simul et auctoritas adsunt." Ibid. §. 12. [["The assembly is also the place to bring charges and initiate trials in capital cases. Penalties are classed according to offence: traitors and deserters they

But when those barbarians had sallied forth from their native forests, and invaded the provinces of the Roman empire, they were soon led to a great improvement in their circumstances. The countries which they conquered had been cultivated and civilized under the Roman dominion; and the inhabitants, though generally in a declining state, were still acquainted with husbandry and a variety of arts. It was to be expected, therefore, that, while the Gothic invaders, during a long course of bloody wars, defaced the monuments of ancient literature, and wherever they came planted their own barbarous customs, they should, on the other hand, suddenly catch a degree of knowledge from the conquered people; and make a quicker progress in agriculture, and some of the coarser handicrafts connected with it, than they could have done in the natural course of things, had they been left to their own experience and observation. By their repeated victories, different heads of families, or *barons,* were enabled to seize great landed estates. They also acquired many captives in war, whom they reduced into servitude, and by whom they were put into a condition for managing their extensive possessions. <175>

---

hang from trees, but the cowardly and unwarlike and those who disgrace their bodies they submerge in the mud of a marsh, with a wicker frame thrown over it.—Likewise in these assemblies are chosen the leaders who administer justice in the cantons and hamlets; each has a hundred associates from the commons, who provide influence as well as advice." Rives trans.]]

"Quum bellum civitas aut inlatum defendit, aut infert; magistratus, qui ei bello praesint, ut vitae necisque habeant potestatem, deliguntur. In pace, nullus est communis magistratus; sed principes regionum atque pagorum inter suos jus dicunt, controversiasque minuunt—ubi quis ex principibus in concilio dixit se ducem fore; qui sequi velint, profiteantur; consurgunt ii, qui et causam et hominem probant, suumque auxilium pollicentur; atque ab multitudine conlaudantur: qui ex iis secuti non sunt, in desertorum ac proditorum numero ducuntur; omniumque iis rerum postea fides derogatur." Caesar, de bell. Gall. 6. §. 23. [["When a state makes or resists aggressive war, officers are chosen to direct it, with the power of life and death. In time of peace there is no general officer of state, but the chiefs of districts and cantons do justice among their followers and settle disputes.—When any of the chiefs has said in public assembly that he will be the leader, [he proclaims,] "Let all those who will follow declare it," and then all who approve the cause and the man rise together to his service and promise their own assistance, and win the general praise of the people. Any of them who have not followed, after their promise, are reckoned as deserters and traitors, and in all things afterwards trust is denied them." Edwards, trans.]]

After the settlement of those nations was completed, the members of
every large family came to be composed of two sorts of people; the slaves,
acquired for the most part by conquest; and the free men, descended from
a common ancestor, and maintained out of his estate. The former were
employed chiefly in cultivating their masters grounds: the latter supported
the interest and dignity of their leader, and in their turn were protected by
him.

The authority of the baron was extremely absolute over all the members
of his family; because they entirely depended upon him for subsistence. He
obliged his slaves to labour at pleasure, and allowed them such recompence
only as he thought proper. His kindred were under the necessity of following his banner in all his military expeditions. He exercised over both a supreme jurisdiction, in punishing their offences, as well as in deciding their
differences; and he subjected them to such regulations as he judged convenient, for removing disorders, or preventing future disputes.

These barons, though in a great measure independent, were early united
in a larger society, under circumstances which gave rise to a very peculiar
set of institutions. The effect of that union, whence proceeded the system
of feudal government in Europe, will fall to be considered in a subsequent
part of this discourse. <176>

The Authority of a Sovereign, and of Subordinate Officers, over a Society Composed of Different Tribes or Villages

SECTION I

The constitution of government arising from the union of different tribes or villages.

The improvement of agriculture, as it increases the quantity of provisions, and renders particular tribes more numerous and flourishing, so it obliges them at length to send out colonies to a distance, who occupy new seats wherever they can find a convenient situation, and are formed into separate villages, after the model of those with which they are acquainted. Thus, in proportion as a country is better cultivated, it comes to be inhabited by a greater number of distinct societies, whether derived from the same or from a different original, agreeing in their manners, and resembling each other in their institutions and customs.

These different communities being frequently at war, and being exposed to continual invasions from their neighbours, are in many cases determined, by the consideration of their mutual interest, to unite against their common enemies, and to form a va-<177>riety of combinations, which, from the influence of particular circumstances, are more or less permanent. Having found the advantage of joining their forces in one expedition, they are naturally disposed to continue the like association in another, and by degrees are encouraged to enter into a general alliance. The intercourse which people, in such a situation, have maintained in war will not be entirely dissolved even in time of peace; and though the different villages should be originally strangers to each other, yet, having many opportunities of assembling in their military enterprises, they cannot fail to contract an acquaintance, which will become an inducement to their future correspondence. They have frequent opportunities of meeting in their common sports and diversions: the leading men entertain one another with rustic hospitality and magnificence: intermarriages begin to take place between their respective families; and the various connexions of society are gradually multiplied and extended.

An alliance for mutual defence and security is a measure suggested by such obvious views of expediency, that it must frequently take place, not only among tribes of husbandmen, but also among those of shepherds, and even of mere savages. Many instances of it are, accordingly, to be found in Tartary, upon the coast of Guinea, in the history of the ancient Germans, and among the Indians of America. But such alliances are not <178> likely to produce a permanent union, until the populousness of a country has been increased by agriculture, and the inhabitants, in consequence of that employment, have taken up a fixed residence in the same neighbourhood.

From a confederacy of this kind, a very simple form of government is commonly established. As every village, or separate community, is subjected to its own leader, their joint measures fall naturally under the direction of all those distinguished personages; whose frequent meeting and deliberation gives rise, in a short time, to a regular council, or senate, invested with a degree of power and authority corresponding to what each of its members has acquired over his own particular domestics and retainers.

The same considerations, however, which determine the individuals of a single tribe to be guided by a particular person in their smaller expeditions, must recommend a similar expedient in conducting a numerous army, composed of different clans, often disagreeing in their views, and little connected with each other. While every chief has the conduct of his own dependents, it is found convenient that some one leader should be intrusted with the supreme command of their united forces; and as that dignity is commonly bestowed upon the person who, by his opulence, is most capable of supporting it, he is frequently enabled to maintain it during life, and even in many cases to render it <179> hereditary. In this manner a great chief, or *king,* is placed at the head of a nation, and is permitted to assume the inspection and superintendence of what relates to its defence and security.

But, notwithstanding the rank and pre-eminence enjoyed by this primitive sovereign, it may easily be conceived that his authority will not be very considerable. His advancement can hardly fail to excite the jealousy of chiefs unaccustomed to subordination, who will be disposed to take every opportunity of curbing his pretensions, and to allow him no higher prerogatives than are sufficient to answer the purposes for which he was created. His interpositions, in matters of public concern, will depend very much upon times and circumstances, and being directed by no previous rules, will be frequently made in an irregular and desultory manner. In a day of battle, when placed at the head of his army, he may venture, perhaps, to rule with a high hand, and it may be dangerous for any of his followers to disobey his orders; but upon other occasions his power is usually confined within a narrower compass, and frequently extends no further than to the members of his own clan. After the conclusion of a military enterprise, when the other tribes have retired to their separate places of abode, they are in a great measure withdrawn from his influence, and are placed under the immediate jurisdiction and authority of the respective chiefs by whom they are protected. As it is neces-<180>sary that these leading men should give their consent to every public measure of importance, they are usually convened for that purpose by the king; who at the same time is accustomed to preside in all their deliberations.

Such, as far as can be collected from the scattered hints delivered by travellers, is the state of government in many rude kingdoms, both upon the coast of Africa, or in those parts of Asia, where a number of distinct tribes or villages have been recently and imperfectly united.*

In the Odyssey, Alcinous, king of the Pheacians, says expressly, "There are twelve chiefs who share dominion in the kingdom, and I am the thir-

---

* Histoire generale des voyages, 4to. tom. 3. liv. 8. chap. 3. § 4.—Ibid. tom. 4. liv. 9. chap. 7. § 8.—liv. 10. chap. 2. 6.—See also Calendar's collection of voyages, vol. 1. p. 67, 68.

teenth."* He is accordingly obliged to call a council of his nobles, before he can venture to furnish Ulysses with a single ship, in order to transport him to his native country.

In the island of Ithaca, the power of the chiefs, who usually deliberated in council upon the affairs of the nation, is equally conspicuous. <181>

> 'Twas silence all, at last Aegyptius spoke;
> Aegyptius, by his age and sorrows broke:—
> Since great Ulysses sought the Phrygian plains,
> Within these walls inglorious silence reigns.
> Say then, ye Peers! by whose commands we meet?
> Why here once more in solemn council sit?
> Ye young, ye old, the weighty cause disclose:
> Arrives some message of invading foes?
> Or say, does high necessity of state
> Inspire some patriot, and demand debate?
> The present Synod speaks its author wise;
> Assist him, Jove! thou regent of the skies!†

From the early history of all the Greek states, we have reason to believe that their government was of a similar nature. The country of Attica, in particular, is said to have been peopled by colonies which were brought, under different leaders, from Egypt and some of the neighbouring countries, and which formed a number of distinct tribes or villages, independent of one another.‡ The first association among these little societies happened in the time of Cecrops,[1] the founder of Athens, who became their general, and who made a considerable reformation in their police and manners.

---

* Δώδεκα γὰρ κατὰ δῆμον ἀριπρεπέες βασιλῆες
Ἀ’ρχοὶ κραίνουσι, τρισκαιδέκα ος δ’ ἐγὼ αὐτός
[["For twelve distinguished kings have we had in our land as rulers, and I am
the thirteenth."]]

Odyss. lib. 8. v. 390.

† Pope's Odyss. book 2. l. 19.

‡ See Thucydides' history of the Peloponnesian war, book 1. 2.

1. Cecrops, traditionally the first king of Attica, was a mythic figure who interacted with the gods and was portrayed as having the body of a man above the waist and that of a snake below. He was associated with the institution of marital, funerary, and property customs.

They were afterwards more intimately united in the reign of Theseus, when the nobility, or principal inhabitants of the several towns or villages, <182> were persuaded to settle at Athens, and composed a senate, or national council, which exercised an authority over the whole country, and obtained the chief direction of religious matters, together with the privilege of electing magistrates, and of teaching and dispensing the laws.*

The resemblance between this and the ancient Roman constitution is sufficiently obvious. The foundation of that mighty empire was laid by a few tribes of barbarians, originally distinct from one another, who at first inhabited different quarters of the city, and who appear to have lived under the jurisdiction of their respective chiefs.† This was, in all probability, the origin of that connexion between the poor and the rich, which remained in after ages, and which has been commonly ascribed to the policy of Romulus. People of the lower class at Rome were all attached to some particular patron of rank and distinction; and every patrician had a number of clients, who, besides owing him respect and submission, were bound to portion his daughters, to pay his debts, and to ransom his per-<183>son from captivity; as, on the other hand, they were entitled to his advice and protection.‡ Of these leading men, who had an extensive influence over the populace, was formed the primitive senate, or council of the sovereign; which appears to have had the absolute determination of peace and war; and which, in the first instance, had not only the privilege of deliberating upon all public regulations, but also, upon the death of a king, that of naming a successor to the royal dignity.§

It must not be overlooked, however, that in the Roman, as well as in many of the Greek governments, there was originally a considerable mix-

---

* Vid. Sigon. de repub. Atheniens. lib. 1. cap. 2.———Thucyd. hist. lib. 2 [[15[2]]].—Plutarch. in vit. Thesei [[24]].

† See the account which is given of the *forum originis,* by the author of the historical law-tracts; whose acute and original genius has been employed in uniting law with philosophy, and in extending the views of a gainful profession to the liberal pursuits of rational entertainment. [[Lord Kames,]] Historical Law-tracts, chap. of courts [[I:363–67]].

‡ Dion. Halicarn. antiq. Rom. lib. 2. § 10.

§ Dion. Halicarn. antiq. Rom. lib. 2. [[§ 3.]]—Polyb. hist. lib. 6. [[13–17.]]—Hein. antiq. Rom. [[Hein I.II.46.]]

ture of democracy, arising from the peculiar circumstances of the people. The different tribes, or families, united in the formation of Rome, or of the independent cities which arose in Peloponnesus and some of the neighbouring countries, had very little property, either in moveables or in land; and their poverty must have prevented the growth of authority in their respective leaders. The influence of a chief, in each of those petty states, depended, in all probability, upon the personal attachment of his followers, and their admiration of his abilities, more than upon his superiority in wealth; and the power which that influence enabled him to assume <184> was, therefore, far, from being absolute. For this reason, under the kingly government of Rome, the authority of the senate, composed of all the chiefs, was not alone sufficient for making general laws, or transacting business where dissension might be apprehended, but its decrees, in such cases, were usually confirmed by an assembly consisting of the whole people. The same practice obtained in Athens and Sparta, and probably in most of the other states of Greece.

The particulars related by Caesar concerning the inhabitants of ancient Gaul may be considered as affording the most authentic evidence of the state of government in any rude country. We learn from this author that the whole of that country was divided into a number of separate states, independent of each other, and differing considerably in the degrees of their power, as well as in the extent of their territories. In the several towns, villages, or families, belonging to each nation, there were certain leading persons, possessed of great influence and authority, by whom their respective followers were governed and protected. The affairs of a whole nation were conducted by a king, or chief magistrate, assisted by a national council; and when different nations were engaged in a common enterprise, they made choice of a general to command their united forces.* <185>

---

* "In Gallia non solum in omnibus civitatibus, atque pagis, partibusque, sed pene etiam in singulis domibus, factiones sunt: earumque factionum sunt principes, qui summam auctoritatem eorum judicio habere existimantur: quorum ad arbitrium, judiciumque, summa omnium rerum consiliorumque redeat. Idque ejus rei causa antiquitus institutum videtur, ne quis ex plebe contra potentiorem auxilii egeret. Suos enim opprimi quisque, et circumveniri non patitur; neque, aliter si faciat, ullam inter suos habeat auctoritatem. Haec eadem ratio est in summa totius Galliae. Namque omnes civitates in

The German nations who, about the fifth century, over-ran and subdued the provinces of the Western empire, were in a different situation from any other people with whose history we are acquainted. While they remained in their own country, those nations had made considerable advances in the pastoral state, and had thereby acquired a good deal of wealth in herds and flocks. By their settlement in the Roman provinces, they had an opportunity, as has been already observed, of acquiring large estates in land, which tended to augment the authority of different leaders in proportion to their riches.

The inhabitants of a large tract of country were, at the same time, associated for their mutual defence, and in their common expeditions, were conducted by a great chief, or king, whose rank and dignity, like that of every subordinate leader, was supported by his own private estate. There were two circumstances which rendered the associations <186> made upon this occasion much more extensive than they commonly are among nations equally barbarous.

As each of the nations who settled in the Western empire, though seldom large, was, by the rapid progress of its arms, and by a sudden improvement in agriculture, enabled to occupy a prodigious quantity of land, the different proprietors, among whom that land was divided, were placed at a great distance from one another, and spread over a wide country. But many of these proprietors consisting of kindred or acquaintance, and all of them having been accustomed to act under one commander, they were still inclined, how remote soever their situation, to maintain a correspondence, and to unite in their military enterprises.

---

duas partes divisae sunt." [["In Gaul there are factions not only in each state, canton, and district, but indeed in nearly every house, and the leaders of these factions are those who are esteemed by the judgments of their compatriots to have the greatest authority; they are those individuals to whose judgment and will the most important matters and counsels are referred. And this seems to have arisen from ancient institutions, that no one of the people should be lacking in strength against someone more powerful. For no one wants those close to him to be cheated and oppressed, for if he allows this he will have no authority among them. This holds for all of Gaul as well. For all the states are divided into two parts."]] Caes. de bell. Gall. lib. 6. [[11.]] See Treasurie of auncient and moderne Times. Pub. 1619. [["Chapter 6: Of the Ancient Gaules," in Mexia et al., *Archaio-ploutos*, 17.]]

The state of the Roman provinces was another circumstance which promoted an extensive association among the conquerors. Each province of the Roman empire constituted, in some measure, a separate government, the several parts of which had all a dependence upon one another. The inhabitants, not to mention their ancient national attachment, had usually a set of laws and customs peculiar to themselves, and were governed by the same officers civil and military. They were accustomed on public occasions to act in concert, and to consider themselves as having a common interest. The capital, which was the seat of the governor, became the centre of government, to which <187> the gentry of the province resorted in expectation of preferment, or with a view of sharing in the pleasures of a court; and from thence, to the most distant parts of the country, innumerable channels of communication were opened, through the principal towns, where trade was carried on, where taxes were levied, or where justice was administered.

The connexions, which had thus subsisted for ages between the several districts of large territory, were not entirely destroyed when it came under the dominion of the barbarians. As the ancient inhabitants were no where extirpated, but either by submitting to servitude, or by entering into various treaties of alliance, were incorporated and blended with the conquerors, the habits of intercourse, and the system of political union which remained with the former, was, in some degree, communicated to the latter. When different tribes, therefore, though strangers to each other, had settled in the same province, they were easily reduced under one sovereign; and the boundaries of a modern kingdom, came frequently, in the western part of Europe, to be nearly of the same extent with the dominions which had been formerly subject to a Roman governor.

In proportion to the number of tribes, or separate families, united in one kingdom, and to the wideness of the country over which they were scattered, the union between them was loose and feeble. <188> Every proprietor of land maintained a sort of independence, and notwithstanding the confederacy of which he was a member, assumed the privilege of engaging in private wars at pleasure. From the violent disposition to theft and rapine which prevailed in that age, neighbouring proprietors, when not occupied in a joint expedition, were tempted to commit depredations upon each other; and mutual injuries between the same individuals being often repeated, became the source of family quarrels, which were prosecuted with implacable animosity and rancour. There was no sufficient authority in the public for repressing these disorders. If, upon great provocation, the king had been excited to humble and punish an opulent baron, he found in many cases that the whole force of the crown was requisite for that purpose, and by the hazard and difficulty of the attempt, was commonly taught to be cautious, for the future, of involving himself in such disputes.

As individuals, therefore, in those times of violence and confusion, were continually exposed to injustice and oppression, and received little or no protection from government, they found it necessary to be constantly attentive to their own safety. It behoved every baron, not only to support his own personal dignity, and to maintain his own rights against the attacks of all his neighbours, but also to protect his retainers and dependents; and he was <189> led, upon that account, to regulate the state of his barony in such a manner, as to preserve the union of all its members, to secure their fidelity and service, and to keep them always in a posture of defence. With this view, when his relations, who had hitherto lived about his house, were gradually permitted to have families of their own, he did not bestow upon them separate estates, which would have rendered them independent; but he assigned them such portions of land as were thought sufficient for their maintenance, to be held upon condition, that whenever they were called upon, they should be ready to serve him in war, and that, in all their controversies, they should submit to his jurisdiction. These grants were made for no limited time, but might be resumed at pleasure; so that, though the master was not likely, without some extraordinary offence, to deprive his kinsmen of their possessions, yet his power in this respect being indisputable, it could hardly fail to keep them in awe, and to produce an implicit obedience to his commands.

The military tenants, supported in this manner, were denominated *vassals;* and the land held by any person upon such terms has been called a *fief;* though many writers, in order to distinguish it from what afterwards went under the same name, have termed it a *benefice.*

When the estate of a baron became extensive, <190> the slaves, by whom it was cultivated, were likewise sent to a distance from the house of their master, and were placed in separate families, each of which obtained the management of a particular farm; but that they might, in those disorderly times, be more easily protected by the owner, and might be in a condition to defend and assist one another, a number of them were usually collected together, and composed a little village. Hence they received the appellation of *villani,* or villains.

The whole of a kingdom was thus divided into a number of baronies, of greater or smaller extent, and regulated nearly in the same manner. The king was at the head of a barony similar in every respect to those of his subjects, though commonly larger, and therefore capable of maintaining a greater number of vassals and dependents. But the land which belonged to the barons, was held in the same independent manner with that which belonged to the king. As each of those warlike chiefs had purchased his demesnes by his own activity and valour, he claimed the absolute enjoyment and disposal of them, together with the privilege of transmitting them to his posterity; and as he had not been indebted to the crown for his original possession, neither was he obliged to secure the continuance of it, by serving the king in war, or by submitting to his jurisdiction. Their property, therefore, was such as has been called *allodial,* in contradistinc-<191>tion to that feudal tenure enjoyed by their respective military tenants.* <192>

* Different authors have entertained very different opinions concerning the primitive state of landed property, and the origin of feudal tenures, in the modern nations of Europe. The antiquaries who first turned their attention to researches on this subject, those of France in particular, living under an absolute monarchy, appear to have been strongly prepossessed by the form of government established in their own times, and their conjectures, with regard to the early state of the feudal institutions, were for a long time almost implicitly followed by later writers. They suppose that, when any of the German nations settled in a Roman province, the king seized upon all the conquered lands: that, retaining in his own possession what was sufficient to maintain the dignity of the crown, he distributed the remainder among the principal officers of his army, to be held precariously upon condition of their attending him in war: and that these officers afterwards bestowed part of their estates upon their dependents or followers, under similar conditions of military service.

This account seems liable to great objections. 1st, It may be asked how the king came to possess so much power as would enable him, at once, to acquire the entire property of the conquered lands? For it must be remembered that the conquest extended over the

These peculiarities, in the state of the kingdoms which were formed upon the ruins of the Roman empire, had a visible effect upon their constitution of government. According to the authority possessed by the barons, each over his own barony, and their independence with respect to each other, and with respect to the king, was their joint power <193> and influence over that great community of which they were members. The supreme powers of government in every kingdom were, therefore, exercised by an assembly composed of all those proprietors, and commonly summoned by the king on every great emergency.

Two meetings of this great council appear to have been regularly held in a year, for the ordinary dispatch of business; the first, after the seed-time, to determine their military operations during the summer; the second, before the harvest, in order to divide the booty. In those meetings it was customary also to rectify abuses by introducing new regulations, and to decide

---

ancient inhabitants of the country, not over his own followers; and with respect to these last, the accounts given by Caesar and Tacitus of the German nations, represent their princes as possessing a very limited authority.

2dly, Upon the supposition that all the conquered lands were originally held of the king during pleasure, his authority, immediately upon the settlement of these nations, must have been rendered altogether despotical. If the king had a power of dispossessing all his subjects of their landed estates, he must have been more absolute than any monarch at present upon the face of the earth. But the early history of the modern European nations, gives an account of their government very different from this, and informs us that the nobility of each kingdom enjoyed great independence, and a degree of opulence, in many cases, little inferior to that of the monarch.

The idea that the king became originally proprietor of all the conquered lands seems now, upon a fuller examination of facts, to be in a great measure relinquished; and several writers of late have made it at least extremely probable that the land in the conquered provinces was at first occupied, according to circumstances, by different individuals, or distributed by lot among the warriors of each victorious tribe; and that each possessor became the full proprietor of that portion of land which had fallen to his share. See Le droit publique de France, eclairci par les monumens de l'antiquité. Par M. Bouquet. [[12.]] See also observations sur l'histoire de France. Par M. L'Abbé de Mably. [[I:50–52.]]

It is true that, in the modern kingdoms of Europe, the proprietors of lands were early understood to be under an obligation of going out to war as often as the public interest required it. But this was a duty which they owed to the community as citizens, not to the king as vassals; and their attendance was required, not by an order of the monarch, but in consequence of a determination of the national assembly, of which they themselves were the constituent members.

those law-suits which had arisen between independent proprietors of land. Such was the business of the early parliaments in France, of the Cortes in Spain, of the Wittenagemote in England; and in each of the feudal kingdoms, we discover evident marks of a national council, constituted in the same manner, and invested with similar priveleges.* <194>

These observations may serve to show the general aspect and complexion of that political constitution which results from the first union of rude tribes, or small independent societies. The government resulting from that union is apt to be of a mixed nature, in which there is a nobility distinguished from the people, and a king exalted above the nobles. But though, according to that system, the peculiar situation of different nations may have produced some variety in the powers belonging to these different orders, yet, unless in very poor states, the influence acquired by the nobles has commonly been such as to occasion a remarkable prevalence of aristocracy. <195>

---

* In France, under the Merovingian kings, all deeds of any importance, issuing from the crown, usually contained some such expression as these: *Una cum nostris optimatibus pertractavimus. De consensu fidelium nostrorum. In nostra et procerum nostrorum praesentia.* [["Together with our best we have consulted. Of our trustworthy agreement. In us and our trustworthy chiefs present."]] Obser. par M. de Mably. [[I:238.]]. And there is good reason to believe that what is called the Salique Law was laid before the national assembly, and received their approbation. "Dictaverunt Salicam legem Proceres ipsius gentis, qui tunc temporis apud eam erant rectores." Praef. leg. Sal. [["Prologus" 1 § 2: "The Chiefs have spoken the Salic law of the clan, who then at that time were governed by it." The early-sixth-century *Lex Salica* was the legal code of the Salian Franks. It is the only extant Germanic, pre-Christian legal code still in relatively pristine form. It is particularly important in French history as it was used to legitimate claims of royal succession, for example from the Capetians to the House of Valois.]] See lettres historiques sur les fonctions essentielles du parlement. Boulainvilliers let. sur le parl. de France. [[I:39, 126. There were references to both Hume's and Robertson's histories in this note in earlier editions of the *Ranks*.]]

SECTION II

The natural progress of government in a rude kingdom.

The continued union of rude tribes, or small societies, has a tendency to produce a great alteration in the political system of a people. The same circumstances, by which, in a single tribe, a chief is gradually advanced over the different heads of families, contribute, in a kingdom, to exalt the sovereign above the chiefs, and to extend his authority throughout the whole of his dominions.

As the king is placed at the head of the nation, and acts the most conspicuous part in all their public measures, his high rank and station reflect upon him a degree of splendour, which is apt to obscure the lustre of every inferior chief; and the longer he has remained in a situation where he excites the admiration and respect of the people, it is to be supposed that their habits of submission to him will be the more confirmed.

From the opulence, too, of the sovereign, which is generally much greater than that of any other member of the community, as well as from the nature of his office, he has more power to reward and protect his friends, and to punish or depress those who have become the objects of his resent-<196>ment or displeasure. The consideration of this must operate powerfully upon individuals, as a motive to court his favour, and, of consequence, to support his interest. It is therefore to be concluded that, from the natural course of things, the immediate followers and dependents of the king will be constantly increasing, and those of every inferior leader will be diminishing in the same proportion.

In a government so constituted as to introduce a continual jealousy between the crown and the nobles, it must frequently happen that the latter, instead of prosecuting a uniform plan for aggrandizing their own order, should be occupied with private quarrels and dissensions among themselves; so that the king, who is ready to improve every conjuncture for extending his power, may often employ and assist the great lords in destroying each other, or take advantage of those occasions when they have been weakened by their continued struggles, and are in no condition to oppose his demands.

According as the real influence and authority of the crown are extended, its prerogatives are gradually augmented. When the king finds that the original chiefs have become in a great measure dependent upon him, he is not solicitous about consulting them in the management of public affairs; and the meetings of the national council, being seldom called, or being attended only by such <197> members as are entirely devoted to the crown, dwindle away from time to time, and are at last laid aside altogether. The judicial power of the heads of different tribes is gradually subjected to similar encroachments; and that jurisdiction, which they at first held in virtue of their own authority, is rendered subordinate to the tribunal of the monarch, who, after having established the right of appeal from their courts to his own court, is led to appoint the judges in each particular district. The power of making laws, as well as that of determining peace and war, and of summoning all his subjects to the field, may come in like manner to be exercised at the discretion of the prince.

This progress of government, towards monarchy, though it seems to hold universally, is likely to be accompanied with some diversity of appearances in different countries; and, in particular, is commonly more rapid in a small state than in a large one; in which point of view the ancient Greeks and Romans are most remarkably distinguished from the greater part of the feudal kingdoms in Europe.

The Roman and Greek states were originally of small extent, and the people belonging to each of them being, for the most part, collected in one city, were led in a short time to cultivate an acquaintance. The police, which was easily established in such a limited territory, put a stop to the divisions so prevalent among neighbouring tribes of barbarians. Those who belonged to different <198> families were soon restrained from injuring one another, and lived in security under the protection of the government. By conversing together almost every day, their ancient prejudices were eradicated; and their animosities, being no longer cherished by reciprocal acts of hostility, were allowed to subside, and left no traces behind. The whole people, being early engaged in violent struggles with the petty states around them, were obliged to hold an intimate correspondence, and acquired an high sense of public interest. In proportion as they were thus incorporated in a larger community, they lost all inferior distinctions. The members of each particular tribe had no reason to maintain their peculiar connexions, or to preserve their primitive attachment to their respective chiefs. The power of the nobility, therefore, which depended upon those circumstances, was quickly destroyed; and the monarch, who remained at the head of the nation without a rival to counterbalance his influence, had no difficulty in extending his influence over the whole of his dominions.

For this reason, the ancient jurisdiction and authority of the chiefs is not very distinctly marked in the early history of those nations, among whom it was in a great measure destroyed before they were possessed of historical records. At Rome, so early as the reign of Servius Tullius, the practice of convening the people according to their tribes, or *curiae,* was almost entirely laid aside; <199> and the public assemblies were held in such a manner, that every individual was classed according to his wealth.[2]

The great extent, on the other hand, of those modern kingdoms which, upon the downfall of the Roman empire, were erected in the western part of Europe, was formerly mentioned; and the political consequences, which appear to have been immediately derived from that circumstance, were likewise taken notice of. The numerous tribes, or separate families, that were associated under a sovereign, far from being collected in a single town, were spread over a large territory, and living at a distance from each other, were for a long time prevented from having much intercourse, or from acquiring the habits of polished society. Strangers to regular government, and little restrained by the authority of the public magistrate, they were devoted to their several chiefs, by whom they were encouraged to rob and plunder their neighbours, and protected from the punishment due to their offences. Mutual depredations became the source of perpetual animosity and discord

---

2. This was known as the Servian Constitution. The divisions based on wealth were traditionally attributed to the semimythical Servius, sixth king of Rome.

among neighbouring barons, who, from jealousy, from an interference of interest, or from resentment of injuries, were, for the most part, either engaged in actual hostilities, or lying in wait for a favourable opportunity to oppress and destroy one another. Thus every kingdom was composed of a great variety of parts, loosely combined together, and for several centuries may be regarded as a collection of small in-<200>dependent societies, rather than as one great political community. The slow advances which were afterwards made by the people towards a more complete union, appear to have been productive of that feudal subordination which has been the subject of so much investigation and controversy.

In those times of license and disorder, the proprietors of small estates were necessarily exposed to many hardships and calamities. Surrounded by wealthier and more powerful neighbours, by whom they were invaded from every quarter, and held in constant terror, they could seldom indulge the hope of maintaining their possessions, or of transmitting them to their posterity. Conscious, therefore, of their weakness, they endeavoured to provide for their future safety, by soliciting the aid of some opulent chief, who appeared most capable of defending them; and, in order to obtain that protection which he afforded to his ancient retainers or vassals, they were obliged to render themselves equally subservient to his interest; to relinquish their pretensions to independence, to acknowledge him as their leader, and to yield him that homage and fealty which belonged to a feudal superior.

The nature of these important transactions, the solemnities with which they were accompanied, and the views and motives from which they were usually concluded, are sufficiently explained from the copies or forms of those deeds which have been collected and handed down to us. The vas-<201>sal promised, in a solemn manner, to submit to the jurisdiction of the superior, to reside within his domain, and to serve him in war, whether he should be engaged in prosecuting his own quarrels, or in the common cause of the nation. The superior, on the other hand, engaged to exert all his power and influence, in protecting the vassal, in defending his possessions, or in avenging his death, in case he should be assassinated. In consequence of these mutual engagements, the vassal, by certain symbols expressive of the agreement, resigned his property, of which he again received the investiture from the hands of the superior.*

It is probable, however, that the extension of particular baronies, by the voluntary submission of allodial proprietors, contributed to ascertain the right of the vassal, and to limit that property with which the superior was originally invested. The ancient <202> military tenants, who were the kindred and relations of the superior, and who had received their lands as a pure gratuity, never thought of demanding to be secured in the future possession; and while they continued to support the interest of the family, which they looked upon as inseparable from their own interest, they had no apprehension that they should ever be deprived of their estates. Thus, according to the more accurate ideas of later times, they were merely tenants

---

* Fidelis Deo propitio ille, ad nostram veniens praesentiam suggessit nobis, eo quod propter simplicitatem suam, causas suas minimè possit prosequi, vel admallare, clementiae regni nostri petiit, ut inlustris vir ille omnes causas suas in vice ipsius, tam in pago, quam in palatio nostro admallandum prosequendumque recipere deberet, quod in praesenti per fistucam eas eidem visus est commendasse. Propterea jubemus, ut dum taliter utriusque decrevit voluntas, memoratus ille vir omnes causas lui, ubicumque prosequi vel admallare deberet, ut unicuique pro ipso, vel hominibus suis; reputatis conditionibus, et directum faciat, et ab aliis similiter in veritate recipiat. Sic tamen quamdiu amborum decrevit voluntas. Formul. Marculsi. 21.—Vid. Ibid. Formul. 13. [["Trusting in gracious God, he, coming to our presence, has supplicated us, (for this reason) because on account of his simplicity he is little able to attend to his affairs or to represent himself legally, [and] he sought the clemency of our royal authority that this illustrious man in the place of the petitioner, both in the small town and in our palace, ought to undertake to represent legally and to attend to all his affairs because at the present time the petitioner seems to entrust his affairs to this same man because he has sworn *per fistucam* (i.e., taken a solemn, formal oath while grasping a stick [see *Lex Salica*, CXII]). On account of this, we order, because, as the will of each and both have decreed, the illustrious man having been reminded that all his affairs be discharged whenever he ought to attend to or legally represent him, that for each personally or for those represented he both do so directly and receive likewise from others. Once the conditions have been taken into consideration, however, this decree is valid for as long as both consent to it." Marculfus's *Formulae Marculfi Libri Duo* was a seventh-century formulary, i.e., a set of formulaic legal contracts that could be used in a variety of circumstances. See Karl Zeumer, ed., *Monumenta Germaniae historica. Legum section V. Formulae* (Hannover, 1886).]]

See also L'Esprit de Loix, liv. 31. chap 8. [[Montesquieu discussed Formula I.13 as part of his general comparison of Frankish constitutions and laws. Millar's general point derives from Montesquieu, namely that Franks and Romans eagerly sought to become vassals as a means of protecting themselves from the chaos of the times.]]

at will; though from the affection of their master, and from their inviolable
fidelity to him, they were commonly permitted to enjoy their lands during
life; and in ordinary cases the same indulgence was even shown to their
posterity.

But it was not to be expected that those who submitted to a foreign
superior, and who gave up their allodial property as an equivalent for the
protection which was promised them, would repose so much confidence
in a person with whom they had no natural connexion, or be willing to
hold their lands by the same precarious tenure. They endeavoured, by express stipulations, to prevent the arbitrary conduct of the master; and, according as they found themselves in a condition to insist for more favourable terms, they obtained a grant of their estates, for a certain limited time,
for life, or to their heirs. By these grants the right of property, instead of
being totally vested in the superior, came to be, in some measure, divided
between him and his vassals. <203>

When a superior had entered into such transactions with his new retainers, he could not well refuse a similar security to such of his ancient
vassals as, from any casual suspicion, thought proper to demand it; so that
from the influence of example, joined to uninterrupted possession in a series of heirs, the same privileges were, either by an express bargain, or by a
sort of tacit agreement, communicated, at length, to all his military tenants.

This alteration gave rise to what were called the *incidents* of the feudal
tenures. The ancient military tenants, who were the kindred of the superior,
might be removed by him at pleasure, or subjected to what burdens he
thought proper to impose upon them; and there was no occasion to specify
the services that might be required of them, or the grounds upon which
they might forfeit their possessions. But when the vassal had obtained a
permanent right to his estate, it became necessary to ascertain the extent
of the obligations which he came under, and the penalty to which he was
subjected upon his neglecting to fulfil them; so that, from the nature of the
feudal connexion, he in some cases incurred a forfeiture, or total loss of the
fief, and in others was liable for the payment of certain duties, which produced an occasional profit to the superior.

1. Thus when the vassal died without heirs; when he violated his duty
by the commission of a crime, or by neglecting to perform the usual ser-

<204>vice; in either of these cases his lands returned to the superior. The emolument arising from this forfeiture, or termination of the fief, was called *an escheat*.

2. When a person was admitted to hold a fief, he engaged by an oath to fulfil the duties of *homage* and *fealty* to the superior. Even after fiefs became hereditary, this ceremony was repeated upon every transmission of the feudal right by succession; so that while the heir of a vassal neglected to renew the engagement, he was not entitled to obtain possession, and the superior, in the mean time, drew the rent of the lands. Hence the incident of *non-entry*.

3. Though the heir of a vassal might claim a renewal of the feudal investiture, this was understood to be granted in consideration of his performing military service. When by his nonage, therefore, the heir was incapable of fulfilling that condition, the superior himself retained the possession of the lands; at the same time that he was accustomed, in that case, to protect and maintain his future vassal. This produced the incident of *wardship*.

4. Upon the death of a vassal, it was usual for the representative of his family to make a present to the superior, in order to obtain a ready admittance into the possession of the lands. When fiefs became hereditary, it was still found expedient to procure by means of a bribe, what could <205> not easily be extorted by force; and the original arbitrary payment was converted into a regular duty, under the name of *relief*.

5. From the original nature of the feudal grants, the vassal could have no title to sell, or give away to any other person, the lands which he held merely as a tenant, in consideration of the service which he was bound to perform. But when fiefs had been granted to heirs, and when of consequence the right of the vassal approached somewhat nearer to that of property, it became customary to compound with the superior for the privilege of alienating the estate, upon payment of a sum of money. This gave rise to a perquisite, called the *fine of alienation*.

6. From the disorders which prevailed in the feudal times, when different families were so frequently at war, it was of great consequence that the vassals should not contract an alliance with the enemy of their Liege Lord; which might have a tendency to corrupt their fidelity. When fiefs therefore

came to be granted for life, or to heirs, it was still held a sufficient ground of forfeiture that the vassal married without the superior's consent. This forfeiture was afterwards converted into a pecuniary penalty, called the incident of *marriage.*

7. According to the usual policy of the feudal nations, the superior levied no taxes from his retainers, but was maintained from the rent of his <206> own estate. In particular cases, however, when his ordinary revenue was insufficient, his vassals were accustomed to supply him by a voluntary contribution. When fiefs were precarious, what was given on those occasions depended upon the will of the superior, who might even seize upon the whole estate of his tenants. But when the vassal had obtained a more permanent right, it became necessary to settle the cases when those contributions were to be made, as well as the quantity that might be demanded; and in this manner, *aid* or *benevolence* came to be enumerated among the duties payable to a superior.

The conversion of allodial into feudal property, by a voluntary resignation, as it proceeded from the general manners and situation of the people, continued to be a frequent practice, while those manners and that situation remained. The smaller barons were thus, at different times, subjected to their opulent neighbours; the number of independent proprietors was gradually diminished; their estates were united and blended together in one barony; and large districts were brought under the dominion of a few great lords, who daily extended their influence and authority, by increasing the number of their vassals.

These changes, by exalting a small part of the nobility over the great body of the people, had, for some time, a tendency to abridge, instead of enlarging the power of the crown, and to render <207> the government more aristocratical. Whenever an independent proprietor had resigned his allodial property, and agreed to hold his land by a feudal tenure, he was no longer entitled to a voice in the national assembly, but was bound to follow the direction of the person to whom he had become liable in homage and fealty. This appears to be the reason of what is observed in France, that the national assembly was originally much more numerous than it came to be afterwards, when its constituent members were all persons of high rank and great opulence.* It would seem also that in England, under the later princes of the Saxon line, the great affairs of the nation were transacted in a meeting composed of a few great barons; and we discover no marks of those numerous assemblies which are taken notice of in a former period.†

But the same circumstances, by which the estates of different small proprietors were united in one barony, contributed afterwards to incorporate these larger districts, and to unite all the inhabitants of a kingdom in the same feudal dependency. As the <208> barons were diminished in number, and increased in power and opulence, they became more immediate rivals to each other. In their different quarrels, which were prosecuted with various success, the weaker party was often obliged to have recourse to the king, who alone was able to screen him from the fury of his enemy; and, in order to procure that succour and protection which his situation required, he became willing to surrender his property, and to hold his estate upon condition of his yielding that obedience, and performing that service, which a superior was accustomed to demand from his vassals. From the various disputes which arose, and the accidental combinations that were formed among the great families, the nobles were all, in their turns, reduced to difficulties from which they were forced to extricate themselves by the like compliances; and the sovereign, who laid hold of every opportunity to extend his influence, established his superiority over the barons by the same means which they themselves had formerly employed for subjecting the proprietors of smaller estates.

Thus, by degrees, the feudal system was completed in most of the countries of Europe. The whole of a kingdom came to be united in one great

* "Tous les Francs indistinctement continuerent d'y avoir entrée; mais dans la suite leur nombre s'étant accru, la distinction entre les Gaulois et les Francs s'étant insensiblement effacé, chaque canton s'assembloit en particulier; et l'on n'admit plus guéres aux assemblées generales, que ceux qui tenoient un rang dans l'etat." Let. hist. sur les parl. [["All the Franks without distinction continued to accede to it; but subsequently, as they grew in number, and the distinction between Gauls and Franks had blurred, each canton gathered in its own assembly; thus no one was any longer admitted to the general assemblies who did not occupy a high rank in the State" ("Lettre III," II:70).]]

† In early times the Wittenagemote is called "infinita fidelium multitudo." [[Literally, "unlimited throng of trustworthy men."]]

fief, of which the king was the superior, or lord paramount, having in some measure the property of all the land within his dominions. The great barons became his immediate vassals, and, accord-<209>ing to the tenure by which they held their estates, were subject to his jurisdiction, and liable to him in services of the same nature with those which they exacted from their own retainers or inferior military tenants.

The precise period when this revolution was finally accomplished, as in most other gradual changes which happen in a country, is involved in doubt and uncertainty. From a comparison of the opinions of different authors who have written upon this subject, and of the facts which they bring in support of their several conjectures, it appears most reasonable to conclude, that in France the great barons continued their allodial possessions during the kings of the first and second race, and about the beginning of the Capetian line were, for the most part, reduced into a state of feudal subjection to the monarch.* <210>

In England it would seem that, in like manner, the nobles maintained their independence during the time of the Saxon princes, and were re-

---

* Many of the French antiquaries and historians have believed that the feudal system was completed under their kings of the first race. (See Mezeray, hist. de France [[84, 36–37, 114, 277, 280]].—Loyseau, traité des seigneuries [[I.1.15, 17–18; I.3.51]].—Salvaing de l'usage des fiefs [[I:2.14]].—) Others have supposed that military tenures were unknown during this early period, and were introduced, either about the time of Charlemagne, or towards the end of the second race of kings, or about the time of Hugh Capet. (See Boulainvilliers, lettres sur les parlemens de France. [[I:98–99, 108–9, 112, 118.]]—Chantereau de Fevre, traité des fiefs. [[I:6.]]—Henault, abr. de l'hist. de France. [[I:103.]]—Bouquet, droit public de France, &c. [[1:2–3.]]) These various opinions appear to have arisen from a different view of the facts relating to the subject; and here, as in most other disputes, the truth probably lies in a middle between the opposite extremes. To those authors who observed that, soon after the settlement of the Franks in Gaul, the king and the great lords had a considerable number of vassals dependent upon them for protection, and liable in military service, it seemed a natural inference, that the whole land in the country was held by military tenure. Those on the contrary who discovered that, under the kings of the first and second race, the great lords were in possession of allodial estates, and who observed, that, after the reign of Hugh Capet, many of the perquisites incident to the feudal tenures were established, thought they had reason from thence to conclude that the feudal system was not introduced before this period. [[Hugh Capet (938–96) was the founder of the Capetian line, the kings who ruled France until the death of Charles IV in 1328.]]

duced to be the vassals of the crown in the reign of William the Conqueror.* <211>

This opinion is confirmed by observing the changes which, from those two periods, began to take place in the government of these kingdoms. From the reign of Hugh Capet, the dominions of France appear more

---

* From similar circumstances it has been a subject of controversy, whether the feudal system took place in England under the government of the Saxon monarchs, or whether it was not first introduced in the reign of William the Conqueror. See *Wright's Introduction to the law of tenures,* chap. 2. and the authorities quoted by him upon both sides of the question.

Sir Henry Spelman having said in his Glossary, v. *feodum,* that fiefs were brought into England by William the Conqueror; and the judges of Ireland, in their argument in the case of *defective titles,* having pointed out that opinion as erroneous, this industrious antiquary was thence excited to write a treatise upon the subject, in which he explains his meaning to be nothing more but that, in England, fiefs were not rendered *hereditary* before the Norman conquest. Thus, after having stated the question, in the beginning of his treatise, he goes on as follows: "A FEUD is said to be *usufructus quidam rei immobilis sub conditione fidei* [[literally, "a type of usufruct of an immovable thing under the condition of trust"]]. But this definition is of too large extent for such kind of *feuds* as our question must consist upon: for it includeth two members or species greatly differing the one from the other; the one *temporary* and *revocable* (as those at will or for years, life or lives); the other *hereditary* and *perpetual.* As for *temporary feuds,* which (like wild fig-trees) could yield none of the feudal fruits of *wardship, marriage, relief, &c.* unto their lords, they belong nothing unto our argument."—And a little after he adds, "But this kind of *feud* (we speak of) and no other, is that only whereof our law taketh notice, though time hath somewhat varied it from the first institution, by drawing the property of the soil from the lord unto the tenant. And I both conceive and affirm under correction, That this our kind of feuds being perpetual and hereditary, and subject to wardship, marriage, and relief, and other feudal services were not in use among our Saxons, nor our law of tenures (whereon they depend) once known unto them." (Spelman's treat. on feuds and tenures by knight-service, chap. 1.) [[In Gibson, ed., *English Works,* I:2. Spellman's *Glossarium Archaiologium* (1664) was one of the main sources for volume I of Millar's *Historical View.*]] The same author, in another part of his treatise, proceeds to shew that, in England among the Saxons, the estates of the nobility were denominated *Boc-land,* and were held in full property, but that *Folc-land,* or the land of the lower people, was held under condition of customary services, at the will of their lord the *Thane.* Ibid., chap. 5.

It is hoped the above remark will appear not improper; because the authority of Spelman, upon this point, has been considered as of much weight; and also because some writers appear to have mistaken his opinion by consulting the passage in his glossary, without attending to the subsequent treatise [[i.e., "The Original, Growth, Propagation and Condition of Feuds and Tenures by Knight-Service, in England"]], published among his posthumous works by Dr. Gibson.

firmly united; they were no longer split upon the death of the sovereign, and shared among his children; the monarch was from this period capable of acting with more vigour, and continued to extend his prerogative till the <212> reign of Lewis XI. who exercised the power of imposing taxes, as well as of making laws independent of the convention of estates.* The same progress, though with some accidental interruptions, may be traced in England, from the Norman conquest to the accession of the Tudor family, under which the powers and prerogatives of the crown were exalted to a height that seemed equally incompatible with the rights of the nobility and the freedom of the people.

The authors, who have written upon the feudal law, seem to have generally considered that system as peculiar to the modern nations of Europe; and from what has been observed above, it appears evident that the circumstances of the Gothic nations, who settled in the western provinces of Rome, rendered such a set of regulations more especially useful for the defence and security of the people. It is highly probable that, from those <213> parts of Europe where the feudal law was first established, it was in some degree communicated, by the intercourse of the inhabitants and the force of example, to some of the neighbouring countries. But it merits particular attention that the same sort of policy, though not brought to the same perfection as in Europe, is to be found in many distant parts of the world, where it never could be derived from imitation; and perhaps there is reason to think that similar institutions, by which small bodies of men are incorporated in larger societies under a single leader, and afterwards linked together in one great community, have been suggested in every extensive kingdom, founded upon the original association of many rude tribes or families.

The kingdom of Congo, upon the southern coast of Africa, is divided into many large districts or provinces, the inhabitants of which appear to have made some progress in agriculture. Each of these districts comprehends a multitude of small lordships, which are said to have been formerly independent, but which are now united together, and reduced under a single chief or governor, who exercises absolute authority over them. The great

---

* See Boulainvilliers, lettres sur les parl. de France. [[Lettre III, II:98.]]

lords, or governors of provinces, are in like manner dependent upon the king, and owe him the payment of certain annual duties. This monarch is understood to have an unlimited power over the goods of all his subjects; he is the proprietor of all the lands in the kingdom, which return to <214> the crown upon the death of the possessors; and, according to the arbitrary will of the prince, are either continued in the same, or bestowed upon a different family. All the inhabitants are bound to appear in the field whenever they are required by the sovereign, who is able in a short time to raise a prodigious army upon any sudden emergency. Every governor has a judicial power in his own district, and from his sentences there lies an appeal to the king, who is the supreme judge of the nation. Similar accounts are given of the constitution in the neighbouring kingdoms of Angola, Loango, and Benin.*

The same form of government may be discovered in several part of the East Indies, where many great lords, who have acquired extensive dominions, are often reduced into a sort of feudal dependence upon a single person.

Among the natives of Indostan, there are a great number of families who have been immemorially trained up to arms, and who enjoy a superior rank to most of the other inhabitants. They form a militia capable of enduring much hardship, and wanting nothing to make good soldiers but order and discipline. These hereditary warriors are subject to the authority of chiefs, or Rajahs, from whom they receive lands, upon condition of their per-<215>forming military service. It would seem that those different families were originally independent of each other. By degrees, however, many of the poorer sort have become subordinate to their opulent neighbours, and are obliged to serve them in war in order to obtain a livelihood. In like manner, the leaders of more wealthy families have been gradually subdued by a certain Rajah, who mounted the throne, and whose influence became more and more extensive. This, in all probability, gave rise to the political constitution at present established in that country. The Rajahs, or nobility, are now for the most part retained by the Great Mogul in a situation re-

---

* Histoire generale des voyages, 4to. tom. 4. 5. [[6]] liv. 13. chap. 2, [[3,]] 4.—Ibid. tom. 4. liv. 11. chap. 1. 6. § 2.—Modern Universal History [[3,]] vol. 16. p. 81.

sembling that of the crown vassals in Europe. At the same time there are
some of those chiefs who still maintain an independency even in the heart
of the empire. In the reign of Aureng-zebe, there were about an hundred,
dispersed over the whole country, several of whom were capable of bringing
into the field 25,000 horse, better troops than those of the monarch.*

In the kingdom of Pegu, which was formerly an independent monarchy,
the king is said to have been the sole heir of all the landed estates of his
subjects. The nobility, or chiefs, had lands and towns assigned them, which
they held of the crown, upon condition of their maintaining a cer-
<216>tain number of troops in time of peace, and bringing them into the
field in case of a war. Besides these military services, they were also bound
to the performance of several kinds of work, which the sovereign rigorously
exacted from them, in token of their subjection. This country is now an-
nexed to the kingdom of Ava, in which, as well as in that of Laos and of
Siam, the same regulations appear to be established.†

"Travellers who make observations on the Malays," says the judicious
M. Le Poivre, "are astonished to find, in the centre of Asia, under the
scorching climate of the line, the laws, the manners, the customs, and the
prejudices of the ancient inhabitants of the north of Europe. The Malays
are governed by feudal laws, that capricious system, conceived for the defence of the liberty of a few against the tyranny of one, while the multitude
is subjected to slavery and oppression.

"A chief, who has the title of king, or sultan, issues his commands to his
great vassals, who obey when they think proper. These have inferior vassals,
who often act in the same manner with regard to them. A small part of the
nation live independent, under the title of *Oramcay,* or *noble,* and sell their
services to those who pay <217> them best; while the body of the nation
is composed of slaves, and lives in perpetual servitude.

"With these laws, the Malays are restless, fond of navigation, war, plunder, emigrations, colonies, desperate enterprises, adventures, and gallantry.
They talk incessantly of their honour, and their bravery, while they are
universally regarded, by those with whom they have intercourse, as the most

* Modern Universal History, vol. 6. p. 254.
† Modern Universal History, vol. 7. p. 54, 62, 64, 127, 188, 190, 225, 263, 273.

treacherous, ferocious people on the face of the globe; and yet, what appeared to me extremely singular, they speak the softest language of Asia. What the Count de Forbin has said, in his Memoirs, is exactly true, and is the reigning characteristic of all the Malay nations. More attached to the absurd laws of their pretended honour, than to those of justice or humanity, you always observe, that among them, the strong oppress the weak: their treaties of peace and friendship never subsisting beyond that self-interest by which they were induced to make them. They are almost always armed, and either at war among themselves, or employed in pillaging their neighbours."*

The remains of this feudal policy are also to be found in Turkey. The Zaims and Timariots, in the Turkish Empire, are a species of vassals, who possess landed estates upon condition of their upholding a certain number of soldiers for the service < 218 > of the grand seignior. The Zaims have lands of greater value than the Timariots, and are obliged to maintain a greater number of soldiers. The estates of both, are, in some cases, held during pleasure, and in others hereditary. It was computed, in the last century, that the whole militia maintained in this manner, throughout the Turkish empire, amounted to an hundred thousand men.†

In the history of the ancient Persians, during the wars which they carried on with the Roman emperors, we may also discover some traces of a similar constitution of government; for it is observed that this nation had no mercenary troops, but that the whole people might be called out to war by the king, and upon the conclusion of every expedition, were accustomed to return, with their booty, to their several places of residence.‡

When a great and polished nation begins to relapse into its primitive rudeness and barbarism, the dominions which belonged to it are in danger of falling asunder; and the same institutions may become necessary for preventing the different parts of the kingdom from being separated, which had been formerly employed in order to unite the several members of an extensive society. This was the case among the Romans in the later periods

---

* Les voyages d'une Philosophe. [[Pierre Poivre, *The Travels of a Philosopher*, 63.]]
† See Ricault's State of the Ottoman Empire. [[Rycault, *The Present State*, III. 3. 342.]]
‡ Herodian. hist. lib. 6. [[5.3–4.]]

of the empire. When the provinces became in a great measure independent, and the government was no <219> longer able to protect them from the repeated invasions of the barbarians, the inhabitants were obliged to shelter themselves under the dominion of particular great men in their neighbourhood, whom the emperor put in possession of large estates, upon condition of their maintaining a proper armed force to defend the country. Thus, in different provinces, there arose a number of chiefs, or leaders, who enjoyed estates in land, as a consideration for the military service which they performed to the sovereign. The Abbé Du Bos has thence been led to imagine that the feudal policy of the German nations was copied from those regulations already established in the countries which they subdued.* But it ought to be considered, that the growth and decay of society have, in some respects, a resemblance to each other; which, independent of imitation, is naturally productive of similar manners and customs. <220>

---

* Histoire critique de l'etablissement de la monarchie Françoise dans les Gaules. [[II:381–83, 464, 466.]]

The Changes Produced in the Government of a People, by Their Progress in Arts, and in Polished Manners

SECTION I

Circumstances, in a polished nation, which tend to increase the power of the Sovereign.

The advancement of a people in the arts of life, is attended with various alterations in the state of individuals, and in the whole constitution of their government.

Mankind, in a rude age, are commonly in readiness to go out to war, as often as their circumstances require it. From their extreme idleness, a military expedition is seldom inconvenient for them; while the prospect of enriching themselves with plunder, and of procuring distinction by their valour, renders it always agreeable. The members of every clan are no less eager to follow their chief, and to revenge his quarrel, than he is desirous of their assistance. They look upon it as a privilege, rather than a burden, to attend upon him, and to share in the danger, as well as in the glory and profit of all his undertakings. By the numberless acts of hostility in which they are engaged, they < 221 > are trained to the use of arms, and acquire experience in the military art, so far as it is then understood. Thus, without any trouble or expence, a powerful militia is constantly maintained, which, upon the slightest notice, can always be brought into the field, and employed in the defence of the country.

When Caesar made war upon the Helvetii they were able to muster against him no less than ninety-two thousand fighting men, amounting to a fourth part of all the inhabitants.*

Hence those prodigious swarms which issued, at different times, from the ill cultivated regions of the north, and over-ran the several provinces of the Roman empire. Hence too, the poor, but superstitious princes of Europe, were enabled to muster such numerous forces under the banner of the cross, in order to attack the opulent nations of the east, and to deliver the holy sepulchre from the hands of the infidels.

The same observation will, in some measure, account for those immense armies which we read of in the early periods of history; or at least may incline us to consider the exaggerated relations of ancient authors, upon that subject, as not entirely destitute of real foundation.

These dispositions, arising from the frequent disorders incident to a rude society, are of course <222> laid aside when good order and tranquillity begin to be established. When the government acquires so much authority as to protect individuals from oppression, and to put an end to the private wars which subsisted between different families, the people, who have no other military enterprises but those which are carried on in the public cause of the nation, become gradually less accustomed to fighting, and their martial ardour is proportionably abated.

The improvement of arts and manufactures, by introducing luxury, contributes yet more to enervate the minds of men, who, according as they enjoy more ease and pleasure at home, feel greater aversion to the hardships and dangers of a military life, and put a lower value upon that sort of reputation which it affords. The increase of industry, at the same time, creates a number of lucrative employments which require a constant attention, and gives rise to a variety of tradesmen and artificers, who cannot afford to leave their business for the transient and uncertain advantages to be derived from the pillage of their enemies.

In these circumstances, the bulk of a people become at length unable or unwilling to serve in war, and when summoned to appear in the field, according to the ancient usage, are induced to offer a sum of money instead

* De bell. Gall. lib. i. [[29.]]

of their personal attendance. A composition of this kind is readily accepted by the sovereign or chief magistrate, as it <223> enables him to hire soldiers among those who have no better employment, or who have contracted a liking to that particular occupation. The forces which he has raised in this manner, receiving constant pay, and having no other means of procuring a livelihood, are entirely under the direction of their leader, and are willing to remain in his service as long as he chooses to retain them. From this alteration of circumstances, he has an opportunity of establishing a proper subordination in the army, and according as it becomes fitter for action, and, in all its motions capable of being guided and regulated with greater facility, he is encouraged to enter upon more difficult enterprises, as well as to meditate more distant schemes of ambition. His wars, which were formerly concluded in a few weeks, are now gradually protracted to a greater length of time, and occasioning a greater variety of operations, are productive of suitable improvements in the military art.

After a numerous body of troops have been levied at considerable expence, and have been prepared for war by a long course of discipline and experience, it appears highly expedient to the sovereign that, even in time of peace, some part of them, at least, should be kept in pay, to be in readiness whenever their service is required. Thus, the introduction of mercenary forces is soon followed by that of a regular standing army. The business of a soldier becomes a distinct profession, <224> which is appropriated to a separate order of men; while the rest of the inhabitants, being devoted to their several employments, become wholly unaccustomed to arms; and the preservation of their lives and fortunes is totally devolved upon those whom they are at the charge of maintaining for that purpose.

This important revolution, with respect to the means of national defence, appears to have taken place in all the civilized and opulent nations of antiquity. In all the Greek states, even in that of Sparta, we find that the military service of the free citizens came, from a change of manners, to be regarded as burdensome, and the practice of employing mercenary troops was introduced. The Romans too, before the end of the republic, had found it necessary to maintain a regular standing army in each of their distant provinces.

In the modern nations of Europe, the disuse of the feudal militia was

an immediate consequence of the progress of the people in arts and manufactures; after which the different sovereigns were forced to hire soldiers
upon particular occasions, and at last to maintain a regular body of troops
for the defence of their dominions. In France, during the reign of Lewis
XIII. and in Germany, about the same period, the military system began
to be established upon that footing, which it has since acquired in all the
countries of Europe.

The tendency of a standing mercenary army to <225> increase the power
and prerogative of the crown, which has been the subject of much declamation, is sufficiently obvious. As the army is immediately under the conduct of the monarch; as the individuals of which it is composed depend
entirely upon him for preferment; as, by forming a separate order of men,
they are apt to become indifferent about the rights of their fellow-citizens;
it may be expected that, in most cases, they will be disposed to pay an implicit obedience to his commands, and that the same force which is maintained to suppress insurrections, and to repel invasions, may often be employed to subvert and destroy the liberties of the people.

The same improvements in society, which give rise to the maintenance
of standing forces, are usually attended with similar changes in the manner
of distributing justice. It has been already observed that, in a large community, which has made but little progress in the arts, every chief or baron
is the judge over his own tribe, and the king, with the assistance of his great
council, exercises a jurisdiction over the members of different tribes or baronies. From the small number of law-suits which occur in the ages of poverty and rudeness, and from the rapidity, with which they are usually determined among a warlike and ignorant people, the office of a judge
demands little attention, and occasions no great interruption to those pursuits in which a man of rank and distinction is common-<226>ly engaged.
The sovereign and the nobility, therefore, in such a situation, may continue
to hold this office, though, in their several courts, they should appoint a
deputy-judge to assist them in discharging the duties of it. But when the
increase of opulence has given encouragement to a variety of tedious liti-
gation, they become unwilling to bestow the necessary time in hearing
causes, and are therefore induced to devolve the whole business upon inferior judges, who acquire by degrees the several branches of the judicial

power, and are obliged to hold regular courts for the benefit of the inhabitants. Thus the exercise of jurisdiction becomes a separate employment,
and is committed to an order of men, who require a particular education
to qualify them for the duties of their office, and who, in return for their
service, must therefore be enabled to earn a livelihood by their profession.

A provision for the maintenance of judges is apt, from the natural course
of things, to grow out of their employment; as, in order to procure an
indemnification for their attendance, they have an opportunity of exacting
fees from the parties who come before them. This is analogous to what
happens with respect to every sort of manufacture, in which an artificer is
commonly paid by those who employ him. We find, accordingly, that this
was the early practice in all the feudal courts of Europe, and that perquisites
drawn by the judges, in different tribunals, yielded a considerable revenue
both <227> to the king and the nobles. It is likely that similar customs, in
this respect, have been adopted in most parts of the world, by nations in
the same period of their advancement. The impropriety, however, of giving
a permission to these exactions, which tend to influence the decisions of a
judge, to render him active in stirring up law-suits, and in multiplying the
forms of his procedure, in order to increase his perquisites; these pernicious
consequences with which it is inseparably connected, could not fail to at-
tract the notice of a polished people, and at length produced the more
perfect plan of providing for the maintenance of judges by the appointment of a fixed salary in place of their former precarious emoluments.

It cannot be doubted that these establishments, of such mighty importance, and of so extensive a nature, must be the source of great expence to
the public. In those early periods, when the inhabitants of a country are in
a condition to defend themselves, and when their internal disputes are decided by judges who claim no reward for their interpositions, or at least no
reward from government, few regulations are necessary with respect to the
public revenue. The king is enabled to maintain his family, and to support
his dignity, by the rents of his own estate; and, in ordinary cases, he has no
farther demand. But when the disuse of the ancient militia has been succeeded by the practice of hiring troops, these original funds are no longer
<228> sufficient; and other resources must be provided in order to supply
the deficiency. By the happy disposition of human events, the very circum-

stance that occasions this difficulty appears also to suggest the means of removing it. When the bulk of a people become unwilling to serve in war, they are naturally disposed to offer a composition in order to be excused from that ancient personal service which, from long custom, it is thought they are bound to perform. Compositions of this nature are levied at first, in consequence of an agreement with each individual: to avoid the trouble arising from a multiplicity of separate transactions, they are afterwards paid in common by the inhabitants of particular districts, and at length give rise to a general *assessment,* the first considerable taxation that is commonly introduced into a country.

If this tax could always be laid upon the people in proportion to their circumstances, it might easily be augmented in such a manner as to defray all the expences of government. But the difficulty of ascertaining the wealth of individuals makes it impossible to push the assessment to a great height, without being guilty of oppression, and renders it proper that other methods of raising money should be employed to answer the increasing demands of the society. In return for the protection which is given to merchants in carrying their goods from one country to another, it is apprehended that some recompence is due to the government, and that certain duties < 229 > may be levied upon the exportation and importation of commodities. The security enjoyed by tradesmen and manufacturers, from the care and vigilance of the magistrate, is held also to lay a foundation for similar exactions upon the retail of goods, and upon the inland trade of a nation. Thus the payment of *customs,* and of what, in a large sense, may be called *excise,* is introduced and gradually extended.

It is not proposed to enter into a comparison of these different taxes, or to consider the several advantages and disadvantages of each. Their general effects in altering the political constitution of a state are more immediately the object of the present enquiry. With respect to this point, it merits attention that, as the sovereign claims a principal share at least, in the nomination of public officers, as he commonly obtains the chief direction in collecting and disposing of the revenue which is raised upon their account, he is enabled thereby to give subsistence to a great number of persons, who, in times of faction and disorder, will naturally adhere to his party, and whose interest, in ordinary cases, will be employed to support and to extend his authority. These circumstances contribute to strengthen the hands of the monarch, to undermine and destroy every opposite power, and to increase the general bias towards the absolute dominion of a single person. <230>

Other circumstances, which contribute to advance the
privileges of the people.

After viewing those effects of opulence and the progress of arts which favour the interest of the crown, let us turn our attention to other circumstances, proceeding from the same source, that have an opposite tendency,
and are manifestly conducive to a popular form of government.

In that early period of agriculture when manufactures are unknown,
persons who have no landed estate are usually incapable of procuring subsistence otherwise than by serving some opulent neighbour, by whom they
are employed, according to their qualifications, either in military service,
or in the several branches of husbandry. Men of great fortune find that the
entertaining a multitude of servants, for either of these purposes, is highly
conducive both to their dignity and their personal security; and in a rude
age, when people are strangers to luxury, and are maintained from the simple productions of the earth, the number of retainers who may be supported upon any particular estate is proportionably great.

In this situation, persons of low rank, have no opportunity of acquiring
an affluent fortune, or of <231> raising themselves to superior stations; and
remaining for ages in a state of dependence, they naturally contract such
dispositions and habits as are suited to their circumstances. They acquire a
sacred veneration for the person of their master, and are taught to pay an
unbounded submission to his authority. They are proud of that servile obedience by which they seem to exalt his dignity, and consider it as their duty
to sacrifice their lives and their possessions in order to promote his interest,
or even to gratify his capricious humour.

But when the arts begin to be cultivated in a country, the labouring part
of the inhabitants are enabled to procure subsistence in a different manner.

They are led to make proficiency in particular trades and professions; and, instead of becoming servants to any body, they often find it more profitable to work at their own charges, and to vend the product of their labour. As in this situation their gain depends upon a variety of customers, they have little to fear from the displeasure of any single person; and, according to the good quality and cheapness of the commodity which they have to dispose of, they may commonly be assured of success in their business.

The farther a nation advances in opulence and refinement, it has occasion to employ a greater number of merchants, of tradesmen and artificers; and as the lower people, in general, become thereby more independent in their circumstances, they be-<232>gin to exert those sentiments of liberty which are natural to the mind of man, and which necessity alone is able to subdue. In proportion as they have less need of the favour and patronage of the great, they are at less pains to procure it; and their application is more uniformly directed to acquire those talents which are useful in the exercise of their employments. The impressions which they received in their former state of servitude are therefore gradually obliterated, and give place to habits of a different nature. The long attention and perseverance, by which they become expert and skilful in their business, render them ignorant of those decorums and of that politeness which arises from the intercourse of society; and that vanity which was formerly discovered in magnifying the power of a chief, is now equally displayed in sullen indifference, or in contemptuous and insolent behaviour to persons of superior rank and station.

While, from these causes, people of low rank are gradually advancing towards a state of independence, the influence derived from wealth is diminished in the same proportion. From the improvement of arts and manufactures, the ancient simplicity of manners is in a great measure destroyed; and the proprietor of a landed estate, instead of consuming its produce in hiring retainers, is obliged to employ a great part of it in purchasing those comforts and conveniencies which have become objects of attention, and which are thought suitable to his <233> condition. Thus while fewer persons are under the necessity of depending upon him, he is daily rendered less capable of maintaining dependents; till at last his domestics and servants are reduced to such as are merely subservient to luxury and pageantry, but are of no use in supporting his authority.

From the usual effects of luxury and refinement, it may at the same time be expected that old families will often be reduced to poverty and beggary. In a refined and luxurious nation those who are born to great affluence, and who have been bred to no business, are excited, with mutual emulation, to surpass one another in the elegance and refinement of their living. According as they have the means of indulging themselves in pleasure, they become more addicted to the pursuit of it, and are sunk in a degree of indolence and dissipation which renders them incapable of any active employment. Thus the expence of the landed gentleman is apt to be continually increasing, without any proportional addition to his income. His estate, therefore, being more and more incumbered with debts, is at length alienated, and brought into the possession of the frugal and industrious merchant, who, by success in trade, has been enabled to buy it, and who is desirous of obtaining that rank and consequence which landed property is capable of bestowing. The posterity, however, of this new proprietor, having adopted <234> the manners of the landed gentry, are again led, in a few generations, to squander their estate, with a heedless extravagance equal to the parsimony and activity by which it was acquired.

This fluctuation of property, so observable in all commercial countries, and which no prohibitions are capable of preventing, must necessarily weaken the authority of those who are placed in the higher ranks of life. Persons who have lately attained to riches, have no opportunity of establishing that train of dependence which is maintained by those who have remained for ages at the head of a great estate. The hereditary influence of family is thus, in a great measure, destroyed; and the consideration derived from wealth is often limited to what the possessor can acquire during his own life. Even this too, for the reasons formerly mentioned, is greatly diminished. A man of great fortune having dismissed his retainers, and spending a great part of his income in the purchase of commodities produced by tradesmen and manufacturers, has no ground to expect that many persons will be willing either to fight for him, or to run any great hazard for promoting his interest. Whatever profit he means to obtain from the labour and assistance of others, he must give a full equivalent for it. He must buy those personal services which are no longer to be performed either from attachment or from peculiar connexions. Money, therefore, becomes more and more the only means of procuring <235> honours and dignities; and the sordid pursuits of avarice are made subservient to the nobler purposes of ambition.

It cannot be doubted that these circumstances have a tendency to introduce a democratical government. As persons of inferior rank are placed in a situation which, in point of subsistence, renders them little dependent upon their superiors; as no one order of men continues in the exclusive possession of opulence; and as every man who is industrious may entertain the hope of gaining a fortune; it is to be expected that the prerogatives of the monarch and of the ancient nobility will be gradually undermined, that the privileges of the people will be extended in the same proportion, and that power, the usual attendant of wealth, will be in some measure diffused over all the members of the community.[1] <236>

---

1. This paragraph and the one preceding it are perhaps the most succinct description to be found in eighteenth-century political theory of the growth of commerce and opulence, and of the subsequent democratization and breakdown of static hierarchies of ranks. But as is apparent from the next section, Millar thought that opulence in large nations tended to give more power to the sovereign than to the people.

SECTION III

Result of the opposition between
these different principles.

So widely different are the effects of opulence and refinement, which, at the same time that they furnish the king with a standing army, the great engine of tyranny and oppression, have also a tendency to inspire the people with notions of liberty and independence. It may thence be expected that a conflict will arise between these two opposite parties, in which a variety of accidents may contribute to cast the balance upon either side.

With respect to the issue of such a contest, it may be remarked that, in a small state, the people have been commonly successful in their efforts to establish a free constitution. When a state consists only of a small territory, and the bulk of the inhabitants live in one city, they have frequently occasion to converse together, and to communicate their sentiments upon every subject of importance. Their attention therefore is roused by every instance of oppression in the government; and as they easily take the alarm, so they are capable of quickly uniting their forces in order to demand redress of their grievances. By repeated experiments they become sensible of their strength, and <237> are enabled by degrees to enlarge their privileges, and to assume a greater share of the public administration.

In large and extensive nations, the struggles between the sovereign and his people are, on the contrary, more likely to terminate in favour of despotism. In a wide country, the encroachments of the government are frequently overlooked; and, even when the indignation of the people has been roused by flagrant injustice, they find it difficult to combine in uniform and vigorous measures for the defence of their rights. It is also difficult, in a great nation, to bring out the militia with that quickness which is requisite in case of a sudden invasion; and it becomes necessary, even before the country has been much civilized, to maintain such a body of mercenaries as is capable of supporting the regal authority.

It is farther to be considered that the revenue of the monarch is commonly a more powerful engine of authority in a great nation than in a small one. The influence of a sovereign seems to depend, not so much upon his absolute wealth, as upon the proportion which it bears to that of the other members of the community. So far as the estate of the king does not exceed that of the richest of his subjects, it is no more than sufficient to supply the ordinary expence of living, in a manner suitable to the splendour and dignity of the crown; and it is only the surplus of that estate which can be di-<238>rectly applied to the purposes of creating dependence. In this view the public revenue of the king will be productive of greater influence according to the extent and populousness of the country in which it is raised. Suppose in a country, like that of ancient Attica, containing about twenty thousand inhabitants, the people were, by assessment or otherwise, to pay at the rate of twenty shillings each person, this would produce only twenty thousand pounds; a revenue that would probably not exalt the chief magistrate above many private citizens. But in a kingdom, containing ten millions of people, the taxes, being paid in the same proportion, would in all probability render the estate of the monarch superior to the united wealth of many hundreds of the most opulent individuals. In these two cases, therefore, the disproportion of the armies maintained in each kingdom should be greater than that of their respective revenues; and if in the one, the king was enabled to maintain two hundred and fifty thousand men, he would, in the other, be incapable of supporting the expence of five hundred. It is obvious, however, that even five hundred regular and well disciplined troops will not strike the same terror into twenty thousand people, that will be created, by an army of two hundred and fifty thousand, over a nation composed of ten millions.

Most of the ancient republics, with which we are acquainted, appeared to have owed their liberty <239> to the narrowness of their territories. From the small number of people, and from the close intercourse among all the individuals in the same community, they imbibed a spirit of freedom even before they had made considerable progress in arts; and they found means to repress or abolish the power of their petty princes, before their effeminacy or industry had introduced the practice of maintaining mercenary troops.

The same observation is applicable to the modern states of Italy, who, after the decay of the western empire, began to flourish in trade, and among whom a republican form of government was early established.

In France, on the other hand, the introduction of a great mercenary army, during the administration of Cardinal Richelieu, which was necessary for the defence of the country, enabled the monarch to establish a despotical power. In the beginning of the reign of Lewis XIII. was called the last convention of the states general which has ever been held in that country: and the monarch has, from that period, been accustomed to exercise almost all the different powers of government. Similar effects have arisen from the establishment of standing forces in most of the great kingdoms of Europe.

The fortunate situation of Great Britain, after the accession of James I. gave her little to fear from any foreign invasion, and superseded the ne- <240>cessity of maintaining a standing army, when the service of the feudal militia had gone into disuse. The weakness and bigotry of her monarchs, at that period, prevented them from employing the only expedient capable of securing an absolute authority. Charles I. saw the power exercised, about this time, by the other princes of Europe; but he did not discover the means by which it was obtained. He seems to have been so much convinced of his divine indefeasible right as, at first, to think that no force was necessary, and afterwards, that every sort of duplicity was excuseable, in support of it. When at the point of a rupture with his parliament, he had no military force upon which he could depend; and he was therefore obliged to yield to the growing power of the commons.

The boldness and dexterity, joined to the want of public spirit, and the perfidy of Oliver Cromwell, rendered abortive the measures of that party, of which he obtained the direction; but the blood that had been shed, and the repeated efforts that were made by the people in defence of their privileges, cherished and spread the love of liberty, and at last produced a popular government, after the best model, perhaps, which is practicable in an extensive country.

Many writers appear to take pleasure in remarking that, as the love of

liberty is natural to man, it is to be found in the greatest perfection among
<241> barbarians, and is apt to be impaired according as people make pro-
gress in civilization and in the arts of life. That mankind, in the state of
mere savages, are in great measure unacquainted with government, and unaccustomed to any sort of constraint, is sufficiently evident. But their independence, in that case, is owing to the wretchedness of their circumstances, which afford nothing that can tempt any one man to become
subject to another. The moment they have quitted the primitive situation,
and, by endeavouring to supply their natural wants, have been led to accumulate property, they are presented with very different motives of action,
and acquire a new set of habits and principles. In those rude ages when the
inhabitants of the earth are divided into tribes of shepherds, or of husbandmen, the usual distribution of property renders the bulk of the people
dependent upon a few chiefs, to whom fidelity and submission becomes
the principal point of honour, and makes a distinguishing part of the national character. The ancient Germans, whose high notions of freedom
have been the subject of many a well-turned period, were accustomed, as
we learn from Tacitus, to stake their persons upon the issue of a game of
hazard, and after an unlucky turn of fortune, to yield themselves up to a
voluntary servitude. Whereever men of inferior condition are enabled to
live in affluence by their own industry, and, in procuring their livelihood,
have little occasion to court <242> the favour of their superiors, there we
may expect that ideas of liberty will be universally diffused. This happy
arrangement of things is naturally produced by commerce and manufactures; but it would be as vain to look for it in the uncultivated parts of the
world, as to look for the independent spirit of an English waggoner among
persons of low rank in the highlands of Scotland. <243>

The Authority of a Master
over His Servants

SECTION I

The condition of Servants in the primitive ages of the world.

In the foregoing chapters we have surveyed the principal distinctions of rank which occur among the free inhabitants of a country, and have endeavoured to mark the progress of society, with regard to the power of the husband, the father, and the civil magistrate. It may now be proper to consider the state of the servants, and to observe the degrees of authority which the laws and customs of different nations have bestowed upon the master.

From the situation of mankind in rude and barbarous countries, we may easily conceive in what manner any one person is, at first, reduced to be the servant of another. Before the manners of men are civilized, and a regular government has been established, persons of small fortune are subject to great inconveniencies from the disorder and violence of the times, and are frequently obliged to solicit the assistance and protection of some <244> powerful neighbour, by whom they are entertained in the station of vassals or military dependents. But those who, from their idleness, have acquired nothing, or who, by accident, have been deprived of their possessions, are necessarily exposed to much more severe calamities. They have no room or encouragement for the exercise of those beneficial trades and professions, the effects of luxury and refinement, by which, in a polished nation, a multitude of people are enabled to live in a comfortable manner. In many cases, therefore, they are under the necessity of serving some opulent person, who, upon account of their labour, is willing to maintain them; and as they are entirely dependent upon him for their subsistence, they are engaged, according to his circumstances, and according to the qualifications they possess, in all the mean and servile occupations which may be requisite for the convenience and support of his family.

In early ages, when neighbouring tribes or nations are almost continually engaged in mutual hostilities, it frequently happens that one of the parties is totally reduced under the power of another. The use that is made of a victory, upon these occasions, is such as might be expected from a fierce and barbarous people, who have too little experience or reflection to discover the utility of carrying on the trade of war with some degree of humanity. The vanquished are often put to death, <245> in order to gratify a spirit of revenge; or, if they are spared, it is only from the consideration that their future labour and service will be of more advantage to the conqueror. As in those times every individual goes out to battle at his own charges, so he claims a proportional share of the profits arising from the expedition; and of consequence obtains the absolute disposal of the captives whom he has procured by his valour, or who, in a division of the booty, are bestowed upon him as the reward of his merit.

This ancient acquisition of servants by *captivity* gave rise, in subsequent periods, to another method of acquiring them, by the *sentence of a judge*. In the primitive state of society, the public was not invested with sufficient power to punish the crimes that were committed; and when a difference arose between individuals, the injured party had frequently no other way of procuring redress than by making war upon the offender, and reducing him into captivity. In more civilized ages, when the magistrate was enabled to restrain these disorders, he sometimes afforded the same redress by his own authority, and assigned the labour and service of the criminal as an indemnification to the sufferer for the loss he had sustained.

By these three methods, by captivity, by the voluntary submission of the indigent, or by the sentence of a judge, many are reduced into a state of unlimited subjection, and become the servants of <246> those who are opulent and prosperous.[1] It may be questioned, in such a case, how far a person is entitled to make use of that power which fortune has put into his hands. It is difficult to ascertain the degree of authority which, from the principles of justice and humanity, we are, in any situation, permitted to assume over our fellow-creatures. But the fact admits of no question, that people have commonly been disposed to use their power in such a manner as appears most conducive to their interest, and most agreeable to their predominant passions. It is natural to suppose that the master would set no bounds to his prerogative over those unhappy persons who, from their circumstances, were under the necessity of yielding an implicit obedience to his commands. He forced them to labour as much, and gave them as little in return for it, as possible. When he found them negligent of their employment, he bestowed upon them such correction as he thought proper; and, actuated by the boisterous dispositions of a savage, he was in some cases provoked to chastise them with a degree of severity, by which they might even be deprived of their life. When he had no use for their work, or when a good opportunity was presented, he endeavoured by a sale to dispose of them to the highest advantage. When he chose to increase the number of his servants, he sometimes encouraged and directed their multiplication; and the same authority which he exercised over the parents was <247> extended to their offspring, whom he had been at the trouble of rearing, and who were equally dependent upon him for their subsistence.

To be a servant, therefore, in those primitive times, was almost universally the same thing as to be a slave. The master assumed an unlimited jurisdiction over his servants, and the privilege of selling them at pleasure. He gave them no wages beside their maintenance; and he allowed them to have no property, but claimed to his own use whatever, by their labour or by any other means, they happened to acquire.

Thus the practice of domestic slavery appears to have been early established among the nations of antiquity; among the Egyptians, the

1. Smith presented five different ways of acquiring slaves in his lectures (LJ [A] iii.145–47), all of which fit into Millar's neater threefold division.

Phoenicians, the Jews, the Babylonians, the Persians, the Greeks, and the Romans.

The same practice obtains at present among all those tribes of barbarians, in different parts of the world, with which we have any correspondence.

There are indeed but few slaves among the greater part of the savages of America; because, from the situation of that people, they have no opportunity of accumulating wealth for maintaining any number of servants. As, in ordinary cases, they find it burdensome to give subsistence to an enemy whom they have subdued, they are accustomed to indulge their natural ferocity by putting him to death, even in cold blood. If ever they behave with humanity to their captives, it is only when, <248> being greatly reduced by the calamities of war, or by uncommon accidents, they are under the immediate necessity of recruiting their strength; and as this rarely happens, the persons whose lives have been thus preserved, are not distinguished from the children of the family into which they are brought, but are formally adopted into the place of the deceased relations, whose loss they are intended to supply.*

The Tartars, on the other hand, who have great possessions in herds and flocks, find no difficulty in supporting a number of domestics. For this reason they commonly preserve their captives, with a view of reaping the benefit that may arise from their labour; and the servitude established among that people disposes them to treat their enemies with a degree of moderation, which otherwise could hardly be expected from their fierce and barbarous dispositions.†

The same observation may be extended to the negroes upon the coast of Guinea, who, from their intercourse with the nations of Europe, derive yet greater advantages from sparing the lives of their <249> enemies. At the same time it cannot be doubted, that, as the encounters of those bar-

---

* These captives are worse treated by some of the American nations than by others; but in fact they are always retained in the condition of slaves. See Lafitau, Moeurs de Sauvages Ameriquains, 4to. tom. 2. p. 308.

† See the accounts which are given of the conquests made by Genghizkhan. Histoire generale des voyages, tom. 9. liv. 3. chap. 3. § 11.

barians have upon this account become less bloody, their wars have been rendered more frequent. From the great demand for slaves to supply the European market, they have the same motives to seize the person of their neighbours, which may excite the inhabitants of other countries to rob one another of their property.* <250>

* Histoire generale des voyages, tom. 3. 4. 5.

The usual effects of opulence and civilized manners,
with regard to the treatment of Servants.

These institutions and customs are such as might be expected from the limited experience, as well as from the rude manners of an early age. By reducing his servants into a state of slavery, the master appears, at first sight, to reap the highest advantage from their future labour and service. But when a people become civilized, and when they have made considerable progress in commerce and manufactures, one would imagine they should entertain more liberal views, and be influenced by more extensive considerations of utility.

A slave, who receives no wages in return for his labour, can never be supposed to exert much vigour or activity in the exercise of any employment. He obtains a livelihood at any rate; and by his utmost assiduity he is able to procure no more. As he works merely in consequence of the terror in which he is held, it may be imagined that he will be idle as often as he can with impunity. This circumstance may easily be overlooked in a country where the inhabitants are strangers to improvement. But when the arts begin to flourish, when the wonderful effects of industry and skill in cheapening commodities, and in bringing them <251> to perfection, become more and more conspicuous, it must be evident that little profit can be drawn from the labour of a slave, who has neither been encouraged to acquire that dexterity, nor those habits of application, which are essentially requisite in the finer and more difficult branches of manufacture.

This may be illustrated from the price of labour in our West-India islands, where it will not be doubted that the inhabitants are at great pains to prevent the idleness of their slaves. In Jamaica, the yearly labour of a field-negro, when he is upheld to the master, is rated at no more than nine pounds, currency of that island. When a negro has been instructed in the trade of a carpenter, the value of his yearly labour will amount at the utmost to thirty-six pounds; whereas a free man is capable of earning seventy pounds yearly in the very same employment.* <252>

It is further to be observed, that, in a polished nation, the acquisition of slaves is commonly much more expensive than among a simple and barbarous people.

After a regular government has been established, the inhabitants of a country are restrained from plundering one another; and, under the authority of the magistrate, individuals of the lowest rank are sufficiently secured from oppression and injustice. In proportion to the improvement of commerce and manufactures, the demand for labour is increased, and greater encouragement is given to industry. The poor have more resources for procuring a livelihood, by such employments as are productive of little subjection or dependence. By degrees, therefore, people of inferior condition are freed from the necessity of becoming slaves in order to obtain subsistence; and the ancient agreement by which a free person resigned his liberty, and was reduced under the power of a master, being rendered more and more unusual, is at length regarded as inconsistent with the natural rights of a citizen.

---

* In North America, where slaves are said to be much better treated than in the West-India islands, it is believed, the expence of a negro-slave, for common labour, is not much inferior to that of a free labourer. In the Jerseys, and in New York, the expence of a negro-slave may be stated as follows:

The original price, about 100 l. currency, for which double interest allowed, at 7 *per cent.*	£ 14
Yearly expence of clothing	6
For medicines. &c.	3
For maintenance	15
In all	£. 38 yearly.

A free labourer, in those provinces, when hired by the year, receives from 24 l. to 30 l. yearly; to which may be added 15 l. for maintenance. And in balancing this account we must take in the risk that the negro, when purchased, may not be fit for the purpose, and that his labour may be of little value.

Thus among the Romans, during the common-<253>wealth, and even under the emperors, no free citizen was allowed, by contract, to become the slave of another.* It was consistent with the refined laws of that people, which rescinded those unequal contracts where one party had gained an undue advantage, or even obtained an unreasonable profit at the expence of the other, to declare that a bargain by which a man surrendered all his rights to a master, and consequently received nothing in return, should have no support or encouragement from the civil magistrate.

As men begin to experience the happy effects of cultivating the arts of peace, and are less frequently employed in acts of hostility, they have less occasion to acquire any number of slaves by captivity. The influence of civilization upon the temper and dispositions of a people has at the same time a tendency to produce a total revolution in the manner of conducting their military operations. That ancient institution, by which every one who is able to bear arms is required to appear in the field at his own charges, becomes too heavy a burden upon those who are enervated with pleasure, or engaged in lucrative professions; and the custom of employing mercenary troops in defence of <254> the country is therefore gradually established. As an army of this kind is maintained by the government; as the soldiers receive constant pay, which is understood to be a full equivalent for their service; they appear to have no title to the extraordinary emoluments arising from the spoil of the enemy; and therefore the captives, though reduced into servitude, are no longer held as belonging to those particular persons by whom they have been subdued, but to the public, at whose expence and hazard the war is supported.†

We may take notice of a similar change in the acquisition of slaves by the sentence of a judge. In rude times, the chief aim of punishment was

---

* See Hein. Ant. Rom. lib. l. tit. 5. §. 6. This regulation, however, admitted of an exception, where a man fraudulently suffered himself to be sold in order to share in the price; in which case he became the slave of the person whom he had defrauded. L. 3 Dig. quib. ad libert. proclam. non licet. [[XL. 13 Quibus ad libertatem proclamare non licet.]]

† It is accordingly held, in the later Roman law, that a soldier is entitled to no part of the plunder acquired in war, unless from the special donation of the emperor. L. 20. §. 1. Dig. de capt. et postl. [[*Digest* XLIX.15 "De Captivis et de postliminio et redemptis ab hostibus."]] l. 36. §. 1. c. de donat. [[*Digest* XXXIX.5 "De donationibus."]]

to gratify the resentment of the private party: and if a person accused of a crime had been found guilty, he was, for that reason, frequently delivered up as a slave to the plaintiff. But upon greater improvement of manners, the interpositions of the magistrate came to be influenced more by considerations of general utility; and as the crimes of individuals were principally considered in the light of offences against the society, it was agreeable to this idea that a criminal should become the slave of the public, and should either be employed in public works, or disposed of in the manner most advantageous to the revenue of the community. <255>

The inhabitants of a civilized country, being thus in a great measure deprived of the primitive modes of acquisition, are obliged to acquire the bulk of their slaves, either by a purchase from their poorer and more barbarous neighbours, or by propagating and rearing from the original stock which they possess. In such a situation, therefore, when we compute the expence attending the labour of a slave, not only the charge of his maintenance, but also the money laid out in the first acquisition, together with all the hazard to which his life is exposed, must necessarily be taken into the account.

When these circumstances are duly considered, it will be found that the work of a slave, who receives nothing but a bare subsistence, is really dearer than that of a free man, to whom constant wages are given in proportion to his industry.[2]

Unhappily, men have seldom been in a condition to examine this point with proper attention, and with sufficient impartiality. The practice of slavery being introduced in an early age, is afterwards regarded with that blind prepossession which is commonly acquired in favour of ancient usages: its inconveniencies are overlooked, and every innovation, with respect to it, is considered as a dangerous measure. The possession of power is too agreeable to be easily relinquished. Few people will venture upon a new experiment; and, amidst the general prejudices of a country, fewer still are ca-<256>pable of making it with fairness. We find, accordingly, that this institution, however inconsistent with the rights of humanity, however per-

2. This passage, and much of the argument following it, parallels Smith's "economic" argument against slavery in LJ (A) iii.112–17, LJ (B) 138, and *Wealth of Nations*, III.ii.9.

nicious and contrary to the true interest of the master, has generally remained in those countries where it was once established, and has been
handed down from one generation to another, during all the successive
improvements of society, in knowledge, arts, and manufactures.

The advancement of a nation, in these particulars, is even frequently
attended with greater severity in the treatment of the slaves.[3] The simplicity
of early ages admits of little distinction between the master and his servants,
in their employments or manner of living; and though, from the impet-
uosity and violence of his temper, they may, on some occasions, be subjected to hardships, he enjoys no great superiority over them, in their dress,
their lodging, or ordinary entertainment. By the introduction of wealth
and luxury, this equality is gradually destroyed. The various refinements
which tend to multiply the comforts and conveniencies of life; whatever
contributes to ease, to pleasure, to ostentation, or to amusement, is in a
great measure appropriated to the rich and the free, while those who remain
in a state of servitude are retained in their primitive indigence. The slaves
are no longer accustomed to sit at the same table with their master. They
must look upon him as a being of a superior order, whom they are seldom
permitted to approach, <257> and with whom they have hardly any thing
in common; who beholds with indifference the toil and drudgery to which
they are subjected, and from whom they can with difficulty procure a scanty
subsistence.

> Ipse dominus dives operis, et laboris expers,
> Quodcunque homini accidit libère, posse retur:
> Aequom esse putat: non reputat laboris quid sit:
> Nec, aequom anne iniquom imperet, cogitabit.*

---

* Plaut. Amphitr. [[ll. 170–73:

> Your wealthy master who takes no part in wealth nor toil,
> Presumes that whatever happens to occur to a man can be satisfied,
> He reckons that fair and doesn't take account of how much work it is,
> nor will he think whether he orders something fair or unfair.]]

3. "We may observe that the state of slavery is a much more tolerable one in [a] poor
and barbarous country than in a rich and polished one" (Smith, LJ [A] iii.105).

What a painful and humbling comparison, what mortifying reflections does this afford to those wretches who are reduced into a state of bondage! reflections which cannot fail to sour their temper, to inspire them with malevolent dispositions, and to produce an untoward and stubborn behaviour; for it is impossible that man, by any system of management, should be so inured to oppression as, like a beast of burden, to submit entirely to the yoke, and not, on some occasions, to feel and testify resentment against the oppressor. A more severe discipline is thus rendered necessary, to conquer the obstinacy of persons, unwilling to labour in their employments. Besides, from the number of slaves which are usually maintained in a wealthy and luxurious nation, they become formidable to the state; and it is requisite that they should be strictly watched, and kept in the utmost subjection, <258> in order to prevent those desperate attempts to which they are frequently instigated in revenge of their sufferings. This is at least the pretence for that shocking barbarity to which the negroes in our colonies are frequently exposed, and which is exhibited even by persons of the weaker sex, in an age distinguished for humanity and politeness.

The prodigious wealth acquired by the Romans towards the end of the commonwealth, and after the establishment of despotism, gave rise to a degree of cruelty and oppression, in the management of their slaves, which had been unknown in former times.

> —Hic frangit ferulas, rubet ille flagellis,
> Hic scutica: sunt quae tortoribus annua praestant.
> Verberat, atque obiter faciem linit, audit amicas,
> Aut latum pictae vestis considerat aurum,
> Et caedit, donec lassis caedentibus, exi
> Intonet horrendum, jam cognitione peracta:
> Praefectura domus Sicula non mitior aula.*

---

* Juven. Sat. 6. [[479–86: "One will have a rod broken over his back, another will be bleeding from a strap, a third from the cat; some women engage their executioners by the year. While the flogging goes on the lady will be daubing her face, or listening to her lady friends, or inspecting the widths of a gold embroidered robe. While thus flogging and flogging, she reads the lengthy Gazette, written right across the page, till at last, the floggers being exhausted, and the inquisition ended, she thunders out a

It was to be expected, however, that particular enormities of this kind would at length excite the attention of the public, and would be in some <259> measure restrained by the gradual progress of government. Although the institution of slavery was permitted to remain, regulations came to be made, by which the master was prevented from such wanton exercise of his power as must have been highly prejudicial to his interest, and could only be regarded as an absurd abuse of his property.

In the Jewish law, we meet with some regulations for this purpose at an early period.

"If a man smite his servant, or his maid, with a rod, and he die under his hand, he shall surely be punished.

"Notwithstanding, if he continue a day or two, he shall not be punished: for he is his money.

"And if a man smite the eye of his servant, or the eye of his maid, that it perish; he shall let him go free for his eye's sake.

"And if he smite out his man-servant's tooth, or his maid-servant's tooth; he shall let him go free for his tooth's sake."*

At Athens, the slaves who had been barbarously treated by their master were allowed to fly for sanctuary to the temple of Theseus, and to com- <260>mence a suit at law against their master, who, if their complaint appeared well founded, was laid under the necessity of selling them.†

---

gruff, "Be off with you!" Her household is governed as cruelly as a Sicilian court." Ramsay, trans.]]

Vedius Pollio, a Roman citizen, is said to have fed the fishes in his fish-ponds with the flesh of his own slaves. Donat. ad Terentii Phorm. act 2. scen. 1. [[This refers to Aelius Donatus's fourth-century commentary on Terence's comedies, *Commentum Terenti*. The story goes back to Seneca *De Irae* III.40. There are nearly identical citations in LJ (A) iii.92–93, LJ (B) 135, and *Wealth of Nations*, IV.7.77.]]

With regard to the treatment of the Roman slaves, see Mr. Hume's learned essay on the populousness of ancient nations. [["Of the Populousness of Ancient Nations," in *Essays*, 391–94 (II.xi.8–13).]]

* Exodus, chap. xxi. ver. 20, 21, 26, 27. It has been a question whether the last quoted laws, in ver. 26 and 27, related to the slaves acquired from foreign nations, or only to such of the Israelites as had been reduced into a state of servitude. Grotius is of the latter opinion. Vide Grot. com. ad cit. cap. [[Grotius, *Annotationes in Vetus Testamentum*, XXI: 27.]]

† See Potters' Antiquities of Greece, book 1. chap. 10.

Various equitable laws, upon this subject, were made by the Roman emperors. At Rome, the absolute power of the master was first subjected to any limitation in the reign of Augustus, who appointed that the *Praefectus urbi* should afford redress to such of the slaves as had been treated with immoderate severity. In the reign of the emperor Claudius, it was enacted, that if a master abandoned the care of his slaves during their sickness, he should forfeit the property of them; and that if he put them to death, he should be held guilty of homicide. Soon after, the inhuman practice of obliging the slaves to fight with wild beasts, which was carried to a prodigious height, and which appears to have afforded a favourite entertainment to men of all ranks, was in some measure restrained. Other statutes were afterwards made, in the reigns of Adrian, of Antoninus Pius, and of Constantine, by which it was finally established, that the master who killed his own slave by design, and not from the accidental excess of chastisement, should suffer the ordinary punishment of murder.* <261>

* Vide Hein. antiq. Rom. lib. 1. tit. 8.

SECTION III

Causes of the freedom acquired by the labouring people in the modern nations of Europe.

By what happy concurrence of events has the practice of slavery been so generally abolished in Europe? By what powerful motives were our fore-fathers induced to deviate from the maxims of other nations, and to abandon a custom so generally retained in other parts of the world?

The northern barbarians, who laid the foundation of the present European states, are said to have possessed a number of slaves, obtained either by captivity or by voluntary submission, and over whom the master enjoyed an unlimited authority.* <262>

* The following account is given by Tacitus, concerning the state of the slaves among the ancient Germans, "Aleam," says he, speaking of that people, "sobrii inter seria exercent, tanta lucrandi perdendique temeritate ut cum omnia defecerunt, extremo ac novissimo jactu, de libertate, et de corpore contendant. Victus voluntariam servitutem adit. Quamvis junior, quamvis robustior, alligare se ac venire patitur; ea est in re prava pervicacia: ipsi fidem vocant: servos conditionis hujus per commercia tradunt, ut se quoque pudore victoriae exsolvant. [["Surprisingly, gambling for them is a serious matter, in which they engage when sober; so recklessly do they win and lose that when all is gone they stake their bodily freedom on the last and final throw. The loser willingly becomes a slave; although perhaps the younger and stronger, he suffers himself to be bound and sold. Such is their persistence in a thoroughly bad business: they themselves call it honour. Slaves of this sort they exchange in trade, to free themselves from the shame of victory" (XXIV.2, Rives, trans.).]]

"Ceteris servis, non in nostrum morem descriptis per familiam ministeriis, utuntur. Suam quisque sedem, suos penates regit. Frumenti modum dominus, ut colono injungit: et servus hactenus paret. Cetera domus officia, uxor ac liberi exsequuntur. Verberare servum, ac vinculis et opere coercere rarum. Occidere solent, non disciplina et severitate, sed impetu et ira, ut inimicum, nisi quod impune."[["The other slaves they do not use as we do, with designated duties throughout the household; each one controls his own holding and home. The master requires from him, as from a tenant, some amount of

When these nations invaded the Roman empire, and settled in the different provinces, they were enabled by their repeated victories to procure an immense number of captives, whom they reduced into servitude, and by whose assistance they occupied landed estates of proportionable extent. From the simple manner of living to which those barbarians had been accustomed, their domestic business was usually performed by the members of each family; and their servants, for the most part, were employed in cultivating their lands.

It appears that, upon the settlement of these invaders in the Roman empire, no immediate change was produced in their notions with respect to slavery, and that the slaves which they gradually acquired by the success of their arms were, at first, in the same condition with those which they had anciently possessed. The master exercised an unlimited power of chastising them, and might even put them to death with impunity. They were liable to be alienated, or impledged by the master at pleasure, and were incapable, either of marrying, or of entering into any other contract, without his consent. They were so much his property, that he might claim them from every possessor, by the ordinary action which was given for the recovery <263> of his goods; and in consequence of this, it was held they could have no civil rights; so that whatever was acquired by their labour belonged to the master, from whom they usually received nothing but a precarious subsistence. In a public capacity, the people of this class were viewed in a light no less humiliating; they enjoyed none of the privileges of a citizen, and were seldom permitted to give evidence against a free man in a court of justice.*

The situation, however, of these bond-men, and the nature of the employment in which they were usually engaged, had a tendency to procure them a variety of privileges from their master, by which, in a course of ages, their condition was rendered more comfortable, and they were advanced to higher degrees of consideration and rank.

---

grain or livestock or clothing, and only so far must the slave submit; the wife and children perform the other domestic chores. Seldom do they beat a slave or punish him: not through hard discipline, but in a fit of rage as they would a foe, except that the deed is unpunished" (XXV.1, Rives, trans.).]] Tacit. de mor. German. § 24, 25.

* Potgiesserus de statu servorum, lib. 2. cap. 1, 3, 4, 5, 9. Ibid. cap. 10. § 3, 7, 8. Ibid. lib. 3. § 1, 3.

As the peasants belonging to a single person could not be conveniently maintained in his house, so in order to cultivate his lands to advantage, it was necessary that they should be sent to a distance, and have a fixed residence in different parts of his estate. Separate habitations were therefore assigned them; and particular farms were committed to the care of individuals, who from their residing in the neighbourhood of one another, and forming small villages or hamlets, received the appellation of "villains." <264>

It may easily be imagined that, in those circumstances, the proprietor of a large estate could not oversee the behaviour of his servants, living in separate families, and scattered over the wide extent of his demesnes; and it was in vain to think of compelling them to labour by endeavouring to chastise them upon account of their idleness. A very little experience would show that no efforts of that kind could be effectual; and that the only means of exciting the industry of the peasants would be to offer them a reward for the work which they performed. Thus, beside the ordinary maintenance allotted to the slaves, they frequently obtained a small gratuity, which, by custom, was gradually converted into a regular hire; and, being allowed the enjoyment and disposal of that subject, they were at length understood to be capable of having separate property.

After the master came to reside at a distance from the bulk of his servants, and had embraced the salutary policy of bribing them, instead of using compulsion, in order to render them active in their employment, he was less apt to be provoked by their negligence; and as he had seldom occasion to treat them with severity, the ancient dominion which he exercised over their lives was at length entirely lost by disuse.

When a slave had been for a long time engaged in a particular farm, and had become acquainted with that particular culture which it required, he <265> was so much the better qualified to continue in the management of it for the future; and it was contrary to the interest of the master that he should be removed to another place, or employed in labour of a different kind. By degrees, therefore, the peasants were regarded as belonging to the stock upon the ground, and came to be uniformly disposed of as a part of the estate which they had been accustomed to cultivate.

As these changes were gradual, it is difficult to ascertain the precise period at which they were completed. The continual disorders which prevailed in the western part of Europe, for ages after it was first over-run by the German nations, prevented for a long time the progress of arts among the new inhabitants. It was about the twelfth century that a spirit of improvement, in several European countries, became somewhat conspicuous; and it may be considered as a mark of that improvement, with respect to agriculture, that about this time, the villains had obtained considerable privileges; that the master's power over their life was then understood to be extinguished; that the chastisement to which they had been formerly subjected was become more moderate; and that they were generally permitted to acquire separate property.* <266>

The effect of the foregoing circumstances is even observable in the history of the Greeks and Romans, among whom the peasants were raised to a better condition than the rest of their slaves. They were indeed bound to serve the proprietor during life, and might have been sold along with the ground upon which they were employed; but their persons were not subject to the absolute jurisdiction of their master; they had the privilege of marrying without his consent; they received wages in return for their labour, and were understood to have a full right of property in whatever goods their industry had enabled them to accumulate.†

It should seem, however, that the limited territory possessed by these ancient nations prevented the farther extension of the privileges bestowed upon their peasants: seven acres were originally the utmost extent of landed property which a Roman citizen was permitted to enjoy; a portion which he was able to cultivate with his own hands, or with no other assistance but

---

* Potgiesserus de statu serv. lib. 2. cap. 1. § 24. A singular proof of the moderation of the masters in correcting their slaves, about this period, is mentioned by the same author, as follows:

"Quae tamen coercitio aliquando eo modo emollita fuit, ut servi non nisi fustibus crassitiem et latitudinem unius veru adaequantibus coercerentur, sicuti in codice membranaceo Werdinensi vetusto me observasse reminiscor." Ibid. [["Indeed punishment was lessened at some time in such a way, that slaves were not punished unless by a cudgel the thickness and breadth of one spear, thus I remember to have noted in the ancient vellum codex of Werdensis."]]

† Vide Hein. antiq. Rom. lib. 1. tit. 3. § 8.—1. un cod. de colon. Thrac. 1. 21. [[*Codex* XI.52 "De colonis Thracensibus."]] cod. de agric. et censit. novell. 162. cap. 3. [[*Codex* XI.48 "De agricolis censitis vel colonis."]]

that of his own <267> family; and there is reason to believe that, for several centuries, no individual acquired such an estate as gave occasion to his retaining many servants for the management of it, or could render the inspection and government of those whom he employed a matter of great trouble or difficulty.*

But after the wide and populous countries under the Roman dominion were subdued and laid waste by the small tribes of the Germans, very extensive landed estates, together with an adequate number of slaves, were immediately acquired by particular persons. As the people retained their primitive simplicity of manners, and were in a great measure strangers to commerce, these large possessions remained for ages without being dismembered. And thus, during all the successive improvements of agriculture, the proprietor of an estate, embarrassed with the multitude of his villains, was obliged to repose a confidence in them, and came by degrees to discover more clearly the utility of exciting them to industry by the prospect of their own private advantage.

The same motives, by which the master was induced to reward his slaves for their labour, determined him afterwards to increase his bounty in proportion to the work which they performed. Having no opportunity of looking narrowly into their management, he was commonly led to esti- <268> mate their diligence according to their success; and therefore, when they brought him a good crop, he made an addition to their wages, at the same time that he allowed them to expect a suitable compensation for their future labour and economy. This at length gave rise to an express stipulation, that their profits should depend upon the fertility of their different farms, and that, in all cases, they should be permitted to retain a certain share of the produce, in consideration of their labour.

* See Dr. Wallace, on the numbers of mankind. [[Wallace for the most part seems to have argued against the position Millar is advocating; for example, "almost every page of antient history demonstrates the great multitude of slaves; which give occasion to a melancholy reflection, that when the world was best peopled, it was not a world of free men, but of slaves" (92). Wallace generally stressed household slavery (90), and this may be why Millar invokes him here. Hume's "Of the Populousness of Ancient Nations," which Millar cited in the first and second editions of *Ranks* and whom Wallace argued amiably against, seems a much better support for his claim. Cf. Hume, *Essays,* 387–88 (II.ix.13).]]

An expedient so obvious and well calculated for promoting the industry of the peasants, could hardly fail to be generally embraced in all the countries of Europe, as soon as the inhabitants became attentive to the improvement of their estates. The remains of this practice are still to be found in Scotland, where, in some cases, the landlord is accustomed to stock the farm, and the tenant pays him a rent in kind, consisting of a certain proportion of the fruits.*

By this alteration, the villains entered into a sort of copartnership with their master; and having always a prospect of gain, according to the vigour or talents which they exerted, they were enabled to earn a more comfortable subsistence, and were even gradually raised to affluence. The acqui-<269> sition of wealth paved the way to a farther extension of their privileges. Those who had obtained something considerable found themselves in a condition to stock their own farms, and to offer a fixed rent to the master, upon condition of their being allowed to retain the surplus for their own emolument. An agreement of this kind, so advantageous to both parties, was concluded without any difficulty. As the tenant secured to himself the whole profit arising from his industry, the landlord was freed from the hazard of accidental losses, and obtained not only a certain, but frequently an additional revenue from his lands.[4]

Thus, by degrees, the ancient villanage came to be entirely abolished. The peasants, who cultivated their farms at their own charges, and at their own hazard, were of course emancipated from the authority of their master, and could no longer be regarded as in the condition of servants. Their personal subjection was at an end. It was of no consequence to the landlord how they conducted themselves; and, provided they punctually paid his rent, nothing farther could be required of them. There was no reason to insist that they should remain in the farm longer than they pleased; for the profits it afforded made them, commonly, not more willing to leave it than

* The stock which is delivered by the master to his tenant goes under the name of "steel-bow goods" in the law of Scotland. At the end of the lease the tenant is bound to restore the same in quantity and quality to the master. [[See Stair, *Institutions of the Laws of Scotland,* I.11.4. Smith discussed "steel-bow" tenants in LJ (A) iii.123–26, LJ (B) 292–93, and *Wealth of Nations,* III.ii.13–14.]]

4. See Smith, LJ (A) 128–33, LJ (B) 141, and *Wealth of Nations,* III.ii.12.

the proprietor was to put them away. When agriculture became so beneficial a trade, when the state of those who followed that profession had been rendered so comfortable, no <270> person had any difficulty to procure a sufficient number of tenants to labour his estate. It was, on the contrary, sometimes difficult for the farmer to obtain land sufficient for the exercise of his employment; and, after he had been at pains to improve the soil, he was in danger of being dispossessed by the proprietor, before he was indemnified for the trouble and expence which he had sustained. This made it necessary to stipulate that he should be allowed to remain for a certain time in the possession, and gave rise to leases, for a term of years, and even sometimes for life, or for a longer period, according to the circumstances or inclination of the parties.

The modern nations of Europe continued for a long time to be almost entirely unacquainted with manufactures; and, as they had no other slaves but those which were employed in agriculture, the privileges acquired by the villains had therefore a tendency to produce a total extinction of servitude. By degrees, however, as the people began to improve their circumstances, and to multiply the comforts and conveniencies of life, their attention was more and more diverted to other employments. At the same time that the villains were engaged in cultivating the ground, they were also bound to perform any other services which the master thought proper to require, and were often called to assist him in practice of those few mechanical arts which were then understood. Particular persons acquiring a singular dexterity in these occupa-<271>tions, were distinguished upon that account, and came to be more frequently employed than their neighbours. In proportion to the liberty which they enjoyed as peasants, they were enabled with more advantage to prosecute this collateral business; and while they received a reward for the crop which they produced upon their farms, they were not restrained from working, for hire, in that peculiar trade or profession which they were qualified to exercise. As the progress of luxury and refinement multiplied these occupations, and rendered the profits which they afforded superior in many cases to those which were derived from agriculture, individuals were gradually led to quit the latter employment, and to attach themselves entirely to the former. In that state of the country, the children of farmers were frequently bred to manufactures; and a number of tradesmen and artificers, having arisen in different villages, were advanced to consideration and esteem, in proportion as their assistance became more essentially necessary in supplying the wants of mankind. According to the wealth which this new order of men had accumulated, they purchased immunities from their master; and, by permitting him to levy tolls and duties upon their commerce, they were enabled to secure his patronage and protection. Thus the privileges acquired by the peasants appear to have given rise to domestic freedom, which was communicated to the trading part of the inhabitants; while the em-<272> ployment of the latter became, on the other hand, the source of great opulence and contributed, as has been formerly observed, to raise the people of inferior rank to political independence.

Other circumstances may be mentioned, which, in a subordinate manner, have, perhaps, contributed something to this remarkable change of European manners.

The establishment of Christianity has been supposed by many to be the principal circumstance which rooted out the practice of slavery, so universally permitted and encouraged among all the heathen nations. There is no doubt that the spirit of this religion, which considers all mankind as children of the same Father, and as all equally the objects of his paternal care and affection, should inspire them with compassion for the miseries of each other, and should teach the opulent and the proud to consider those who are depressed with labour and penury as creatures of the same species, to treat them with mildness and humanity, and to soften the rigours to which their severe and unequal fortune has unavoidably subjected them. But it does not seem to have been the intention of Christianity to alter the civil rights of mankind, or to abolish those distinctions of rank which were already established. There is no precept of the gospel by which the authority of the master is in any respect restrained or limited; but, on the contrary, there are several passages from which it <273> may be inferred that slaves, even after they had embraced the Christian religion, were not absolved from any part of the duties formerly incumbent upon them.*

---

* Thus Onesimus, notwithstanding his conversion to Christianity, is understood by the apostle Paul to continue still the slave of Philemon [[Onesimus was a runaway slave

We accordingly find that slavery remained all over Europe for several centuries after Christianity became the established religion: not to mention that this institution is still retained in Russia, in Poland, in Hungary, and in several parts of Germany; and that it is at present admitted without limitation, in the colonies which belong to the European nations, whether in Asia, Africa, or America. The Quakers of Pennsylvania, are the first body of men in those countries, who have discovered any scruples upon that account, and who seem to have thought that the abolition of this practice is a duty they owe to religion and humanity.*

It has likewise been imagined that the state of the clergy, their great influence and ambition, to-<274>gether with that opposition between the civil and ecclesiastical powers, which subsisted for a long time in most of the nations of Europe, were favourable to the lower ranks of men, and contributed to limit and destroy the ancient practice of villanage. The learning, the ideas of policy, and, above all, the peaceable manners of ecclesiastics, naturally produced an aversion to the disorders incident to the feudal governments, and disposed them to shelter the weak and defenceless from the tyranny of their superiors.

In those dark and superstitious ages, the church was, at the same time, most successful in establishing her authority over the lowest and most ignorant of the people, and was therefore led, in a particular manner, to exert

---

whom Paul met in prison and converted to Christianity]]; and it is not supposed that the master, who was also a Christian, was under an obligation to relinquish any part of his authority, far less to give liberty to his servant. See St. Paul's epistle to Philemon. See also, to the same purpose, Rom. chap. xiii ver. 1, &c.—Ephes. chap. vi. ver. 5.—Coloss. chap. iii. ver. 22.—1 Tim. chap. vi. ver. 1, 2.—Tit. chap. ii. ver. 9, 10.—1 Pet. chap. ii. ver. 18.—1 Cor. chap. vii. ver. 21, 22. [[See Smith's similar discussion of the role of Christianity in the abolition of slavery at LJ (A) iii.127–28 and LJ (B) 142.]]

* See the publications on this subject by Anthony Benezet. [[A Philadelphia Quaker of French extraction, Anthony Benezet (1713–84) was the most important activist and pamphleteer of the early antislavery movement. See particularly: *Observation on the inslaving, importing and purchasing of Negroes; A short account of that part of Africa, inhabited by the negroes; A caution and warning to Great Britain and her colonies, in a short representation of the calamitous state of the enslaved Negroes in the British dominions; Some historical account of Guinea, its situation, produce and the general disposition of its inhabitants.*]]

her power and abilities in protecting that order of men by which she was
most firmly supported. As dying persons were frequently inclined to make
considerable donations for pious uses, it was more immediately for the interest of churchmen, that people of inferior condition should be rendered
capable of acquiring property, and should have the free disposal of what
they had acquired.

The progress of ecclesiastical rapacity seems at length to have produced
a custom that villains, who obtained their liberty by the influence of the
clergy, should reward their benefactors; and that the manumission should,
for this reason, be confirmed by the church. In these circumstances, <275>
the ministers of religion did not fail to recommend the manumission of
slaves, as an action highly proper to atone for the offences of a sinner; and
ecclesiastical censures were, in some cases, inflicted upon the master, when
he refused to allow his villains the liberty of alienating their goods by a
testament. So much does this appear to have been an object of attention,
that a bull was published by Pope Alexander III exhorting the Christian
world to a general emancipation of the villains.*

It was not, however, to be expected that, from such interested views, the
clergy would be disposed to strike at the root of servitude, or to employ
their casuistry in overthrowing an institution upon which so great a part
of their own property depended. Like physicians, they were far from thinking it necessary to swallow that medicine which they had prescribed to the
people; and while they appeared so extremely liberal with regard to the
estates of the laity, they held a very different conduct with relation to the
villains in their own possession. These being appropriated to pious uses,
and being only held in usufruct, were not to be alienated by the present
incumbent. Thus we meet with many ecclesiastical regulations, both in
France and Germany, by which it is provided that no bishop, or priest, shall

* See Boulainvil. sur les Parl. de France. let. 4. Potgiesserus de stat. serv. lib. 2. cap.
10. § 12.—Ibid. cap. 11. § 2. [[Millar is referring to Alexander III's order in 1167 to the
Muslim ruler of Valencia not to enslave Christian subjects. See *Wealth of Nations,*
III.ii.12.]]

manumit a slave in the patrimony of <276> the church, without purchasing two others of equal value to be put in his place.*

The state of the civil government, in most of the countries of Europe, may be regarded as another circumstance which had some influence in abolishing domestic slavery. From the aristocratical constitution established in these kingdoms, the sovereign was engaged in long and violent <277> struggles with his barons; and being often incapable of carrying his measures by direct force, he was obliged to employ every artifice that his situation would admit, in order to humble his rivals, and reduce them under subjection. For this purpose he frequently exerted his authority in protecting the villains from the tyranny of the master; and thus endeavoured to undermine

---

* See the different decrees of councils referred to by Potgiesserus de stat. serv. lib. 4. cap. 2. § 4, 5.

In one of these it is enacted, "Episcopus liberos ex familiis ecclesiae, ad condemnationem suam facere non praesumat. Impium enim est, ut qui res suas ecclesiae Christi non contulit, damnum inferat, et ejus ecclesiae rem alienare contendat. Tales igitur libertos successor episcopus revocabit, quia eos non aequitas, sed improbitas absolvit." [["Under penalty of condemnation, the bishop should not presume to make men free from the families of the church (i.e., his parish). Indeed it is sacrilegious that someone who does not contribute property to the church of Christ, should harm it and may hasten to sell off the property of his church. Therefore each successor bishop will recall such freed men [to servitude], because the initial act of freeing them was wicked."]]

In another it is said, "Mancipia monachis donata ab abbate non liceat manumitti. Injustum est enim, ut monachis quotidianum rurale opus facientibus, servi eorum libertatis otio potiantur." [["Slaves given to the monks ought not to be freed by an abbot. Indeed it is unjust that while the monks are doing their daily rural work, their slaves take possession of the leisure of liberty." That is, since the abbot does not work he has no right to take away a working monk's slave.]]

It is likely, however, that the clergy treated their slaves with greater lenity than was usual among the rest of the people. Mention is made of a bishop of Arles, who, in conformity to the Mosaical institution, never allowed above thirty-nine stripes to be given, at one time, to any of his servants.—"Solebat sanctus vir id accurate observare, ut nemo ex istis qui ipsi parebant, sive ille servi essent, sive ingenui, si pro culpa flagellandi essent, amplius triginta novem ictibus ferirentur. Si quis vero in gravi culpa deprehensus esset, permittebat quidem ut post paucos dies iterum vapularet, sed paucis." Cyprianus in vita S. Caesarii, Cit. Potgiess. lib. 2. cap. 1. § 6. [["The holy man was accustomed to see to it that no one out of those who had appeared before him, neither slaves, nor natives, if they were whipped for a crime, was beaten with more than thirty-nine stripes. But if someone was truly mired in grave sin, it was permitted indeed to flog him again after a few days, but less."]]

the power of the nobles, by withdrawing the submission of their immediate dependents.

While the monarch was, upon this account, endeavouring to protect the villains possessed by his barons, and to raise them to such a condition as might render them less dependent upon their masters, he found means of deriving some revenue from the people of that class, upon pretence of confirming, by royal authority, the privileges that were bestowed upon them. Other reasons, in the mean time, induced the sovereign to give particular encouragement to the bond-men upon his own demesnes; as these, under the shelter of the crown, had been enabled to acquire a degree of opulence, not only by their advances in agriculture, but also by their application to trade and manufactures, and consequently were in a condition to purchase freedom and immunities by pecuniary compositions, or by submitting to regular duties for the support of government. From such political considerations, we find that repeated efforts were made, and many regulations were introduced by different <278> princes of Europe, for extending and securing the liberties and rights of the lower and more industrious part of their subjects.*

In this manner domestic slavery, having gradually declined for ages, has at last been exploded from the greater part of Europe. In several European kingdoms, this has happened, from the natural progress of manners, and without any express interposition of the legislature. Thus in England, the peasants having, in consequence of their situation, acquired successive privileges, many of them were promoted to the rank of vassals or freeholders, while the rest, advancing more slowly, have remained in the condition of those who are called *copy-holders* at present. So late as the reign of Queen Elizabeth it appears that real bond-men were still to be found in many parts of the kingdom.†

In Scotland the slavery of the villains, which was probably of a similar nature to what obtained in the other countries of Europe, appears in like manner to have gone into disuse without any aid of statute; but the period

---

* See Boulanvil. lettres sur les Parl. des France. let. 4, 5.

† See observations on the statutes, chiefly the more ancient: 1 Rich. II. A. D. 1377. Smith's Commonwealth of Eng. B. 3 chap. 10.

when this change was effected has not been ascertained by lawyers or historians.* <279>

The remains of bondage which are still to be found in the case of colliers and salters in Scotland, and of those who work in the mines in some other parts of Europe, are sufficient to point out the chief circumstance, from which, in all other cases, the ancient institution has been so generally abolished. In a coal-work, as the different workmen are collected in one place, instead of being scattered, like the ordinary peasants, over an extensive territory, they were capable of being put under the care of an overseer, who might compel them to labour; and the master did not so immediately feel the necessity of resigning that authority over them with which he was invested.†

After domestic liberty had been thus, in a great measure, established in those European nations which had made the greatest improvement in agriculture, America was discovered; the first settlers in which, from their distance, and from the little attention that was paid to them by the government of their mother countries, were under no necessity of conforming to the laws and customs of Europe. The acquisition of gold and silver was the great object by which the Spaniards were directed in their settlements

* With regard to the state of the villains, while they existed in Scotland, see *Regiam Majestatem.* lib. 2. cap. 11, 12, 13, 14. *Quoniam Attachiamenta.* cap. 56. [[*Regiam Majestatem* was a compilation of the old Scots law, and *Quoniam Attachiamenta* a manual of court procedure. Although both are fourteenth-century works, they draw together much older Scots law.]]

† The right of the master, with regard to the labour of colliers and salters, is secured by statute, parl. 1606. c. 11. [[The notorious Colliers Act essentially made colliers and salters—coal miners and charcoal producers—serfs, insofar as they were bound to their masters, transferable when the mines they worked were sold, and punishable as slaves for running away (those who aided them were punished as well). The bondage of the colliers was not a vestige of old feudal practice but rather had been instituted to keep skilled laborers from leaving the mines. The act was limited in 1775 and repealed only in 1799. In other words, there was still slavery of a sort in Scotland when the last lifetime edition of the *Ranks* appeared. Recent research, however, has shown that the practice was not as brutal as Millar made out and that the status of colliers did not change much after 1799. See Christopher A. Whatley, "The Dark Side of the Enlightenment? Sorting out Serfdom" in *Eighteenth-Century Scotland: New Perspectives,* ed. T. M. Devine and J. R. Young (East Lothian, Scotland: Tuckwell Press, 1999), 259–74. (Thanks to Richard Sher for the reference.)]]

upon that continent; and the native inhabitants, whom they had conquered, were reduced into slavery and put to work in the mines. <280>
But, these being either exhausted by the severity with which they were
treated, or not being thought sufficiently robust for that kind of labour,
negro-slaves were afterwards purchased for this purpose from the Portuguese settlements on the coast of Africa. When sugar-plantations were
erected, the same people were employed in these, and in most other kinds
of work which came to be performed in that part of the world. Thus the
practice of slavery was no sooner extinguished by the inhabitants in one
quarter of the globe, than it was revived by the very same people in another,
where it has remained ever since, without being much regarded by the public, or exciting any effectual regulations in order to suppress it.*

It merits particular attention, that the chief circumstance which contributed to procure freedom to the slaves in Europe, had no place in our
American plantations. From the manner of working the mines, a number
of slaves are usually collected together, and may therefore be placed under
the command of a single person, who has it in his power to superintend
their behaviour, and to punish their negligence. The same observation is
applicable to the planting of sugar, and to the other occupations in our
colonies, in which the negroes perform the same sort of work which in
Europe is <281> commonly performed by cattle, and in which, of consequence, many servants are kept upon the same plantation. As the slaves are
continually under the lash of their master, he has not been forced to use
the disagreeable expedient of rewarding their labour, and of improving
their condition by those means which were found so necessary, and which
were employed with so much emolument, to encourage the industry of the
peasants in Europe. <282>

---

* See Anderson's history of commerce, vol. 1. p. 336—The first importation of negro-
slaves into Hispaniola was in the year 1508. Ibid.

SECTION IV

Political consequences of Slavery.

In the history of mankind, there is no revolution of greater importance to the happiness of society than this which we have now had occasion to contemplate. The laws and customs of the modern European nations have carried the advantages of liberty to a height which was never known in any other age or country. In the ancient states, so celebrated upon account of their free government, the bulk of their mechanics and labouring people were denied the common privileges of men, and treated upon the footing of inferior animals. In proportion to the opulence and refinement of those nations, the number of their slaves was increased, and the grievances to which they were subjected became the more intolerable.

The citizens of Athens, according to an enumeration of Demetrius Phalerius, are said to have amounted to 21,000, the strangers residing in that city to 10,000, and the slaves possessed by the whole people, to no less than 400,000.* There is reason to believe, however, that, in this enumeration of the free men, none but the heads of families are <283> included, and in that of the slaves, every individual is comprehended; for an account of the former would probably be taken with a view to the taxes imposed upon each head of a family, and the latter, it is most likely, would be numbered, like cattle, in order to ascertain the wealth of each proprietor. Thus, allowing five persons to each family, the Athenian slaves exceeded the free men in the proportion of between two and three to one.†

---

* Athenaeus lib. 6. cap. 20. Under the administration of Pericles the free citizens of Athens were not so numerous. See Plutarch, in Pericles. [[This remark does not appear to correspond to a particular passage in Plutarch's *Life of Pericles.*]]

† Mr. Hume supposes that, in the above enumeration, none but heads of families, either of the slaves or free men, are included; from which it would follow that, throwing

In the most flourishing periods of Rome, when luxury was carried to so amazing a pitch, the proportion of the inhabitants reduced into servitude was in all probability still greater. The number of slaves possessed by particular Roman citizens was prodigious. T. Minucius, a Roman knight, is said to have had 400.* Pliny mentions one Caecilius, who bequeathed in his testament upwards of 4000 slaves.† And Athenaeus takes notice, that the Roman slaves, belonging to individuals, often <284> amounted to 10,000, or even to 20,000; and sometimes, to a greater number.‡

The negro-slaves in the West-Indies are commonly said to exceed the free people nearly as three to one; and it has been supposed that the disproportion between them is daily increasing.

It may in general be observed, that according as men have made greater progress in commerce and the arts, the establishment of domestic freedom is of greater importance; and that, in opulent and polished nations, its influence extends to the great body of the people, who form the principal part of a community, and whose comfortable situation ought never to be overlooked in the provisions that are made for national happiness and prosperity.

In whatever light we regard the institution of slavery, it appears equally inconvenient and pernicious. No conclusion seems more certain than this, that men will commonly exert more activity when they work for their own benefit, than when they are compelled to labour for the benefit merely of another. The introduction of personal liberty has therefore an infallible tendency to render the inhabitants of a country more industrious; and, by producing greater plenty of provisions, must necessarily increase the populousness, as well as the strength and security of a nation.

Some persons have imagined that slavery is conducive to population, on

---

aside the strangers, the slaves exceeded the citizens nearly as twenty to one; and as this disproportion is highly incredible, he is of opinion that the number of slaves should be reduced to 40,000. But the precise reduction to this number is entirely arbitrary; and upon the supposition which I have made, there will be no reason to suspect the account either of exaggeration or inaccuracy. [[Hume, "Of the Populousness of Ancient Nations," *Essays,* 427 (II.xi.III).]]

　* Seneca de tranquillitate, cap. 8.
　† Lib. 33. cap. 10. [[Pliny *Naturalis Historia* XXXIII.47 [135].]]
　‡ [[Athenaeus *History*]] Lib. 6. cap. 20.

account of the frugality <285> with which the slaves are usually maintained, and on account of the attention which is given by the master to their multiplication.

With regard to the former circumstance, it ought to be considered, that the work of a labourer depends very much upon the subsistence which he receives. As by living in too great affluence he may occasion an useless consumption of provisions, so by obtaining too little he is rendered less fit for the exercise of those employments by which mankind are supported. To promote the populousness of a country, the mechanics and labouring people should be maintained in such a manner as will yield the highest profit from the work which they are capable of performing; and it is probable that they will more commonly procure the enjoyments of life according to this due medium, when they provide their own maintenance, than when it depends upon the arbitrary will of a master, who, from narrow and partial views, may imagine that he has an interest to diminish the expence of their living as much as possible. To those who have occasion to know the extreme parsimony with which the negro-slaves in our colonies are usually maintained, any illustration of this remark will appear superfluous.

With respect to the care of the master to encourage the multiplication of his slaves, it must be obvious that this is of little moment, unless it be accompanied with an increase of the means of their <286> subsistence. If slavery be always unfavourable to industry, and tend to hinder the improvement of a country, the number of inhabitants will be proportionably limited, in spite of all the regulations that can be made, and of all the encouragement that can be given to the propagation of the species. It is impossible even to multiply cattle beyond a certain extent, without having previously enriched the pastures upon which they are fed.

But slavery is not more hurtful to the industry than to the good morals of a people. To cast a man out from the privileges of society, and to mark his condition with infamy, is to deprive him of the most powerful incitements to virtue; and, very often, to render him worthy of that contempt with which he is treated. What effects, on the other hand, may we not expect that this debasement of the servants will produce on the temper and disposition of the master? In how many different ways is it possible to abuse that absolute power with which he is invested? And what vicious habits may be contracted by a train of such abuses, unrestrained by the laws, and palliated by the influence of example. It would seem that nothing could exceed the dishonesty and profligacy of the Roman slaves, unless we except the inhumanity and the extravagant vices which prevailed among the rest of the inhabitants.

Various statutes were made to restrain the manumission of slaves, and to prevent the dignity of <287> a Roman citizen from being communicated to such infamous persons. "Such is the confusion of our times," says Dionysius of Halicarnassus, "so much has the Roman probity degenerated into shameful meanness, that some, having gathered money by robberies, prostitutions, and all kinds of wickedness, are enabled to procure their freedom, and to become Romans; others, associating with their masters, in poisonings, murders, and crimes committed both against the gods and the commonwealth, are rewarded in the same manner."*

It has been alledged that, in one respect, the institution of slavery is beneficial to a nation, as it affords the most convenient provision for those who are become unable to maintain themselves. The maintenance of the poor, is doubtless, a very important object, and may be regarded as one of the most difficult branches in the police of a country. In the early periods of society, when family-attachments are widely extended, the rich are commonly willing to take care of their indigent relations; and from the dispositions of a people unacquainted with luxury, those persons who have no other resource may expect relief from the occasional charity of their neighbours. But in a commercial and populous nation, in which the bulk of the people must work hard for their livelihood, many individuals are, by a variety of accidents, reduced to indi-<288>gence; while at the same time, from their numbers, as well as from the prevailing spirit of the age, their misery is little regarded by their fellow-creatures. The cunning impostor, in such a case, may sometimes carry on a profitable trade of begging; but the real object of distress is apt to be overlooked, and without some interposition of the public, would often perish from want. Poors-rates therefore, in some shape or other, must be established; and from the nature of such an establishment, it is usually attended with much expence, and

* Dion. Hal. Antiq. Rom. lib. 3. [[Actually IV.24 [5].]]

liable to many abuses. In a country where slavery is practised, no such inconvenience is felt. As the master may be obliged, in all cases, to maintain his slaves, no assessment is necessary, no charges are incurred in collecting and distributing money, for the benefit of the poor: not to mention, that the nuisance of common begging is thus effectually removed.

It must be owned that this is a frugal regulation; but that it will answer the purpose is far from being so evident. When the same person, who is subjected to a tax, is also entrusted with the application of the money, what security is there that he will ever apply it to the uses for which it is intended? When a master is ordered to support his slaves, after they have become unfit for labour, what measures can be taken to secure their obedience? As it is plainly his interest to get free of this burden, what reason have we to expect that <289> he will submit to it longer than he thinks fit? In a matter of domestic economy, how is it possible for the public to watch over his conduct, or to observe one of a thousand instances in which he may neglect his decayed servants, or withhold from them the common necessaries of life? Instead of maintaining the poor, therefore, this is only a method of starving them in the most expeditious, and perhaps in the most private manner. In perusing the Roman history, with relation to this subject, we meet with enormities which fill the mind with horror. Among that people it appears that, notwithstanding all the laws that were made by emperors, of the best intentions and possessed of absolute power, the master did not even think it necessary to conceal his barbarity, or to show more regard to his slaves, than is usually shown to cattle which, from age or diseases, are no longer of service to the owner.

Considering the many advantages which a country derives from the freedom of the labouring people, it is to be regretted that any species of slavery should still remain in the dominions of Great Britain, in which liberty is generally so well understood, and so highly valued.

The situation of the colliers and salters in Scotland may seem of little consequence, as the number of persons engaged in that employment is not very great, and their servitude is not very grievous. The detriment, however, which arises from thence to the proprietor of such works is manifest. No <290> man would choose to be a slave if he could earn nearly the same wages by living in a state of freedom. Each collier, therefore, must have an additional premium for his labour, upon account of the bondage into which he is reduced: otherwise he will endeavour to procure a livelihood by some other employment.* <291>

Many of the coal-masters begin to be sensible of this, and wish that their workmen were upon a different footing; although, with a timidity natural to those who have a great pecuniary interest at stake, they are averse from altering the former practice, until such alteration shall be rendered universal by an act of parliament. But whatever advantages might accrue to them from a general law abolishing the slavery of the colliers, it seems evident that these advantages would be reaped in a much higher degree by any single proprietor who should have the resolution to give liberty to his workmen, and renounce the privileges which the law bestows upon him, with respect to those who might afterwards engage in his service. If the slavery of the colliers tends to heighten their wages, surely any one master who should be freed from this inconvenience before the rest, would be in the same circumstances with a manufacturer who produces a commodity at less expence

* The following facts, with regard to the comparative price of the labour of colliers in Scotland and England, and of that of colliers in comparison with other labourers, in both countries, have been communicated to the author by a gentleman of great knowledge and observation. [[The "gentleman" is likely Adam Smith, since Smith discussed the colliers at LJ (A) iii.127–30 and LJ (B) 139 and provided documentary evidence of their wages. Millar presumably got this information from Smith's lectures and personal discussion. See also *Wealth of Nations,* I.x.b.15.]]

In Scotland, a collier labouring eight hours in twenty-four, earns, exclusive of all expence, twelve shillings *per* week, or two shillings *per* day. More particularly,

In the county of Mid-Lothian, at an average, about thirteen shillings.
In the county of Fife, about twelve shillings.
In the counties of Linlithgow and Stirling, thirteen shillings.
In the county of Ayr, thirteen shillings and upwards.

It is to be observed, however, that this is not what every collier actually earns, but what every collier who works his regular task gets; and this exclusive of bearers.

The labourers in the lead-mines at Lead-hills, Wanloch-head, &c. in Scotland, working eight hours in twenty-four, earn eight shillings *per* week.

At Newcastle the colliers earn nine shillings *per* week.

Common labour at Newcastle is at six shillings *per* week.—In the county of Mid-Lothian in Scotland five shillings.—In the county of Fife four shillings.—In the counties of Linlithgow and Stirling five shillings.—In the county of Ayr from five shillings and sixpence to six shillings.—At Lead-hills, Wanloch-head, &c. six shillings.

than his neighbours, and who is thereby enabled to undersell them in the market.*

The slavery established in our colonies is an object of greater importance, and is, perhaps, attended with difficulties which cannot be so easily <292> removed. It has been thought, that the management of our plantations requires a labour in which free men would not be willing to engage, and which the white people are, from their constitution, incapable of performing. How far this opinion is well founded, according to the present manner of labouring in that part of the world, seems difficult to determine, as it has never been properly examined by those who are in a condition to ascertain the facts in question. But there is ground to believe that the institution of slavery is the chief circumstance that has prevented those contrivances to shorten and facilitate the more laborious employments of the people, which take place in other countries where freedom has been introduced.

Notwithstanding the connection between our colonies and the mother-country, the instruments proper for some of the most common branches of labour are little known in many parts of the West Indies. In Jamaica the digging of a grave gives full employment to two men for a whole day; as from the want of proper tools it is necessary to make a large hole no way adapted to the human figure. I am informed, that, unless it has been procured very lately, there is hardly a spade in the whole island. In procuring firewood for boiling sugar, &c. a work that takes up about five or six weeks yearly, no use is made of the saw, but the trees are cut with an ax into logs of about 30 inches in length. Instead of a flail the negroes <293> make use of a single stick in threshing the Guinea-corn; so that in this and in winnowing, ten women are capable of doing no more work in a day, than, with our instruments and machinery, two men would perform in two hours. From the want of a scythe or sickle, they are obliged every night to cut with a knife, or pull with their hands, a quantity of grass sufficient to serve their horses, mules, and black cattle.†

* By a late act of parliament such regulations have been made as, in a short time, will probably abolish the remains of that servitude to which this order of men have been so long subjected. [[See note p. 269.]]

† These observations were made about the year 1765, and relate more immediately to the parishes of Vere, Hanover, and St. Thomas in the vale.

With regard to the planting of sugar, experiments have been made, in some of the islands, from which it appears that, in this species of cultivation, cattle might be employed with advantage, and that the number of slaves might be greatly diminished.* But these experiments have been little regarded, in opposition to the former usage, and in opposition to a lucrative branch of trade which this innovation would in a great measure destroy.

At any rate, the interest of our colonies seems to demand that the negroes should be better treated, and even that they should be raised to a better condition. The author of a late elegant account of our American settlements has proposed, that small wages should be given them as an encouragement to industry.⁵ If this measure were once be-<294>gun, it is probable that it would gradually be pushed to a greater extent; as the master would soon find the advantage of proportioning the wages of the slaves to the work which they performed. It is astonishing that so little attention has hitherto been paid to any improvements of this nature, after the good effects of them have been so fully illustrated in the case of the villains in Europe. The owner of a sugar or tobacco plantation, one would think, might easily estimate the average value of the crop which it had formerly yielded, and could run no hazard, whatever profit he might reap, by allowing the people employed in the cultivation to draw a share of any additional produce obtained by their labour and frugality.

It affords a curious spectacle to observe, that the same people who talk in a high strain of political liberty, and who consider the privilege of imposing their own taxes as one of the unalienable rights of mankind, should make no scruple of reducing a great proportion of their fellow-creatures into circumstances by which they are not only deprived of property, but almost of every species of right. Fortune perhaps never produced

---

* See American Husbandry, published in 1775. [[John Mitchell and Arthur Young, *American Husbandry. Containing an Account of the Soil, Climate, Production, and Agriculture of the British Colonies in North-America and the West-Indies* (London: J. Bew, 1775), II:138, 146.]]

5. Benjamin Rush favorably quotes a letter from Granville Sharpe in *An Address to the Inhabitants of the British Settlements, on the Slavery of the Negroes in America,* in which Sharpe suggests that slaves be paid wages one working day every week as a step in the abolition of slavery (Benjamin Rush, *An Address,* pp. 20–21n). Rush's *Vindication,* cited by Millar in the next note, was published in a volume with *An Address.*

a situation more calculated to ridicule a liberal hypothesis, or to show how little the conduct of men is at the bottom directed by any philosophical principles.

In those provinces, however, of North America, where few slaves have ever been maintained, and where slavery does not seem to be recommended <295> by the nature of those employments in which the people are usually engaged, there may be some ground to expect that its pernicious effects upon industry will soon be felt, and that the practice will of course be abandoned. It is said that some of the provincial assemblies in that country have lately resolved to prevent or discourage the importation of negroes; but from what motives this resolution has proceeded, it is difficult to determine.*

The advancement of commerce and the arts, together with the diffusion of knowledge, in the present age, has of late contributed to the removal of many prejudices, and been productive of enlarged opinions, both upon this and upon a variety of other subjects. It has long been held, in Britain, that a negro-slave, imported into this country, obtained thereby many of the privileges of a free man. But by a late judgment in the court of king's-bench, it was found that the master could not recover his power over the servant by sending him abroad at pleasure.†

By a still more recent decision of the chief court in Scotland, it was declared, "That the dominion assumed over this negro, under the law of Jamaica, being unjust, could not be supported in <296> this country to any extent: that therefore the defender had no right to the negro's service for any space of time; nor to send him out of the country against his consent."‡

---

* See [[Benjamin Rush]] a vindication of the address to the inhabitants of the British settlements on the slavery of the negroes in America, by a Pennsylvanian, printed at Philadelphia, 1773.

† In the case of Somerset, the negro, decided in 1772. [[James Somerset was owned by Charles Stewart, a Bostonian. Stewart brought Somerset to England, where he escaped. After Somerset's recapture, Stewart sent him on a ship to Jamaica. Granville Sharpe, the antislavery activist, convinced Lord Mansfield, the Lord Chief Justice, to issue a writ of *habeas corpus.* The ship was stopped, Somerset returned to England, and the case proceeded. Eventually Mansfield ruled in Somerset's favour and Somerset was freed.]]

‡ Joseph Knight, a negro, against John Wedderburn, 15th January 1778. [[Sir John

This last decision, which was given in 1778, is the more worthy of attention, as it condemns the slavery of the negroes in explicit terms, and, being the first opinion of that nature delivered by any court in the island, may be accounted an authentic testimony of the liberal sentiments entertained in the latter part of the eighteenth century.

THE END.

Wedderburn brought his slave Joseph Knight from Jamaica to Scotland where after a few years Knight petitioned the courts for his freedom. Wedderburn made a distinction between perpetual servitude—using the colliers as precedent—and slavery, and won an initial case in 1774. Knight appealed and eventually won the case in 1778.]]

APPENDIX I

Note on the Editions

Millar's *Ranks* went through notable transformations in three lifetime editions and in the fourth, posthumous edition reproduced here. It also was translated into German twice and into French once.

The first edition was divided into five chapters.[1] The second edition added further section headings within the chapters and important new material in the footnotes. For example, the strikingly Humean discussion of liberty concluding the fifth chapter of the third edition was added as a lengthy footnote in the second edition. The third edition had a new title, a new chapter division, and extensive new material. Most notably, Millar thought his discussion of "The Changes Produced in the Government of a People, by their Progress in Arts, and in Polished Manners" to be sufficiently important to merit its own chapter and so separated the fourth chapter in the prior edition into two distinct chapters. He also moved many of the quotations that were in footnotes into the main body of the text and added many additional citations in the final chapter as a result of momentous changes in slavery laws between the publication of the first and the third edition. The fourth, posthumous edition is essentially the third edition with the addition of Craig's "Life." The printings of the three lifetime editions were as follows:

---

1. Chapter I. *Of the rank and condition of women in different ages*
   Chapter II. *Of the jurisdiction and authority of a father over his children*
   Chapter III. *Of the authority of a chief over the members of a tribe or village*
   Chapter IV. *Of the rise of a sovereign over an extensive society, and the advancement of a people in civilization and refinement*
   Chapter V. *Of the condition of servants in different parts of the world*

1. *Observations Concerning the Distinction of Ranks in Society*
By John Millar, Esq.
Professor of Laws in the University of Glasgow.
London:
Printed by W. and J. Richardson,
For
John Murray, No 32, Fleet-Street,
Opposite St. Dunstan's Church.
M.DCC.LXXI.
xv, 242 pp.

1A. *Observations Concerning the Distinction of Ranks in Society*
By John Millar, Esq.
Professor of Laws in the University of Glasgow.
Dublin: Printed by T. Ewing, in Capel-Street
M.DCC.LXXI
xiv, 240 pp.

[The Dublin edition is almost identical to the London edition. The type used is the same; the line spacing is slightly different. Lehmann suggests it may be a pirated volume.]

2. *Observations Concerning the Distinction of Ranks in Society*
By John Millar, Esq.
Professor of Law in the University of Glasgow
The Second Edition, Greatly Enlarged.
London: Printed for J. Murray, No 32, Fleet Street, Opposite St. Dunstan's Church.
M.DCC.LXXIII.
xxii, 312 pp.

3. *The Origin of the Distinction of Ranks; or, An Inquiry into the Circumstances which give rise to Influence and Authority in the Different Members of Society*
By John Millar, Esq. Professor of Law in the University of Glasgow.
The Third Edition,
Corrected and Enlarged.
London
Printed for J. Murray, No. 32, Fleet Street, Facing St. Dunstan's Church.
MDCCLXXXI
viii, 362 pp.

3A. *The Origin of the Distinction of Ranks; or, An Inquiry into the Circumstances which give rise to Influence and Authority in the Different Members of Society.*
By John Millar, Esq. Professor of Law in the University of Glasgow.
Basil:
Printed and sold by J. J. Tourneisen
MDCCXCIII
iv, 284 pp.

[This is a reprint of the third edition.]

There were two German translations:

Johann Millar, Esquire, *Bemerkungen über den Unterschied der Stände in der bürglichen Gesellschaft* (Leipzig: Engelhart Benjamin Schwidert, 1772), iii, 237 pp. [a translation of the first edition].

John Millar, *Aufklärungen über Ursprung und Fortschritte des Unterschieds der Stände und des Ranges, in Hinsicht auf Kultur und Sitten bei den vorzüglichsten Nationen* (Leipzig: Weygand, 1798), viii, 392 pp. [a translation of the third edition].

And one French translation:

John Millar, *Observations sur les commencemens de la société* (Amsterdam: Arkstée et Merkus, 1773), xxiv, 423 pp. [a translation of the second edition, published in Paris under a false imprint; Millar's French translator was the great Jean-Baptiste-Antoine Suard, who translated Hume, Robertson, and Macpherson as well].

Millar's Preface to the First Edition

Millar drastically rewrote his introduction to the *Ranks* for the third edition. The introduction to the first edition is very much worth reading because it is one of the most compact and erudite descriptions ever written of the empiricist attitude in the human sciences. It is reproduced here with Millar's original title of "Preface."

Preface <i>

Those who have examined the manners and customs of nations have had chiefly two objects in view. By observing the systems of law established in different parts of the world, and by remarking the consequences with which they are attended, men have endeavoured to reap advantage from the experience of others, and to make a selection of those institutions and modes of government which appear most worthy of being adopted. <ii>

To investigate the causes of different usages, hath also been esteemed an useful as well as an entertaining speculation. When we contemplate the amazing diversity in the manners of different countries, and even of the same country at different periods; when we survey the distinctions of national characters, and the singular customs that have prevailed; we are led to discover the various dispositions and sentiments with which man is endowed, the various powers and faculties which he is capable of exerting. When at the same time we consider how much the character of individuals is influenced by their education, their professions, and their peculiar circumstances, we are enabled, in some measure, to account for the behaviour of different nations. From the situation of a people in different ages and countries, they are presented with particular views of expediency; they form <iii> peculiar maxims, and are induced to cultivate and acquire a variety of talents and habits. Man is every where the same; and we must necessarily conclude, that the untutored Indian and the civilized European have acted upon the same principles.

Thus, by real experiments, not by abstracted metaphysical theories, human nature is unfolded; the general laws of our constitution are laid open; and history is rendered subservient to moral philosophy and jurisprudence. The manners and customs of people may be regarded as the most authentic record of their opinions, concerning what is right or wrong, what is praise-worthy or blamable, what is expedient or hurtful. In perusing such records, however, the utmost caution is necessary; and we must carefully attend to the circumstances in which they were <iv> framed, in order to ascertain the evidence which they afford, or to discern the conclusions that may be drawn from them. As the regulations of every country may have their peculiar advantages, so they are commonly tinctured with all the prejudices and erroneous judgments of the inhabitants. It is therefore by a comparison only of the ideas and the practice of different nations, that we can arrive at the knowledge of those rules of conduct, which, independent of all positive institutions, are consistent with propriety, and agreeable to the sense of justice.

When these enquiries are properly conducted, they have likewise a tendency to restrain that wanton spirit of innovation which men are apt to indulge in their political reasonings. To know the laws already established, to discern the causes from which they have arisen, and the <v> means by which they were introduced; this preliminary step is essentially requisite, in order to determine upon what occasions they ought to be altered or abolished. The institutions of a country, how imperfect soever and defective they may seem, are commonly suited to the state of the people by whom they have been embraced; and therefore in most cases, they are only susceptible of those general improvements, which proceed from a gradual reformation of the manners, and are accompanied with a correspondent change in the condition of society. In every system of law or government, the different parts have an intimate connection with each other. As it is dangerous to tamper with the machine, unless we are previously acquainted with the several wheels and springs of which it is composed, so there is reason to fear, that the violent alteration of any single part may <vi> destroy the regularity of its movements, and produce the utmost disorder and confusion.

The following observations are intended to illustrate the natural history of mankind in several important articles. This is attempted, by pointing out the more obvious and common improvements in the state of society, and by show-

ing the influence of these upon the manners, the laws, and the government of
a people.

In the first chapter the author has considered the ideas entertained in different
ages, with respect to the rank and condition of the two sexes. From these, the
chief regulations concerning marriage, and the rights of the husband and wife,
are evidently derived. <vii>

He has endeavored, first of all, to show the effects of poverty and barbarism,
with regard to the passions of sex, with regard to the general occupations of a
people, and with regard to the degree of consideration which is paid to the
women as members of society.

He has next proceeded to take notice of the refinements in the state of our
passions, arising from the acquaintance of wealth; first in moveables, by the
invention of pasturing cattle; and afterward in land, by the application of mankind to the cultivation of the earth.

In the third place, he has examined the alterations produced, in the condition
of the fair sex, by the improvement of the more necessary arts and manufactures,
and by the influence of civilization and regular government. <viii>

Lastly, he has attempted to delineate the changes, in this respect, introduced
by the cultivation of the elegant arts, and by the progress of a people in opulence
and luxury.

After the rights of the husband and wife, those that subsist between parents
and their children come next to be examined. In the second chapter, some observations are made, concerning the authority which, in the rudest periods, a
father is accustomed to exercise over his children. The limitations, upon the
branch of jurisdiction, arising from the improvements of a later age, are afterwards considered.

Having reviewed the primitive government of a family, the author has proceeded, in the third chapter, to enquire into the state of a tribe or village, composed of several families; to point out the origin of a chief, who is raised to the
head of their society; <ix> and the various branches of authority assumed by
the early magistrate, according to the different species of property which the
people have had an opportunity of acquiring.

By the union of several tribes, a larger society is formed, requiring a greater
variety of regulations, for securing the rights of individuals, and for maintaining
the publick tranquility. This makes the subject of the fourth chapter; which may
be divided into two parts:

The first relates to the political constitution, derived from a simple confederacy among these independent communities. As in the different governments, produced by an association of this sort, we every where observe a great degree of uniformity; we may also discover certain peculiar circumstances, by which the constitution of some <x> states is particularly distinguished. One of the most remarkable of these is the establishment of the feudal law; which makes so great a figure in the history of Europe, and has been the subject of so much investigation and controversy. Concerning the origin of the feudal institutions, and concerning the time and manner in which they were introduced, the author has ventured to deliver an opinion, which has the appearance of reconciling the different facts, collected by antiquaries and lawyers in support of their various and opposite conjectures.

The second part of that chapter contains remarks upon the alterations in the police and government of a country, arising from the progress of its inhabitants, in manufactures and commerce, and in that refinement of manners which is the natural consequence of affluence and security. <xi>

The consideration of the distinctions of rank, among the free inhabitants of a country, is followed by an enquiry into the state of persons of inferior condition, who, in order to procure subsistence, are obliged to labour in the service of others, and who form the great body of the people. In prosecuting this enquiry, the author has first considered the state of servants, in the primitive ages of the world. He has next attempted to point out those variations in their condition, which have proceeded from the usual improvements of society, in law and government; and, lastly, to give an account of that singular revolution, by which the laws of Europe are, in this respect, so eminently distinguished.

Upon the whole it has been the author's design to explain the causes of various manners and customs, rather than to enter <xii> into any formal discussion concerning the political advantages or disadvantages of which they have been productive; and it appeared unnecessary to give a separate detail of the laws of any one country, or to take notice of particular institutions, further than as they contributed to show the natural progress of human society.

[The final paragraph is identical with the final paragraph of the text of the fourth edition.]

APPENDIX 3

Millar's "Lectures on Government"

As mentioned in the Introduction to this volume, the *Ranks* grew out of Millar's *Lectures on Government*. The university regularly published outlines of the courses. Below is the first section of the course in 1771, the year of publication of the *Ranks*. I have presented the first section of the 1771 course and the section headings of the succeeding topics in order that the reader might see the place of the *Ranks* in Millar's system of teaching and its connection to the *Historical View*. I have followed the 1771 course with the corresponding sections of the course outline twenty years later to indicate how it had changed.

I.

A Course of Lectures on Government; Given Annually in the University. Glasgow. M.DCC.LXXI

Part I.
Of the Origin and Progress of Government in Society.

Lecture 1. The origin of influence and authority among mankind.
    2. The primitive government of a family.
    3. The government of a tribe or village of savages.
    4. The progress of government among independent tribes of shepherds and husbandmen.
    5. The government arising from the union of different tribes, or small societies.
    6. Changes produced in the state of society by the improvement of arts, manufactures, and commerce.

7. Influence of these changes upon the government of a people.

8. — with regard to the provisions that are made for national defence.

9. — with regard to the distribution of justice.

10. — with regard to the exercise of the legislative power.

11. Remarks upon the decline of nations.

Part II.

This subject illustrated from a view of particular Governments.

[Eighteen historical lectures on governments ranging from those of Athens, Sparta, and Rome to that of contemporary Scotland.]

Part III.

Present state of Government in Great Britain.

[Thirteen lectures on British government.]

2.

A Course of Lectures on Government; Given Annually in the University.

By John Millar,
Professor of Law.
Glasgow 1792

Part I.

Of the Origin and Progress of Government in Society.

Lecture 1. Order of the following Lectures—General principles of government.

Lecture 2. —Continuation of the same subject.

Lecture 3. State of government among *savages.*

Lecture 4. Advancement of political society in the *pastoral* ages.

Lecture 5. Progressive improvements in government, arising from the introduction of *agriculture*—In a single independent tribe of *husbandmen.*

Lecture 6. —In a *rude nation,* composed of different tribes.

Lecture 7. Changes produced in the state of society, by the improvement of manufactures, commerce, and the liberal arts—Causes of this improvement—Principal steps in the advancement of manufactures—of commerce—of the liberal arts.

Lecture 8. Effect of these changes upon the *general state* of society.

Lect. 9. Influence of manufactures, commerce, and the arts, upon the *intellectual* improvements—and upon the *morals* of a people.

Lect. 10. Their influence upon the *manners,* the *temper,* and the *deportment* of mankind.

Lect. 11. In what manner the *government* of a people is affected by these changes.

Lect. 12. Effect of these changes upon the *different powers* of government— The *legislative,* or *supreme directing* power.

Lect. 13. —Upon the *ministerial* powers of government.

Lect. 14. —Upon the establishments for the *distribution of justice.*

Lect 15. Remarks upon the decline of nations.

Lect 16. The same subject continued.

Part II.
The History of Government illustrated from a view of the Constitution in particular contries.

[Twenty-one historical lectures on government.]

Part III.
Present state of Government in Great Britain.

[Fourteen lectures on British government.]

BIBLIOGRAPHY

Modern Texts

The following texts are the works that Millar drew on in the footnotes to *Ranks*. They are not necessarily the editions Millar consulted, although I have tried to use the editions he would likely have used whenever I could identify them. I have also included ancient works that Millar cites in a specific contemporary edition, for example, Gillies' *Lysias* or Pope's *Odyssey* and *Iliad*. The remaining ancient works are listed in a separate section.

Anderson, Adam. *An Historical and Chronological Deduction of the Origin of Commerce*. 2 vols. London, 1764.

Anonymous. *A Curious Collection of Voyages, Selected from the Writers of All Nations*. 9 vols. London, 1761.

Anonymous. *Travels of the Jesuits, into various parts of the world: particularly China and the East Indies*. 2nd ed., 2 vols. Trans. Mr. Lockman. London, 1762. [Abridged and translated from *Lettres édifiantes et curieuses écrites des missions étrangères, par quelques missionaires de la Compagnie de Jésus*. 34 vols. Paris, 1703–76.]

Anson, George. *A Voyage Around the World*. Ed. R. Walter. London, 1748.

Arvieux, Laurent de. *The Travels of the Chevalier d'Arvieux in Arabia the desart, written by himself, and published by Mr. De Roque. . . . To which is added, a general description of Arabia, by Sultan Ishmael Abulfeda*. 2nd ed. London, 1732.

Benezet, Anthony. *A caution and warning to Great Britain and her colonies, in a short representation of the calamitous state of the enslaved Negroes in the British dominions*. Philadelphia, 1766.

———. *Observation on the inslaving, importing and purchasing of Negroes*. Germantown, Pa., 1759.

———. *A short account of that part of Africa, inhabited by the negroes*. Philadelphia, 1762.

————. *Some historical account of Guinea, its situation, produce and the general disposition of its inhabitants.* Philadelphia, 1771.

Bossu, Jean-Bernard. *Nouveaux voyages aux Indes Occidentales; contenant une relation des differens peuples qui habitent les environs du grand fleuve Saint-Louis, appellé vulgairement le Mississippi; leur religion; leur gouvernement; leurs moeurs; leurs guerres & commerce.* 2 vols. Paris, 1768.

Boulainvilliers, Henri, comte de. *Histoire des anciens Parlemens de France, ou États Généraux du royaume . . .* London, 1737.

————. *An historical account of the antient parliaments of France, or States-general of the kingdom . . .* 2 vols. London, 1739.

————. *Lettres sur les anciens parlemens de France que l'on nomme États-généraux.* 2 vols. London, 1753.

Bouquet, Pierre. *Le droit public de France, éclairci par les monuments de l'antiquité.* Paris, 1756.

Brisson, Barnabé. *Opera Minorae Varii Argumenta.* Lugduni Batavorum, 1747.

Brosses, Charles de. *Histoire des navigations aux Terres Australes.* 3 vols. Paris, 1756.

Bruce, James. *An Interesting Narrative of the Travels of James Bruce into Abyssinia, to discover the source of the Nile.* 2nd ed. Boston, 1798.

Bynkershoek, Cornelius van. *Opera Omnia.* 2 vols. Lugduni Batavorum, 1767. ["De jure occidendi et exponendi liberos apud veteres Romanos" first appeared in 1723.]

Byron, John. *The Narrative of the Honourable John Byron (Commodore in the Late Expedition around the World) Containing an Account of the Great Distresses Suffered by Himself and His Companions on the Coast of Patagonia From the Year of 1740, till their Arrival in England, 1746.* London, 1768.

Callander, John. *Terra australis cognita; or, voyages to the Terra Australis, or southern hemisphere, during the sixteenth, seventeenth and eighteenth centuries.* 3 vols. Edinburgh, 1766–68. [This is actually Callander's translation, with additions, of de Brosse's *Histoire des navigations aux Terres Australes.*]

Chantereau-Lefebvre, Louis. *Traité des fiefs.* Paris: L. Billaine, 1662.

Chardin, Jean. *Voyage de Paris à Ispahan.* 4 vols. Amsterdam, 1735. [First published in both French and English in 1686.]

Charlevoix, Père Pierre-François-Xavier de. *Histoire et description générale de la Nouvelle-France, avec le Journal historique d'un voyage fait par ordre du roi dans l'Amérique Septentrionale.* 3 vols. Paris, 1744.

Dampier, William. *A new voyage around the world: describing particularly the isthmus of America, several coasts and islands in the West Indies, the isles of Cape Verd, the passage by Terra del Fuego, the South Sea coasts of Chili, Peru, and Mexico, the isle of Guam, one of the Ladrones, Mindanao, and other Philippine and East-India islands near Cambodia, China, Formosa, Luconia, Celebes &c., New Holland, Sumatra, Nicobar Isles, the Cape of Good Hope, and Santa Helena* . . . London, 1697.

De Pauw, Cornelius. *Recherches philosophiques sur les Américains.* 3 vols. Berlin, 1768–70.

Du Halde, Jean-Baptiste. *The general history of China. Containing a geographical, historical, chronological, political and physical description of the empire of China, Chinese-Tartary, Corea and Thibet* . . . 3rd ed., 4 vols. Trans. Richard Brookes. London: J. Watts, 1741. [First published in French in 1735.]

Filmer, Sir Robert. *Patriarchia.* 1680.

Fontenelle, Bernard de. *Oeuvres.* 3 vols. Amsterdam, 1764.

Gillies, John, ed. and trans. *The orations of Lysias and Isocrates, translated from the Greek: with some account of their lives; and A discourse on the history, manners, and character of the Greeks, from the conclusion of the Peloponnesian War, to the Battle of Chaeronea.* London: J. Murray, 1778.

Gmelin, Johann Georg. *Voyage en Sibérie; contenant la description des moeurs & usages des peuples de ce pays.* 2 vols. Trans. M. de Keralio. Paris, 1767. [First published in German in 1751–52.]

Goguet, Antoine-Yves. *The Origin of Laws, Arts and Sciences among the most ancient Nations.* Edinburgh: A. Donaldson & J. Reid, 1761. [First published in French in 1758.]

Grotius, Hugo. *Annotationes in Vetus & Novum Testamentum juxta editionem amstelaedamensem, MDCLXXIX, in compendium redactae.* London, 1727.

Hawkesworth, John, ed. *An account of the voyages undertaken by the order of His present Majesty for making discoveries in the Southern Hemisphere: and successively performed by Commodore Byron, Captain Wallis, Captain Carteret, and Captain Cook, in the* Dolphin, *the* Swallow, *and the* Endeavor, *drawn up from the journals which were kept by the several commanders, and from the papers of Joseph Banks, Esq.* 3 vols. London, 1773.

Heineccius, Johann Gottlieb. *Antiquitatum Romanarum Jurisprudentiam.* 2nd ed. Argentotati, 1724.

———. *Elementa iuris Germanici.* 2 vols. Halae, 1736–37.

Hénault, Charles Jean François. *Nouvel abrégé chronologique de l'histoire de France.* 2nd ed. Paris, 1746.

Herrera y Tordesillas, Antonio de. *The general history of the vast continent and islands of America, commonly call'd, the West-Indies, from the first discovery thereof.* 2nd ed., 6 vols. Trans. Capt. John Stevens. London, 1740.

Hume, David. *Essays and Treatises on Several Subjects.* 2 vols. London, 1768. (*Essays, Moral, Political, and Literary.* Rev. ed. Edited by Eugene F. Miller. Indianapolis: Liberty Fund, 1987.)

Kames (Henry Home), Lord. *Elements of Criticism.* 6th ed. 2 vols. Edinburgh: J. Bell and W. Creech, 1785. (*Elements of Criticism.* Edited by Peter Jones. 2 vols. Indianapolis: Liberty Fund, 2005.)

———. *Historical Law-Tracts.* 2 vols. Edinburgh: A. Kincaid and J. Bell, 1758.

Kolb, Peter. *The present state of the Cape of Good Hope: or, A particular account of the several nations of the Hottentot.* 2 vols. Trans. Mr. Medley. London, 1731. [First published in German in 1719.]

Krasheninnikov, Stepan Petrovitch. *The History of Kamtschatka, and the Kurilski Islands.* Gloucester: T. Jefferys, 1764.

Lafitau, Père Joseph-François. *Moeurs des sauvages Amériquains.* 4 vols. Paris, 1724.

Le Comte, Louis. *Memoirs and observations topographical, physical, mathematical, mechanical, natural, civil, and ecclesiastical made in a late journey through the empire of China.* 3rd ed. London, 1699.

Le Gobien, Père Charles. *Histoire des isles Marianes, nouvellement converties à la religion chrestienne; & du martyre des premiers a-postres qui y ont prêché la foy.* Paris, 1700.

Lockman, John. *Travels of the Jesuits, into various parts of the world: particularly China and the East-Indies.* 2d ed. London: T. Piety, 1762.

Loyseau, Charles. *Traité des seigneuries.* 3rd ed. Paris, 1620.

Mably, Abbé de. *Observations sur l'histoire de France.* 2 vols. Geneva, 1765.

Macpherson, James. *The Poems of Ossian and Related Works.* Ed. Howard Gaskill. Edinburgh: Edinburgh University Press, 1996. [The poems in this volume began to appear in 1762.]

Mexía, Pedro, et al. *Archaio-ploutos. Containing, ten follovving bookes to the former Treasurie of auncient and moderne times: being the learned collections, iudicious readings, and memorable obseruations, not onely diuine, morall, and philosophicall, but also poeticall, martiall, politicall, historicall, astrologicall, &c.* London, 1619.

Mézeray, François Eudes de. *Histoire de France avant Clovis.* Amsterdam: A. Wolfgang, 1692.

Mitchell, John, and Arthur Young. *American Husbandry. Containing an Account of the Soil, Climate, Production and Agriculture of the British Colonies in North-America and the West-Indies.* London: J. Bew, 1775.

Montaigne, Michel de. *Essais.* 8 vols. Paris: Abel l'Angelier, 1604.

Montesquieu, Charles de Secondat, Baron de. *L'Esprit des Loix.* Geneva, 1748.

Noodt, Gerard de. *Julius Paulus, sive De partus expositione et nece apud veteres liber singularis.* Leiden, 1710.

Noort, Olivier van. *Voyage autour du monde, par le d'étroit de Magellan, en 1598.* Amsterdam, 1705.

Perizonius, Jacobus. *Ant. Fil. Dissertationum Septem.* Halae Magdeburgiae, 1722.

Petit, Pierre. *De Amazonibus dissertatio, quâ an verè extiterint, necne, variis ultro citroque conjecturis & argumentis disputatur. Multa etiam ad eam gentem pertinentia, ex antiquis monumentis eruuntur atque illustrantur.* Paris, 1685.

Poivre, Pierre. *The Travels of a Philosopher.* London, 1769. [First published in French in 1768.]

Pope, Alexander, trans. *Homer's Iliad.* 6 vols. London, 1715–20.

———. *Homer's Odyssey.* 5 vols. London, 1760.

Potgieser, Joachim. *Commentariorum iuris Germanici de statu servorum veteri perinde atque novo libri quinque.* Lemgoviae, 1736.

Potter, John. *Archaeologia graeca: or, The antiquities of Greece.* 2 vols. Oxford, 1697.

Potter, R., ed. and trans. *The Tragedies of Aeschylus.* Norwich, 1777.

Prévost d'Exile, Abbé. *Histoire générale des voyages; ou, Nouvelle collection de toutes les relations de voyages par mer et par terre qui ont été publiées jusqu'à present dans les différentes langues de toutes les nations connues . . .* 2 vols. Paris, 1746–89.

Racine, Jean. *Phèdre.* Paris, 1677.

Renneville, Constantin de. *Recueil des voyages qui ont servi a l'établissement et aux progrès de la Compagnie des Indes Orientales, formée dans les Provinces Unies des Païs-Bas.* 7 vols. Amsterdam, 1702–7.

Ricaut, Paul. *The present state of the Ottoman Empire: containing the maxims of the Turkish polity, the most material points of the Mahometan religion, their sects and heresies, their convents and religious votaries, their military discipline: with an exact computation of their forces both by sea and land.* London, 1682.

Richardson, S., et al. *The Modern Part of an Universal History: From the Earliest Account of Time.* 44 vols. London, 1759–66.

Rush, Benjamin. *An address to the inhabitants of the British settlements: on the slavery of the negroes in America. To which is added, A vindication of the address, in answer to a pamphlet entitled, "Slavery not forbidden in Scripture; or, A defence of the West India planters."* 2nd ed. Philadelphia, 1773.

Sainte-Palaye, Jean-Baptiste de La Curne de. *Mémoires sur l'ancienne chevalerie.* 3 vols. Paris: Duchesne, 1759–81.

Salvaing de Boissieu, Denis. *De l'usage des fiefs et autres droits seigneuriaux.* 3rd ed. 1644; Avignon, 1731.

Shaw, Thomas. *Travels or Observations relating to several parts of Barbary and the Levant.* 2nd ed. London, 1757.

Sigonio, Carlo. *De Antiquo Iure Civium Romanorum Libri Duo.* Venice, 1562.

Smith, Adam. *The Theory of Moral Sentiments.* Ed. D. D. Raphael and A. L. Macfie. 1759; Oxford, 1976. (*The Theory of Moral Sentiments.* Edited by D. D. Raphael and A. L. Macfie. Indianapolis: Liberty Fund, 1984.)

Smith, Thomas. *The common-vvelth of England, and maner of gouernment thereof.* London, 1589. [English translation of *De republica anglorum*, 1583.]

Spelman, Sir Henry. *Glossarium archaiologicum: continens latino-barbara, peregrina, obsoleta, & novatae significationis vocabula, quae post labefactatas a gothis, vandalisque res Europaeas, in ecclesiasticis, profanisque scriptoribus, variarum item gentium legibus antiquis municipalibus, chartis, & formulis occurrunt, scholiis & commentariis illustrata, in quibus prisci ritus quam-plurimi, magistratus, dignitates, munera, officia, mores, leges ipsae, &c. consuetudines enarrantur.* 3 vols. London, 1687.

———. *Reliquiae Spellmannianae: The posthumous works of Sir Henry Spelman Kt. Relating to the laws and antiquities of England.* 2 vols. Ed. Edmund Gibson. Oxford/London, 1723.

Stuart, Gilbert. *Historical dissertation concerning the antiquity of the English constitution.* Edinburgh, 1768.

Ulloa, Antonio de, and George Juan. *A Voyage to South America: Describing at Large the Spanish Cities, Towns, Provinces, &c. on that extensive Continent.* 2 vols. London, 1758.

Velly, Abbé Paul François. *Histoire de France, depuis l'établissement de la monarchie Jusqu' au règne de Louis XIV.* 30 vols. Paris, 1755–86.

Wallace, Robert. *A dissertation on the numbers of mankind in antient and modern times: in which the superior populousness of antiquity is maintained. With an appendix, . . . and some remarks on Mr. Hume's Political discourse.* Edinburgh, 1753.

Weber, Friedrich Christian. *The Present State of Russia.* 2 vols. London, 1722–23. [First published in German in 1715.]

Wright, Sir Martin. *An introduction to the law of tenures.* 3rd ed. Dublin: M. Owen, 1750.

Ancient Texts

I have given Roman titles in Latin and Greek titles in English because for the most part Millar did not cite Greek works by Greek titles. Millar cited ancient titles in abbreviated form, but his abbreviations should become evident when compared with this list.

Aelian, *Varia Historia*

Aelius Donatus, *Commentum Terenti*

Aristotle, *Nicomachean Ethics, Politics*

Athenaeus, *History*

Caesar, *De Bello Gallico*

Cicero, *De Senectute, Pro Flacco, In Verrem*

Cornelius Nepos, *De Viris Illustribus*

Diodorus Siculus, *History*

Dionysius of Halicarnassus, *Antiquitates Romanae*

Herodian, *History of the Roman Empire*

Herodotus, *History*

Homer, *Iliad, Odyssey*

Horace, *Sermones* [cited as *Satires*]

Juvenal, *Saturae*

Lucan, *Pharsalia*

Lysias, *Orations*

Ovid, *Metamorphoses*

Plautus, *Amphitryon*

Pliny, *Naturalis Historia*

Plutarch, *Lives of Eminent Men*

Seneca, *De Beneficiis, De Tranquilitate*

Strabo, *Geography*

Suetonius, *De Vita Caesarum*

Tacitus, *De Origine et Situ Germanorum* [Millar knew Tacitus's work as *De Moribus Germanorum* and cited it accordingly.]

Thucydides, *History of the Peloponnesian War*

Valerius Maximus, *Factorum et Dictorum Memorabiliorum*
Virgil, *Aeneid*

Roman, German, and Medieval Legal Works and Other Sources

Besides the omnipresent *Digest, Codex,* and *Institutes* of Justinian, Millar made use of the *Codex Theodosianus,* Gaius's *Institutionem iuris civilis Commentarii,* Ulpian's *Fragments,* the *Lex Salica* and *Lex Burgundionum,* Marculfus's *Formulae,* the Hebrew Bible, and the New Testament.

Translations Used in Preparation of This Edition

Edwards, H. J., trans. and ed. *Julius Caesar: The Gallic War.* Cambridge: Loeb, 1917.

Grene, David, trans. *Herodotus: The History.* Chicago: University of Chicago Press, 1987.

Mandelbaum, Allen, trans. *The Aeneid of Virgil.* Berkeley: University of California Press, 1971.

———. *The Metamorphoses of Ovid.* New York: Harcourt Brace, 1993.

Rackham, H., trans. *Aristotle: Politics.* Cambridge, Mass.: Harvard University Press, 1944.

Ramsay, G. G., trans. and ed. *Juvenal and Persius.* Cambridge: Loeb, 1918.

Rives, J. B., trans. and ed. *Tacitus: Germania.* Oxford: Clarendon Press, 1999.

Rowe, Nicholas, trans. *Lucan: The Civil War.* London: J. M. Dent, 1998. [Reissue of Rowe's edition of 1719.]

Watson, Alan, trans. *The Digest of Justinian.* Philadelphia: University of Pennsylvania Press, 1985.

INDEX

This book is set in Adobe Garamond, a modern adaptation by Robert
Slimbach of the typeface originally cut around 1540 by the French
typographer and printer Claude Garamond. The Garamond face, with
its small lowercase height and restrained contrast between thick and
thin strokes, is a classic "old-style" face and has long been one of the
most influential and widely used typefaces.

Printed on paper that is acid-free and meets the requirements of the
American National Standard for Permanence of Paper for Printed
Library Materials, z39.48-1992. ⊗

Book design by Louise OFarrell
Gainesville, Florida
Typography by Apex Publishing, LLC
Madison, Wisconsin
Printed and bound by Worzalla Publishing Company
Stevens Point, Wisconsin